Comparative Politics

Comparative Politics

A *Theoretical Framework*

Fourth Edition

Gabriel A. Almond
Stanford University

G. Bingham Powell, Jr.
University of Rochester

Kaare Strøm
University of California, San Diego

Russell J. Dalton
University of California, Irvine

PEARSON
Longman

New York   San Francisco   Boston
London   Toronto   Sydney   Tokyo   Singapore   Madrid
Mexico City   Munich   Paris   Cape Town   Hong Kong   Montreal

Vice President and Publisher: Priscilla McGeehon
Executive Editor: Eric Stano
Senior Marketing Manager: Megan Galvin-Fak
Supplements Editor: Kristi Olson
Media Editor: Patrick McCarthy
Production Manager: Joseph Vella
Project Coordination, Text Design, and Electronic Page Makeup: Shepherd Incorporated
Cover Design Manager/Designer: John Callahan
Cover Photo: Courtesy of PhotoDisc, Inc.
Manufacturing Buyer: Roy L. Pickering, Jr.
Printer and Binder: Courier Corp.—Stoughton
Cover Printer: Coral Graphic Services

Library of Congress Cataloging-in-Publication Data

Comparative politics : a theoretical frameword / [edited by] Gabriel A. Almond ... [et al.].—
4th ed.
   p. cm.
   Includes bibliographical references and index.
   ISBN 0-321-08988-5
   1. Comparative government. I. Almond, Gabriel Abraham, 1911–2002

JF51 .C62 2002
320.3—dc21   2002025485

Visit us at www.ablongman.com

ISBN 0-321-08985-5

2 3 4 5 6 7 8 9 10—CRS—06 05 04 03

CONTENTS

PART TWO System, Process, and Policy

CHAPTER 3

Political Culture and Political Socialization   56

CHAPTER 4

Interest Articulation   78

CHAPTER 5

Interest Aggregation and Political Parties   102

PREFACE

Comparative Politics Today: A Theoretical Framework, Fourth Edition, presents in the form of a separate book the chapters of Part One and Part Two of *Comparative Politics Today: A World View,* Eighth Edition (© 2004). These theoretical chapters trace back to the original Almond and Powell, *Comparative Politics: A Developmental Approach* (Little, Brown, 1966) as revised and expanded in *Comparative Politics: System, Process and Policy* (Little, Brown, 1978). Our purpose in making these theoretical chapters separately available is for the convenience of those teachers of comparative politics who find our approach useful, but prefer to make their own selection of exemplary reading materials from the larger literature of country and analytical studies.

This fourth edition, like the last one, begins with the theme of why governments exist, what functions they serve, how they create problems as well as solutions. We explore the debates about the costs and benefits of government in the history of philosophy and in the contemporary exchanges among academics and politicians. The first chapter also introduces the three great challenges that face most states in the world today: (1) building a common identity and sense of community; (2) fostering economic and social development; and (3) securing democracy, human rights, and civil liberties. The second chapter in Part One sketches the concepts needed to compare different politics in very different societies: political system and environment, structures and functions, policy performance, and its consequences.

Part Two elaborates important elements in the system, process and policy framework, discussing the causes and consequences of important aspects of political cultures, interest groups, parties and other aggregation structures, constitutions, key policymaking structures, types of public policies, and their consequences. Tables, figures, and boxes in these five chapters provide examples, compare systems, and discuss important trends, such as value changes, the rise of fundamentalism, democratization, the recruitment of women into leadership roles, the rule of law, and international interdependence.

As with each new edition, both Part One and Part Two have been updated to reflect current data and political events as well as recent political theory. The reshaping of world events following the terrorist attacks on the United States of September 11, 2001, plays a role in many places, as well as in the United States. Since the previous edition there have also been national elections in most democratic countries, including Britain, France, Germany, Japan, Russia and the United States, and particularly dramatic ones in Brazil and Mexico. China has experienced an important leadership change. These and other significant political events help shape this edition.

The Acknowledgments in the Eighth Edition of *Comparative Politics Today: A World View* express our debts and appreciation to those who helped us prepare that edition, which is the basis of this volume also. Rather than repeat those remarks here, we simply refer the reader to page xix of that text. But we do wish to reiterate explicitly our gratitude to the authors of the twelve country studies in that volume—Richard Rose (England), Martin A. Schain (France), Russell J. Dalton (Germany), Frances Rosenbluth and Michael F. Thies (Japan), Thomas F. Remington (Russia), Melanie Manion (China), Wayne A. Cornelius and Jeffrey A. Weldon (Mexico), Frances Hagopian (Brazil), Ann Mosely Lesch (Egypt), Subrata K. Mitra (India), Robert J. Mundt and Oladimeji Aborisade (Nigeria), and Austin Ranney (United States)—who added once more, as they and their predecessors have many times over the years, essential contents and interpretative insights to the basic theoretical framework.

Gabriel Almond passed away in December 2002, just short of his 92nd birthday. His influence upon the study and teaching of comparative politics, and upon each of us, was enormous. He wrote at length about many important political topics, including the types of interest groups, the culture of democracy, the nature of fundamentalism, and the history of political science. One of his greatest achievements was his continuing commitment to finding ways to understand, compare, and explain the most diverse forms of political life. This text is deeply shaped by that commitment, both by his own involvement in writing it and by his influence upon us. And one of his greatest legacies is the generation of students who have learned about comparative politics and our world through the insights he provided.

G. BINGHAM POWELL, JR.
KAARE STRØM
RUSSELL J. DALTON

Comparative Politics

1

Issues in
Comparative Politics

WHAT IS POLITICS?

Some people love politics. They may relish the excitement of political events, such as elections, as they would an exciting athletic contest (a World Series or Super-Bowl, perhaps). Others are fascinated with politics because they care about the issues and their consequences for people in their own communities or around the world. On the other hand, there are those who hate politics, either because it sets groups and individuals against each other, or because it involves abuse of power, deceit, manipulation, treachery, and violence. Finally, there are those who are indifferent to politics, who perhaps find it boring because it has little to do with the things that matter most to them. Most of us react to politics with a mixture of these sentiments, which may change with time and events. Politics has many faces and can be a force for good as well as evil. This book is about the comparative study of politics. In order to make political comparisons, we need to understand what is meant by politics as well as what it means to study it comparatively. The former is the task of this chapter, whereas Chapter 2 will discuss the latter.

Politics has to do with human decisions, and political science is the study of such decisions. Yet, not all decisions are political, and many of the social sciences are concerned with decisions that are of little interest to political scientists. For example, consider a situation in which you go with a friend (a date, perhaps) to an event such as a concert or a soccer match. You have a certain amount of money at your disposal. You can spend this money on your tickets (to get the best seats possible) or on food and drink, or you can save it. Economists might be interested in what sorts of spending decisions you make. Psychologists might wish to know why you were going with this friend and not with someone else, or in how you and your friend decided what to do. Political scientists are not likely to want to study any of these questions, unless perhaps the event you attended turned into a riot (both soccer matches and concerts occasionally do), or the experience somehow changed your political outlook (which may occasionally happen at soccer matches and concerts, too, though you probably should not hold your breath).

1

The main point here is that not all choices or decisions are political. Specifically, political decisions are *public* and *authoritative*. To say that politics has to do with public decisions is to say that politics is inherently social. Politics always involves and has consequences for multiple human beings. There is no such thing as political solitaire, playing politics by yourself. Political decisions always take place within some community that we may call a *political system*. We shall discuss that concept later.

Yet, not all social decisions are public. Most of what happens within families, among friends, or within voluntary associations belongs to the *private* sphere. Actions within this sphere are voluntary, not regulated, and do not bind anyone outside the group involved. In most societies, with whom you go to concerts and what food you buy are private decisions. When many people are indifferent to politics, it is largely because they value this private sphere, in which they may place their family life, friendships, faith, and nature, more highly than they regard the public domain. Societies vary greatly in the scope of the public versus the private sphere. In totalitarian societies, the public sphere is very large and private life very limited. In other societies, the private domain may almost crowd out the public one. To complicate things even more, the boundaries between the public and private spheres get redrawn all the time. A couple of decades ago, the sex lives of U.S. presidents or members of the British royal family were considered private matters, not to be discussed in public and certainly not by politicians. In recent years, this seems to have changed, although in other countries the traditional standards remain. On the other hand, there was a time in British history when certain religious beliefs were in themselves considered treasonous. People who held such beliefs could be executed, as was Thomas More under King Henry VIII. Nowadays, most modern democracies consider religious beliefs to be private matters, though other societies may not. Yet, all societies maintain some distinction between public and private affairs. And although politics may be influenced by what happens in the private domain, it has directly to do only with those decisions that are public.

Also, politics is authoritative. Authority means formal power that is vested in individuals or groups with the expectation that their decisions will be carried out and respected. That is to say that the choices in which we are interested are designed to be binding (compulsory) for those individuals or groups to whom they apply. In some cases, force (coercion) may be applied to ensure that they are implemented. Those who have political authority typically have access to force and to monetary resources so that they can enforce their decisions. We call such resources means of coercion. Authority does not have to be backed up by coercion, but in politics it often is. Nowadays, in most advanced democracies religious authorities, such as the Pope, have few coercive powers. They can only persuade, but rarely compel, their followers. On the other hand, tax authorities, such as the Internal Revenue Service in the United States, can typically not only exhort but also compel.

By politics we thus refer to the activities associated with the control of public decisions among a given people and in a given territory, where this control may be backed up by authoritative and coercive means. Politics refers to the use of these authoritative and coercive means—who gets to employ them and for what purposes.

GOVERNMENTS AND THE STATE OF NATURE

Authority and coercive control are typically exercised by governments. **Governments** are organizations of individuals who are legally empowered to make binding decisions on behalf of a particular community. Governments thus have authoritative and coercive powers. Governments do many things. They wage war or encourage peace, cultivate or restrict international trade, open their borders to the exchange of ideas and art or close them, tax their populations heavily or lightly and through different means, allocate resources for education, health, and welfare, or leave such matters to others.

Governments may take many different forms, and they may be more or less ambitious or expansive. In the nineteenth century, most Western countries had very limited governments built on the model of the **night watchman state:** governments that provided basic law and order, defense, and protection of property rights, but little else (though education was also becoming a major government concern). Twentieth-century political development has produced two much more expansive types of governments. One is the **police state** seen in many authoritarian societies, particularly under communism or fascism. The second is the **welfare state** with programs of social welfare assistance, unemployment benefits, accident and sickness insurance, old age pensions, public education, and the like. German Chancellor Otto von Bismarck's government first began developing such programs in the 1880s in response to Germany's rapid industrialization and urbanization, which had caused widespread social displacement and distress. His programs were soon copied by governments in many other countries and especially democratic ones. The scope and cost of welfare state programs have since grown enormously, particularly from the Great Depression of the 1930s until the 1970s. Yet, welfare state policies differ greatly from country to country. Welfare policies in the United States stress equality of opportunity through public education. In contrast, many Western European countries have given priority to social security and health programs over education.

As government expenditures have grown to between one-third and one-half of the national product in most industrialized democracies, problems have arisen. In some countries the increasing cost and alleged inefficiencies of the welfare state have brought about efforts to prevent further increases in programs and to impose limits on public expenditures. The size of the government budget and its effects on savings, investment, inflation, and employment have become central issues. In effect, the government's role in providing welfare services has become more contested. The **regulatory state** that had developed alongside the welfare state has also come in for criticism and reassessment, and many economic sectors have been deregulated. We shall return to these issues in Chapter 7.

This debate over the welfare state and the regulatory state is far from new. On the contrary, it calls to mind a classic polemic in political philosophy. For centuries, political philosophers have debated whether government is a force for good or evil. In the seventeenth and eighteenth centuries—the time of the English,

French, and American revolutions—much of this debate was couched in arguments concerning the **state of nature**. Philosophers thought about the state of nature as the condition that would obtain if no government existed. In some cases, they may have thought that such a state had actually existed before the advent of the first governments. At any rate, these philosophers used their ideas of a state of nature to identify some ideal social contract (agreement) on which societies could build. We therefore often refer to them as social contract theorists. The age of exploration, the discovery of previously unknown continents, and encounters with unfamiliar societies and cultures fed their imaginations. Even today, many political philosophers find it useful to make such a mental experiment to consider the consequences of political intervention.

Among the social contract philosophers whose reflections on the state of nature have become highly influential are Britons Thomas Hobbes and John Locke, and the Frenchman Jean-Jacques Rousseau. Though the state of nature had a similarly critical place in their respective political philosophies, their ideas about this condition varied dramatically. The contrast between Hobbes and Rousseau is most striking. Hobbes thought of the state of nature as mercilessly inhospitable, a situation of eternal conflict of all against all, and a source of barbarism and continuous fear. Referring to the state of nature, he pessimistically argued that "In such condition, there is no place for Industry; because the fruit thereof is uncertain: and consequently no Culture of the Earth; no Navigation, nor use of the commodities that may be imported by Sea; no commodious Building, . . . no Arts; no Letters; no Society; and which is worst of all, continuall feare, and danger of violent death; And the life of man, solitary, poor, nasty, brutish, and short."[1]

For Rousseau, on the other hand, the state of nature represented humanity before its fall from grace, without all the corruptions that governments have introduced. "Man is born free," Rousseau observed in *The Social Contract*, "and yet everywhere he is in chains." Rousseau saw governments as the source of power and inequality, and these conditions in turn as the causes of human alienation and corruption. "The extreme inequality in our way of life," he argued, "excess of idleness in some, excess of labor in others; . . . late nights, excesses of all kinds, immoderate ecstasies of all the passions; fatigues and exhaustion of mind, numberless sorrows and afflictions . . . that most of our ills are our own work; that we would have avoided almost all of them by preserving the simple, uniform, and solitary way of life prescribed to us by nature."[2]

Finally, John Locke, whose ideas have been particularly important for the development of Western democracies, took a position in between those of Hobbes and Rousseau. Locke did not share Hobbes's dire view of the state of nature. Compared with Hobbes, Locke thought of human beings as more businesslike and less war prone. Yet, like Hobbes he proposed a social contract to replace the state of nature with a system of government. But whereas for Hobbes, the main task for government was to quell disorder and protect against violence and war, Locke saw the state's main role as protecting property and commerce and promoting economic growth. This it would do, in his view, by establishing and enforcing property rights and rules of economic exchange. And whereas Hobbes thought government needed to be a Leviathan, a benevolent dictator to whom the citizens would yield all their power, Locke promoted a limited government.

WHY GOVERNMENTS?

As the social contract philosophers have pointed out, there are many reasons why human beings create governments and prefer to live under such a social order. Later social theorists and politicians have come to add many items to their catalog of useful functions that governments serve. We shall discuss some of these, beginning with activities that help generate a stable community in the first place and proceeding to those that help this community prosper.

Community- and Nation-Building

One of the first purposes that governments can serve is to help create and maintain a stable and peaceful community. While humans may be social beings, it is not always easy to build a community in which large numbers of individuals can communicate, feel at home, and engage in constructive interaction such as settled family life or trade. It is a particular challenge to foster such a common identity among large numbers of people living in an extended area without regular interaction with one another. We commonly call such large-scale communities based on a common perceived identity nations. Governments can help generate such communities in many different ways, for example by teaching a common language, instilling common norms and values, creating common myths and symbols, supporting a national identity, and so forth. Nation-building activities help instill common world views, values, and expectations. Using a concept discussed at greater length in Chapter 3, we can say that such government activities can help homogenize the **political cultures** of their citizens. And the more homogeneous the political culture, the easier it is to live in peaceful coexistence and engage in activities for mutual gain, such as commerce.

Security and Order

Thomas Hobbes believed that governments, and only strong governments, could make society safe for its inhabitants. Providing security, law, and order are indeed among the most essential tasks that governments are called upon to perform. We often distinguish between external and internal security, both of which were important concerns to Hobbes. External security means protection against attacks from other political systems. National defense forces, such as armies, navies, and air forces, are typically created to perform this function. Internal security means protection against theft, aggression, and violence from members of one's own society. In most societies this is the function of the police. The provision of security and order still plays a critical role in modern states, most of which employ military as well as police forces. The German social scientist Max Weber saw a monopoly on the use of force as the defining property of the modern state. Consider this issue for a moment. While governments across the world have privatized many of the services they used to perform—for example, post offices, railroads, telecommunications, health care, and pensions—it is hard to think of governments that have privatized their police or defense forces (though some U.S. states have privatized prisons).

Protecting Property and Other Rights

John Locke saw the establishment and protection of economic and political rights as the most essential purpose of government. Though Locke's greatest concern may have been with economic property rights, there are many other social and political rights that governments, and perhaps only governments, can provide. Among them are freedoms of speech and association and protection against various forms of discrimination and harassment. Nonetheless, Locke considered property rights to be particularly critical to the sustained development of nations and other communities. Without effective protection of property rights, people will not invest much of their goods or energies in productive processes. Also, unless property rights exist and credible contracts can be negotiated and enforced, people will not trust their neighbors enough to engage in much trade and commerce. Therefore, anything beyond the mere subsistence economy requires effective property rights and contracts. Effective property rights must clearly allocate ownership and use and protect against trespass and violations. Such rights must also make the buying and selling ("alienation") of property relatively inexpensive and painless. Finally, citizens must have faith that their property rights will persist and be defended (long-term credibility). The more effective the property rights, the more people will trade, invest, and enter into other long-term agreements that generate sustained economic growth.

Promoting Economic Efficiency and Growth

Governments can thus help promote economic development by establishing and enforcing effective property rights and by facilitating trade. Particularly in the twentieth century, however, economists have come to see many other ways in which government can promote economic development. These are related to market failures in capitalist economies. Neoclassical economics shows that market economies are efficient when property rights are defined and protected, competition rigorous, and information freely available. When one or several of these conditions do not hold, however, market failures may result, and supply may not efficiently meet demand.

Public goods are particularly susceptible to market failure. Public goods have two defining characteristics. One is that if they are provided to one consumer, they cannot be withheld from anyone else. The second is that one person's enjoyment or consumption of the good does not detract from anyone else's. Consider clean air or national defense. It is, for most practical purposes, impossible to provide one person with clean air or defense without also giving it to his or her neighbors. Moreover, my enjoyment of clean air or national security does not mean that my neighbors have any less of it. It is often argued that for these reasons, in a market economy people will not pay for public goods which will therefore be undersupplied. If anyone can benefit from such goods as public parks and lighthouses, why should I (or anyone else) voluntarily pay for them? Only government, it is argued, can by taxing its citizens step in and provide such public goods as parks, roads, lighthouses, national defense, and environmental protection.

A second and related type of market failure is **externalities**, which occur when some economic activity produces costs that are not borne or taken into account by any of the parties. Though externalities need not be bad, some certainly are. Many forms of environmental degradation occur when neither those who produce the goods nor those who consume them bear all the production costs. Polluting factories, waste dumps, prisons, pornographic shops, or major highways can impose large uncompensated costs on those who live near them, and recent years have witnessed a major rise in protest activity among so-called NIMBY ("not-in-my-back-yard") groups. Governments can help protect against the imposition of obnoxious externalities or ensure that burdens are fairly shared.

So-called natural monopolies represent yet another role governments can play in promoting economic growth and efficiency. There are some goods, it is commonly held, for which efficiency dictates that there should be only one supplier. This typically occurs because there are very large start-up costs or because of the prohibitive costs of coordination between different suppliers. The government may then step in and become the monopolist, or it may tightly control a private or semipublic monopolist. In the nineteenth century, for example, many countries created railroad monopolies, which were frequently run by the government. Similarly, telecommunications have commonly been a government monopoly, as have mail services and in many countries strategic defense industries.

Social Justice

Governments can play a role not only in promoting economic growth but also in dividing the fruits of such growth equitably. Many people argue that governments are needed to promote social justice by redistributing wealth and other resources between citizens. In many countries the distribution of income is highly uneven. Land and other wealth are typically even more unequally distributed than income. Moreover, in many societies income and wealth inequalities have been getting worse over time. Brazil, for example, has one of the most severe income inequalities in the world, an inequality that grew in every decade from the 1930s to the 1990s.

Under such circumstances, social justice may dictate a "new deal," especially if existing inequalities deprive many individuals of education, adequate health care, and other basic needs. Government intervention may be needed to redistribute resources from the better-off to the poor. Some theorists of distributive justice argue that such transfers should attempt to equalize the conditions of all citizens. Others would instead prefer governments to redistribute enough to "create a level playing field" and thus equalize opportunities but then let individuals be responsible for their own fortunes. Either way, citizens in many societies would agree that there should be efforts to make the distribution of wealth and income more even. Though many private individuals, organizations, and foundations participate in voluntary efforts to help the poor, they generally do not have the capacity or authority to effect large-scale redistribution. Governments can, at least under some circumstances. Many tax and welfare policies are indeed designed to do just that, though how successful they are, or how far such redistribution should go, is often hotly disputed. But even many individuals who do not think that governments have a general responsibility to redistribute wealth would agree that they should at least provide certain minimum standards of living, a social safety net, for all citizens.

B O X 1 . 1   Tage Erlander and the "People's Home"

In much of Europe, social democratic parties have been a main force behind the expansion of government that has taken place in the twentieth century, and particularly from the Great Depression of the 1930s to the 1970s. The Swedish Social Democratic Party, for example, ruled virtually without interruption from 1932 to 1976. For most of that time Tage Erlander was the party leader and Sweden's prime minister (1946–1969). Under his leadership, Sweden developed one of the most extensive welfare states in the world and virtually eradicated most forms of poverty, though at the cost of the highest tax rates in the Western world.

Tage Erlander referred to the Swedish welfare state as the "people's home" and a "strong society," by which he meant a powerful government guided by a sense of solidarity and community spirit. In a 1954 parliamentary speech, Erlander presented this argument:

> It is a mistake to think that the freedom of human beings, whether in the economic area or the political one, will diminish if they agree to join forces to do such things as they cannot manage by themselves. What is . . . the main part of our political activity other than attempts to organize such cooperation? We want health insurance, but nobody can manage that on his own. We must therefore create the opportunity for a collective solution. The same is true with respect to our wish to provide social security, to improve our roads, schools, defense, etc. All our political activities are filled with our striving to secure community cooperation to solve such tasks, which we can accomplish together, but which we cannot solve by ourselves. For us social democrats, it has been important to try to create a society in which the citizens consider the government's activities as an expression of their own efforts.

Source: Riksdagens Protokoll, January 20, 1954, p.169. Translation by the editors.

Protecting the Weak

We commonly rely on the government to protect individuals and groups, such as future generations, that are not able to speak for themselves. Such groups obviously cannot act to protect their own interests. Governments, however, can protect the interests of the unborn and prevent them from getting saddled with economic debts or environmental degradation. And in recent decades, governments have become much more involved in protecting groups that for various reasons are politically weak or unenfranchised, such as children, the old, and the infirm or disabled, as well as nonhuman parts of the creation—from whales and birds to trees and other parts of our natural environment.

WHEN DOES GOVERNMENT BECOME THE PROBLEM?

Although there are many reasons that governments may be called upon to intervene in and regulate human affairs, such intervention is not always welcomed by all. Whether and when government intervention is necessary and desirable has been one of the greatest issues in twentieth-century politics. Over the course of this century, the role of governments has expanded enormously. At the same time, criticisms of many government policies have persisted and in some cases intensified. Such skepticism has been directed at virtually all government activities. Yet, the critics of governments have been particularly insistent and influential when they have criticized the economic roles that many governments have taken on.

Critics of Government: Anarchists and Libertarians

Critics of government intervention come in many camps and political shades, but two groups are especially outspoken: anarchists and libertarians. Both groups believe that governments do many things that are unnecessary or even harmful. Both see excessive government intervention and regulation as a serious threat to basic human values. They differ, however, in the threats they see as most serious, as well as in their favored alternatives to government intervention. **Libertarians** are *individualists* who see society as composed of individual human beings with fundamental rights that must be protected. Among these are property rights and the freedoms of speech and association. The main problem with government, libertarians argue, is that the more tasks it takes on, the more prone it is to violate such basic rights. While **anarchists** agree that governments impose undesirable effects, they see the ills of governments somewhat differently. Anarchists are *communitarians*. They see societies not as collections of individuals but as naturally close-knit and egalitarian communities. Governments and power corrupt such communities and lead to oppression and alienation. Anarchists see the alternative to government in voluntary cooperation and natural communities. Libertarians, on the other hand, promote a society of unfettered individuals, free to make their own choices and to seek out the groups to which they want to belong. Their differences aside, both libertarians and anarchists find much to criticize in the activities of contemporary governments. Many of these concerns are shared by individuals that are neither anarchists nor libertarians.

Destruction of Community

Whereas some see governments as a way to build community, anarchists argue with Rousseau that governments destroy natural communities. Government, they hold, implies power and inequality between human beings. And power corrupts. In Lord Acton's famous words, "power corrupts, and absolute power corrupts absolutely." While those who have power are corrupted, those without it are degraded and alienated. According to Rousseau, only human beings unfettered by government can form bonds that allow them to develop their full human potential. By imposing an order based on coercion, hierarchy, and the threat of force, governments therefore destroy natural communities. The stronger government becomes, the more it creates inequalities of power that have such pernicious consequences. In more contemporary terms, some would argue that governments create a "client society," in which people learn to be subservient to authorities and to rely

---

B O X 1 . 2 The Anarchist Kropotkin

Prince Petr Alekseevich Kropotkin (1842–1921), a Russian geographer and philosophical anarchist, believed that cooperation rather than competition is the norm in both animal and human life. In such a society based on cooperative norms, government would be replaced by voluntary groups. The economy would be based on need, which would leave citizens much time for leisure and creative activity. Kropotkin was imprisoned under the czars for preaching this philosophy and spent much of his later life in exile in England. His ideas are developed in a book entitled *Mutual Aid*, which was published in 1902.

> The State was established for the precise purpose of imposing the rule of landowners, the employers of industry, the warrior class, and the clergy upon the peasants on the land and the artisans in the city. And the rich perfectly well know that if the machinery of the State ceased to protect them, their power over the laboring classes would be gone immediately. Socialism, we have said—whatever form it may take in its evolution toward communism—must find *its own form* of political organization. . . . This is why socialism *cannot* utilize representative government as a weapon for liberating labor. . . . A new form of political organization has to be worked out the moment that socialist principles shall enter into our life. And it is self-evident that this new form will have to be *more popular, more decentralized, and nearer to the folkmote self-government* than representative government can ever be.

Source: Petr Alekseevich Kropotkin, "Modern Science and Anarchism," in Emile Capouya and Keitha Tompkins, eds., *The Essential Kropotkin* (New York: Liveright, 1975, pp. 85–86). Emphases in the original.

---

on governments to meet their needs, and in which governments patronize and pacify their citizens.

Violations of Basic Rights

At the same time that power allows governments to destroy communities, it also enables them to infringe on the rights of citizens. This is the main concern of many libertarians. Just as governments can help establish and defend many essential rights, they can also use their powers to violate these rights in the most serious manner. The twentieth century has witnessed enormous progress in the extension of political, economic, and social rights in societies all around the world. At the same time, however, basic human rights have probably never before been violated on such a gross scale. The loss of millions of lives to political persecution is only the most serious manifestation of these violations. Such horrors have happened not only in Nazi extermination camps and during Stalin's Great Terror in the Soviet Union, but also on a huge scale in China and Cambodia, and on a smaller scale in such countries as Iraq, Argentina, Guatemala,

B O X   1 . 3   The Libertarian Barry Goldwater

Some might call Barry Goldwater (1909–1998) a libertarian. A businessman and an Air Force officer, he won a seat in the U.S. Senate for Arizona (1953–1965, 1969–1987) and ran for the presidency on the Republican ticket in 1964. In his nomination acceptance address he insisted, "extremism in the defense of liberty is no vice . . . and moderation in the pursuit of justice is no virtue." He is viewed as the founder of modern Republican conservatism, though his libertarian beliefs often put him at odds with other members of his party.

> For the American Conservative, there is no difficulty in identifying the day's overriding political challenge: it is *to preserve and extend freedom.* . . . Throughout history, government has proved to be the chief instrument for thwarting man's liberty. . . . The *legitimate* functions of government are actually conducive to freedom. Maintaining internal order, keeping foreign foes at bay, administering justice, removing obstacles to the free interchange of goods—the exercise of these powers makes it possible for men to follow their chosen pursuits with maximum freedom. But note that the very instruments by which these desirable ends are achieved *can* be the instrument for achieving undesirable ends—that government can, instead of extending freedom, restrict freedom. And note, secondly, that the "can" quickly becomes "will" the moment the holders of government power are left to their own devices.

Source: Barry M. Goldwater, *The Conscience of a Conservative*, Shepherdsville, KY: Victor Publishing, 1960, pp. 14–17. Emphases in the original.

Haiti, and Rwanda. These extreme abuses of government power illustrate a dilemma that troubled James Madison and other founding fathers of the American Revolution: the problem of creating a government strong enough to govern effectively but not so strong that it could destroy the rights of those whom it was designed to serve.

Economic Inefficiency

Many of the most important criticisms of modern governments have come from economists. And the objections that arise out of economic scholarship and research have convinced the citizens of many countries to restrict the role of governments in the economy. Economic problems might arise even if government officials do not actively abuse their power. Critics of government regulation of the economy point out that it may distort the terms of trade and lower people's incentives to produce, thus hurting overall economic performance. When governments not only regulate the economy, but also act as producers in their own right, they may generate further inefficiencies. This is particularly likely if the government is a monopoly producer of an important good, since monopolies generally cause goods to be undersupplied and overpriced. Moreover, government industries may be especially prone to inefficiency and complacency because management and workers often have far better job protection than those in the private sector. Therefore, they may not have to worry about losing their jobs or benefits even if their enterprises perform poorly.

Government for Private Gain

What happens if public officials are neither benevolent nor tyrannical, but simply self-interested? This is a question that economists and other social scientists increasingly raise. If politicians are rational and self-interested, they may be inclined to make decisions from which they would personally profit, regardless of whether this would be the best choice for society as a whole. Such self-interested political pursuit of private gain has become known as **rent seeking**. *Rents* are benefits created through government intervention in the economy—for example, tax revenue or profits created because the government has restricted competition. Rent seeking refers to efforts that individuals, groups, firms, or organizations exert in order to reap such benefits. While the terminology may sound unfamiliar, the idea behind it is really quite simple. Rent seeking occurs when people seek to use governments for their private gain.

B O X 1 . 4   Rent Seeking and the Case of Mobutu Sese Seko

The problem of rent seeking has been the particular concern of economists and political scientists in the public choice tradition, founded in the 1960s by James Buchanan and Gordon Tullock. Until that time, economists had generally assumed that governments intervene only when markets fail. They further assumed that once the government intervenes, it will do so to benefit the economy as a whole. Public choice scholars ask instead, "what if government officials acted in the same ways that economics assumes that other producers and consumers behave?" That is to say, what happens if politicians use their power in their own self-interest, or to benefit individuals or groups that support them? Public choice analysts tend to see the competition of political parties and interest groups over government policy as driven by a pursuit of rents (private benefits generated through government intervention). Once in power, they argue, politicians and organizations seek to benefit themselves and their followers at the expense of their competitors.

President Mobutu Sese Seko (1930–1997) of Zaire offers a tragic example of the costs that rent-seeking politicians can impose on their societies. After seizing power in a 1965 coup, Mobutu ruled the large African state of Congo (which he renamed Zaire) for more than 30 years. Mobutu banned opposition parties and ruled his country as a dictator until he was finally deposed by rebel forces in 1997. During his long rule, President Mobutu used government funds, including aid from Western states such as the United States, to amass a huge personal fortune which he invested abroad. In addition to large sums of money, he is reported to have owned about 30 luxury residences abroad, including a number of palatial estates on the French Riviera. Meanwhile, living standards in Zaire, a poor country with large natural resources, plummeted, and the country was racked with epidemic disease and civil war. Mobutu died of natural causes shortly after his ouster.

Rent seeking is at best a game in which one person's gain is another person's loss. At worst, however, rent seeking can impose large net costs on society, because each party or group is willing to expend large resources in order to control the spoils of government. It may turn into outright corruption, in which influence is traded for money or other advantage. We discuss the problem of corruption at greater length in Chapter 6. Rent seeking may be a particularly serious problem in poor societies, where politics is often the surest or most effective way to get rich, and where the courts and mass media may be too weak to constrain government officials from abusing their power. Besides, many developing societies do not have strong norms against using government for private gain. On the contrary, people often expect those in government to use their power to benefit themselves, their families, kin, and neighbors. Remember also that even in many advanced democratic societies—for example, in Britain—the line between the private property of the monarch and that of the government was not clearly drawn even in the recent past.

Vested Interests and Inertia

The fact that governments create rents also means that they are difficult to change or abolish once established. We speak of individuals, groups, or firms that benefit from specific government jobs, contracts, or policies as having *vested interests* in the existing government. The larger the government and the more attractive the benefits it provides, the more likely it is that those who have such vested interests will resist change (unless change means making their benefits even larger). Therefore, any government will foster a class of people with a vested interest in maintaining or enlarging government benefits. Such groups may become a powerful force against change and in favor of the status quo. This makes it difficult to change government policies or make them more efficient. Instead, once established, agencies and policies tend to live on far beyond their usefulness. When, for example, the Spanish Armada in 1588 threatened to invade, the English government posted a military observation post at Land's End in southwest England. This observation post remained in place in the late twentieth century, long after the Spanish navy had ceased to be a threat. In the United States, many federal programs created during the New Deal of the 1930s remained in place toward the end of the millennium, even though the need for them might have changed dramatically. One example is the Rural Electrification Administration, which was created in 1935 and persisted for almost 60 years, until it was finally merged into the Rural Utilities Service in 1994. Similarly, the U.S. Senate maintained and staffed a Committee on Revolutionary War Claims until well into the twentieth century.

Vested interests are particularly likely to prevail in political systems that contain a lot of safeguards against rapid political change. While the checks and balances in such political systems as the United States are designed to safeguard the rights of individuals, groups, and local communities, they may also end up protecting the privileges of vested interests. Yet, even political systems that contain far fewer such checks may be slow to change. Britain is an excellent example. Until the

Blair government came to power in 1997, for example, the majority of the members of the House of Lords (noblemen, bishops, and judges) represented the social groups (the "estates") that dominated British society before the Industrial Revolution more than 200 years ago.

Alternatives to Government: Markets and Voluntary Coordination

To the extent that governments cannot always be trusted to solve social problems, what can take their place? Here, the answers vary substantially between different camps of government critics. Anarchists and communitarians suggest that many central government functions can instead be performed either through much more local and decentralized governments, or through voluntary cooperation without formal political authority. Radical anarchists reject all forms of private property as well as all formal authority. To the extent that governments have to exist, anarchists argue, they should be as close to the people as possible. That is to say that office holders should have limited terms and few privileges, that decision making should be as transparent as possible, and that ordinary citizens should be given the opportunity to participate extensively in political decision making. Of course, many people who are not anarchists may support such causes. For example, "Green" (environmentalist) political parties, particularly in European countries such as Germany, seek to promote political reforms of these kinds.

While libertarians and market-oriented economists (such as the so-called "Chicago school") support some of these causes (for example, government decentralization), they tend to focus on a different set of reforms. Most libertarians accept the role of governments in protecting security, individual rights, and commerce. Yet, they are sharply critical of government economic regulation and production. A few libertarians go further in their critique of governments and advocate draft resistance, tax resistance, and legalization of all drugs. Building on strands in modern economics, including the influential work of Ronald H. Coase, libertarians argue that much of what appears to be market failure can be solved without government intervention, by strengthening ownership. Their preferred alternative is to rely on free markets and individual property rights.

The debate between the proponents and critics of strong governments continues and is likely to be a key political controversy for a long time. In the past 20 years or so, there has been a clear trend away from extensive government regulation of many economic sectors. Yet, the overall size of governments in advanced industrial countries has not changed very much. Measured as a proportion of the total economy (for example, gross domestic product), the government's share has declined in some countries (e.g., Britain and New Zealand), increased in others (e.g., Japan), and stayed fairly constant in yet others (e.g., the United States). In the former Communist countries and in some developing countries, however, the government's size has shrunk much more dramatically. Since the 1970s especially, there has been a movement in many societies to privatize many economic sectors and to deregulate others, such as telecommunications, transportation (e.g., the airline industry), and banking, which many governments had previously strictly regulated. But whereas government regulation has become less extensive in some areas, it has grown in others—for example, in passing laws protecting the environment or the rights of children.

POLITICAL SYSTEMS

Politics takes place within and between political systems. Since the term **political system** is the main organizing concept of this book, we shall elaborate its meaning below. Any system must necessarily have two properties: (1) a set of interdependent parts, and (2) boundaries towards the outside environment. There are many kinds of systems: mechanical systems such as automobiles, ecological systems (ecosystems) such as the plants and animals coexisting in a single habitat, and social systems such as a family. All have interdependent parts and boundaries. Political systems are a particular type of social system—namely, one involved in the making of authoritative public decisions. To put it slightly differently, the political system is a set of institutions, such as parliaments, bureaucracies, and courts, that formulate and implement the collective goals of a society or of groups within it.

Governments typically require obedience from their citizens, and their authoritative decisions can normally be backed up by coercion (force) if necessary. Yet, most governments much prefer that citizens comply because of legitimacy than due to the threat of force. By legitimacy we mean that those who are ruled believe that the rulers have a "right" (whether by law or by custom) to implement their decisions. The legitimacy of a political system may vary over time. The legitimacy of the U.S. political system was high just after World War II; it declined substantially during and after the Vietnam War but has since then recovered at least somewhat. In Germany, on the other hand, the new democratic system had little support just after World War II but has gradually gained in legitimacy since then. Low legitimacy may result in breakdowns in political organization and public policy failures. Policy failures in turn can cause declining legitimacy. The Soviet system collapsed in 1991 after its legitimacy had been undermined by a failed and costly war in Afghanistan, a nuclear power disaster in Chernobyl, corruption, and declining economic productivity. We discuss legitimacy at greater length in Chapter 3.

Political systems feature governments at their core, but they also encompass important parts of the environment in which governments operate. There is more to politics than authoritative and coercive activities—for example, political organizations such as political parties or interest groups. Such organizations do not have coercive authority, unless they control the government. Likewise, the mass media only indirectly affect elections, legislation, and law enforcement. Then there is a whole host of institutions beginning with the family and including communities, churches, schools, universities, corporations, foundations, and think-tanks, which influence political attitudes and public policy. The term *political system* refers to this whole collection of related, interacting institutions and agencies.

Political systems mold and are molded by a domestic and an international environment. The system receives inputs from these environments and shapes them through its outputs. The boundaries of political systems are defined in terms of persons, territory, and property. Most human beings belong to, and have citizenship rights in, only one country. Similarly, territory is divided between states in ways that are meant to be mutually exclusive. A given piece of land is supposed to belong to one and only one country. Much the same is true with respect to other property rights. Of course, disputes over citizenship, territory, and property are by no means uncommon and have indeed been among the most frequent causes of international conflict all through history.

Comparative politics is the study of political systems, not as isolated cases but through generalizations and comparisons. Chapter 2 discusses how and why we make such comparisons. There are many kinds of political systems, such as cities, states, international organizations, klans, or even influential families. In principle, comparative politics could compare any or all of these types of political systems. In practice, however, although there are important literatures comparing political institutions such as political parties, interest groups, and legislatures, comparative politics focuses on comparisons of *states*, or what we commonly refer to as countries. We shall therefore discuss states and their role in the contemporary world next.

STATES

The twelve political systems that we compare in this book are all *states*. A **state** is a political system that has **sovereignty**—independent legal authority over a population in a particular territory, based on the recognized right to self-determination. Sovereignty rests with those who have the ultimate right to make political decisions. We distinguish between internal and external sovereignty. *Internal sovereignty* means the right, without external intervention, to determine matters having to do with one's own citizens. *External sovereignty* means the right to conclude binding agreements (treaties) with other states. For example, the British government has internal sovereignty in the sense that it can impose whatever taxes it wants on British citizens. Similarly, its external sovereignty means that it can enter into treaties with other states. The city of Edinburgh does not have these rights. Nor does the county of Kent or the principality of Wales. All of them are dependent on the central British government in tax matters and foreign policy. Yet, sovereignty is never absolute, and every state in the real world faces constraints on its internal and external sovereignty. With the increasing integration of the United Kingdom (Britain) into the European Union (EU), the British government has in fact had to give up parts of its sovereignty to the EU, and this loss of sovereignty has been a major topic of political debate.

In the United States we confuse things a bit by calling the 50 constituent units "states," even though they enjoy much less sovereignty than Britain. The states of the United States share the power and authority of the "state" with the central government in Washington, DC. However confusing this usage is today, it does reflect what American government was once like, under the Articles of Confederation. Since then, however, much authority has been shifted from the states to the central (federal) government.

We often think of the world as a patchwork quilt of states with sizable and contiguous territories and a common national identity. We call such cases, in which national identification and the scope of legal authority largely coincide, **nation-states**. In the twentieth century, we have come to think of nation-states as the natural way to organize states, and often as an ideal. The national right to self-determination, the idea that every nation had a right to form its own state if it so wished, was enshrined in the Treaty of Versailles signed at the end of World War I.

But even though this may seem the natural way to organize world politics, it has not always been so. Until about 500 years ago, Europe was comprised of many very small states and a few very large ones, whose territorial possessions were not always very stable or contiguous. Nor did states always consist of people with the same national identity. Most probably knew next to nothing about the political system to which they belonged. Gradually, a set of European nation-states evolved, and the 1648 Treaty of Westphalia established that principle for the political organization of Europe. The eighteenth and nineteenth centuries were the main era during which the concentration of power in the nation-state occurred. Since then, Europe has transformed itself into something approximating a set of nation-states, each of which contains a people with a common identity. This did not happen accidentally—the governments of the emerging nation-states consciously strove to instill a sense of community, a common national identity, among the peoples they controlled. They did so, often heavy-handedly and with massive doses of coercion, by promoting a common language, a common educational system, and often a common religion. While we may in retrospect find many aspects of this *nation-building* process deplorable, it has produced a Europe in which the inhabitants of most states have a strong sense of community.

Many societies in the developing world today face similar challenges. Especially in Africa, the former colonial powers (particularly Britain and France) left the newly independent states with very weak national identities. In many parts of Africa, large-scale national communities simply did not exist before colonization. Even where they did exist, they were rarely reflected in the boundaries that the colonial powers drew between their possessions. These boundaries were frequently drawn according to the strategic and military interests of the colonizers, who often knew and cared little about local identities among the populations they ruled. After independence, many new states have therefore been left with huge nation-building tasks.

There are additional challenges to contemporary states. After World War II, power began shifting from the state downward to local governments, and upward to supranational organizations. The European Union (EU) and the North American Free Trade Agreement (NAFTA) are examples of the latter development. Most of the countries of Western Europe have, after centuries of costly and destructive wars, gradually created a common market economy and in 1999 many of them adopted a common currency, the Euro. Originally consisting of six countries—France, Germany, Italy, Belgium, the Netherlands, and Luxembourg—the European Community has expanded to 15—adding Britain, Denmark, Ireland, Spain, Portugal, Greece, Austria, Finland, and Sweden. An additional 10 countries, mostly in Eastern and Central Europe, have been approved for membership within the next few years.

The **United Nations (UN)**, formed at the end of World War II in 1945, is the most important organization that encompasses almost all the world's states. With the accession of Switzerland and East Timor, the United Nations in 2002 reached a membership of 192 states. There is only a small number of countries (such as Taiwan and the Vatican) that are not members of the UN.[3] The United Nations has acquired new responsibilities in recent years, especially since the collapse of the Soviet Union in 1991. Most dramatically, UN forces have been deployed as peacekeepers in a large number of countries. Many of these are areas stricken by civil war and lawlessness. The UN has acquired increased authority over world security, constraining, supporting, and replacing the unilateral actions of individual states. But while the sovereignty of states may thus be slipping away, they are still the most important political systems around. That, of course, is the main reason that they are the subject of this, and most other, texts on comparative politics.

Old and New States

Just about the entire surface of the world today is covered by close to 200 independent states, and there are some secessionary movements that, if successful, would make our figures obsolete. When the United States declared its independence in 1776, most independent states were European (see Figure 1.1). Much of

F I G U R E   1 . 1   Formation of States Since 1776

Source: For contemporary members, Information Office, United Nations. Data to 1945 from Charles Taylor and Michael Hudson, *World Handbook of Political and Social Indicators* (New Haven, CT: Yale University Press, 1972), pp. 26 ff.

the rest of the world had been parceled out as colonies to some European empire. In the nineteenth and early twentieth centuries, the number of states increased, principally in Latin America where the Spanish and Portuguese empires broke up into 20 independent states. In Europe, newly independent countries emerged in the Balkans, Scandinavia, and the Low Countries. Between the two world wars, national proliferation extended to North Africa and the Middle East; and Europe continued to fragment as Poland, Finland, Czechoslovakia, and Yugoslavia gained their independence from the Russian and Austro-Hungarian empires. At the same time, the three Baltic countries—Lithuania, Latvia, and Estonia—briefly experienced independence but were again swallowed by the Soviet Union from 1939 until its collapse in 1991. Since World War II, the development of new states has really taken off. By 2002, 126 new countries had joined the 68 states that existed in 1945. The largest group of new states is in Sub-Saharan Africa. The 1990s alone witnessed more than 20 new countries—mostly the successor states of the Soviet Union, Yugoslavia, and Czechoslovakia.

First, Second, and Third World, North and South

From the 1950s on, it became customary to divide the states of the world into three categories: the first, second, and third world. The first world consisted of the advanced capitalist democracies; the second world encompassed the communist bloc of countries, at that time led by the Soviet Union; the third world made up the remaining states of the world, those that were neither rich and Western nor communist. Indeed, most of the world's states and population fell into this third category. With the collapse of most communist states and the increasing differences between developing societies, these categories are no longer as useful as they once were. Today, it is common to refer to the developing states collectively as the South and the rich, capitalist democracies as the North. Not all southern states are poor (e.g., Australia), and not all northern states are rich or democratic (e.g., North Korea), but there is still a strong tendency for these characteristics to go together.

Big and Small States

Russia is the largest country in area, encompassing more than 17 million square kilometers. China has the most people, approximately 1.3 billion. There are many countries at the other extreme, but the smallest legally independent political entity in both respects is Vatican City, the headquarters of the Catholic Church, with less than half a square kilometer of turf and under a thousand residents. Table 1.1 reports the widely differing populations and areas of 12 countries we cover in detail in this book.[4] The political implications of these striking contrasts in population size and geographic area are not always obvious. Big countries are not always the most important and do not always prevail over the small ones. Cuba has challenged the United States for 40 years; Israel stands off the Arab world; and tiny Vatican City has great cultural power and influence.

Nor do area and population size determine a country's political system. Both Luxembourg and the United States are democracies. Authoritarian regimes can be found in small, medium, or large countries. These enormous contrasts in size show

T A B L E   1 . 1   Area and Population of Selected Countries

Country	Population (millions in 2000)	Average Annual Growth of Population, 1990–2000	Area 1995 (thousands of square km)
China	1,261	1.1	9,326
India	1,016	1.8	2,973
United States	282	1.2	9,159
Brazil	170	1.4	8,457
Russia	146	−0.2	16,889
Japan	127	0.3	377
Nigeria	127	2.8	911
Mexico	98	1.6	1,909
Germany	82	0.3	349
Egypt	64	2.0	995
Britain	60	0.4	242
France	59	0.4	550

Source: World Bank, *World Development Report: 2002.* (New York, Oxford University Press), 2002, tables 1 and 3, pp. 232–33, and previous editions.

only that the countries now making up the world differ greatly in their physical and human resources. Yet, area and population do affect economic development, foreign policy and defense problems, and many other issues of political significance. For example, with population growth rates double those of the industrialized countries, developing countries have to grow twice as fast economically just to avoid falling further behind.

A state's geographic location has important strategic implications. In the sixteenth through nineteenth centuries, a state located in the center of Europe could not avoid building a large land army to protect itself from its neighbors. It would have difficulty developing free political institutions, since it needed a strong government to extract resources on a large scale and keep its population under control. Britain has historically been protected by the English Channel and could defend itself through its navy. It could do with a smaller army, lower taxation, and less centralization of power. The United States was a similar case. The Atlantic Ocean and the relatively open continent critically shaped U.S. political institutions. Most peoples of Asia, Africa, and Latin America were dominated, and in most cases colonized, by the more powerful Western nations. Those that had the richest natural resources and the most benign climates tended to attract the largest numbers of settlers.

Whether they are old or new, large or small, most of the world's states face a number of common challenges. The first is building community. Most of the world's states do not have a homogeneous population, and instilling a sense of shared identity and interest can be a serious problem. So can creating a sense of allegiance to the government. The second is the ability to foster economic, social, and political development now and in the future, a challenge that confronts even the wealthiest states.

Finally, most states face significant challenges in securing and furthering democracy and civil liberties. These challenges should be familiar from our discussion of the purposes and dangers of governments. In the remainder of this chapter, we shall discuss these challenges successively.

BUILDING COMMUNITY

One of the most important challenges facing political systems all over the world is to build a common identity and a sense of community among the citizens. The absence of such a sense of common identity can have the most severe political consequences. Conflicts over national, ethnic, or religious identities are among the most explosive causes of political turmoil, as we have recently witnessed in Northern Ireland, the former Yugoslavia, Rwanda, Indonesia, the Middle East and elsewhere. But while building community is a pervasive challenge, some countries are in a much more favorable situation than others. Japan, for example, has relatively little to worry about. Its population is ethnically quite homogeneous and shares a language and a long political history. Large majorities of the Japanese share the faiths of Buddhism and Shintoism, and the country is separated by hundreds or thousands of miles of ocean from its most important neighbors. Nigeria, on the other hand, has an extremely diverse population of more than 100 million. The country itself is an accidental and artificial creation of British colonial rule and has no common precolonial history. The population is sharply divided between Muslims and Christians; the Christians are divided equally into Catholics and Protestants. There are some 250 different ethnic groups, speaking a variety of local languages, in addition to English. Obviously, the challenges of building community are much greater in Nigeria than they are in Japan. But although few countries face problems as complicated as those of the Nigerians, the community-building challenge is one of the most serious issues facing many states today.

States and Nations

The word *nation* is sometimes used to mean almost the same as a state, as in the name the United Nations. Strictly speaking, however, we wish to use the term **nation** to refer to a group of people with a common identity. When we speak of a "nation," we thus refer to the self-identification of a people. That common identity may be built upon a common language, history, race, or culture, or simply upon the fact that this group has occupied the same territory. Nations may or may not have their own state or independent government. In some cases, such as Japan, France, or Sweden, there is a close correspondence between the memberships of the state and the nation. Most people who identify themselves as Japanese do in fact live in the state of Japan, and most people who live in Japan identify themselves as Japanese. As mentioned above, we call such states nation-states.

But in the case of most states today or in the past, the correspondence between the nation and the state is not so neat. Nor is it obvious that it should be. In some cases, states are *multinational*—consisting of a multitude of different nations. The

Soviet Union, Yugoslavia, and Czechoslovakia were multinational states that have now broken apart. On the other hand, there are some nations that are much larger than the corresponding states, such as the Germans for most of their history, or the Chinese. Some nations have been divided into two or more states for political reasons, such as Koreans today and the Germans between 1949 and 1990. Some groups with claims to be nations have no state at all, such as the Kurds, the Basques, the Jews in the past, and the Palestinians today. When states and nations do not coincide, it can cause explosive political conflict. On the other hand, the presence of several nations within the same state can also be a source of cultural enrichment.

Nationality and Ethnicity

There is a fine line between nations and *ethnic groups*, which may also have common physical traits, languages, cultures, or history. But whereas we think of nationality as a form of primary identification, **ethnicity** may be of lesser importance to the group involved. Like nationality, ethnicity need not have any objective basis in genetics, culture, or history. In his classic introduction to sociological theory, the German sociologist Max Weber defined ethnic groups as "those human groups that entertain a subjective belief in their common descent because of similarities of physical type or of customs or both, or because of memories of colonization and migration. . . . [I]t does not matter whether or not an objective blood relationship exists."[5] Similarly, groups that are physically quite similar, but differ by language, religion, customs, marriage patterns, and historical memories (for example, the Serbs, Croats, and Muslim Bosnians) may believe themselves to be descended from different ancestors and hence insist on their separate identities. Over centuries, originally homogeneous populations may become substantially intermixed genetically with other populations, even though the culture may continue. This is true, for example, of the Jewish population of Israel, which has come together after more than two millennia of global dispersion.

Ethnic differences have been the source of a large number of political conflicts around the world. Even before the end of the Cold War, ethnic autonomy movements in parts of old countries—such as the United Kingdom (the Scots and Welsh) and Canada (the Quebecois)—sought to break free or achieve greater autonomy. And since the end of the Cold War, many states of the former Soviet bloc have been coming apart at their ethnic and religious seams. In the former Yugoslavia, secession by a number of provinces triggered several wars. The most brutal of these has taken place in Bosnia-Herzegovina, where a new Muslim regime faced rebellion and murderous "ethnic cleansing" by the large Serbian minority, backed by their fellow Serb majority in the remaining Yugoslavian state. Intervention by the UN, NATO, and the United States to contain Serbian aggression has led to an uneasy settlement, but considerable tension remains. Later the Serbs in Yugoslavia undertook to "cleanse" Albanians from the province of Kosovo, even though they were the ethnic majority there. After thousands of Albanians were killed and hundreds of thousands driven from their homes, NATO intervened with a bombing campaign, forcing the Serbs to withdraw their forces and permit the Kosovans to return.

In many developing countries, boundaries established by former colonial powers cut across ethnic lines. In 1947 the British withdrew from India and divided the subcontinent into a northern Muslim area—Pakistan—and a southern Hindu area—India. The immediate consequence was a terrible civil conflict and "ethno-religious" cleansing incidental to the exchange of populations. There still are almost 100 million Muslims in India. Similarly, 30 years ago the Ibo "tribe" of Nigeria fought an unsuccessful separatist war against the rest of Nigeria, resulting in the deaths of millions of people. The Tutsi and Hutu peoples of the small African state of Rwanda have been engaged in a civil war of extermination, with hundreds of thousands of people slaughtered, and millions fleeing the country in fear of their lives.

Vestiges of imperial conquest (by Russia, Britain, France, Spain, Portugal, or the Netherlands) are one source of contemporary division. The migration of labor, forced or voluntary, across state boundaries, is another. The North and South American descendants of Africans forcefully enslaved between the seventeenth and the nineteenth centuries remind us of the largest coercive labor migration in world history. Voluntary migration takes the form, for example, of the many Indians, Bangladeshi, Egyptians, and Palestinians seeking better lives in the oil sheikhdoms around the Persian Gulf; of Mexican and Caribbean migrant workers in the United States; and of Turkish and Algerian migrants in Germany, France, and other European countries. Some migration is politically motivated, triggered by civil war or repression. A recent book refers to the contemporary world as living through an "Age of Migration,"[6] comparable in scale to that of the late nineteenth and early twentieth centuries.

Table 1.2 provides examples of politically significant "ethnicity," broadly defined, in our twelve selected countries. Five sets of traits are included, beginning

T A B L E   1 . 2   Examples of Ethnicity: Its Bases and Their Salience*

	Physical Differences	Language	Norms Against Intermarriage	Religion	Negative Historical Memories
Brazil: Blacks	XX	O	XX	X	X
Britain: Scots	O	O	O	X	X
China: Tibetans	X	XX	XX	XX	XX
Egypt: Copts	O	O	XX	XX	X
France: Algerians	X	X	XX	XX	XX
Germany: Turks	X	XX	XX	XX	O
India: Muslims	O	X	XX	XX	XX
Japan: Buraku-min	O	O	XX	O	XX
Mexico: Mayan	X	X	XX	X	XX
Nigeria: Ibo	O	X	XX	XX	XX
Russia: Chechens	X	XX	XX	XX	XX
United States: Africans-Americans	XX	X	XX	O	XX

*Salience is estimated at the following levels: O = none or almost none; X = some; XX = much importance in affecting political differences.

with physical differences, then language, norms against intermarriage, religion, and negative historical memories. The table illustrates the importance of each distinction to ethnic identity and shows that ethnicity may or may not be based on objective differences. The most important bases of distinction lie in intermarriage, religion, and historical memories. Language differences are of great importance in three cases and of some importance in five; and finally, and perhaps surprisingly, physical differences are of great importance in only two cases.

Recent migration has made such previously homogeneous states as France, Japan, and Germany more multiethnic. Other countries such as the United States, Britain, and Canada have long been multiethnic and have become even more so. The political problems resulting from ethnic diversity range from demands for recognition, civil rights, and equality of treatment, through struggles for autonomy or national independence, to ethnocentric demands for ethnic cleansing.

Language

Language can be source of social division that may or may not be associated with ethnicity. There are approximately 5,000 different languages in use in the world today, and a much smaller number of language families. Most of these languages are spoken by relatively small tribal groups in North and South America, Asia, Africa, or Oceania. Only 200 languages have a million or more speakers, and only eight may be classified as world languages. English is the most truly international language. There are approximately 350 million people who speak English at home, and 1.8 billion who live in countries where it is an official language. Other international languages include Spanish (more than 300 million home speakers), Arabic (200 million), Russian (165 million), Portuguese (165 million), French (100 million), and German (100 million). The language with the largest number of speakers, though in several varieties, is Chinese (1.2 billion). The major languages with the greatest international spread are those of the former colonial powers— Great Britain, France, Spain, and Portugal.[7]

Linguistic divisions can create particularly thorny political problems. It has been said that "constitutions can be blind but not dumb." That is to say that while political systems can choose to ignore racial, ethnic, or religious differences among their citizens, they cannot avoid committing themselves to one or several languages. Linguistic conflicts typically show up in controversies over educational policies, or over language use in the government. Occasionally, language regulation is more intrusive, as in Quebec, where English-only street signs are prohibited and larger corporations are required to conduct their business in French.

Religious Beliefs and Fundamentalism

States vary in their religious characteristics. In some such as Israel, the Irish Republic, and Pakistan, a common faith can be a basis of national identity for a majority of the population. In other societies, such as Poland under communism, religious authorities can serve as rallying points for opponents of authoritarian regimes. In many Latin American countries clergy have spoken out as advocates of the poor

---

B O X   1 . 5   Osama Bin Laden, Al Qaeda, and the Taliban

Osama bin Laden was born in Riyadh, Saudi Arabia in 1957, the scion of a powerful and wealthy Saudi family. In his early twenties, he recruited a group of Arab volunteers to fight against the Soviet occupation of Afghanistan. Later, when Egypt, Algeria, and Yemen accused him of supporting subversive activities in their countries, the Saudi authorities deprived him of his passport. He ultimately fled to Afghanistan and to the protection of the Taliban. It was in this struggle in the 1980s and 1990s, and in opposition to the Saudi-American alliance and stationing of American air bases and troops in Saudi Arabia, that he developed his anti-American, radical Islamic ideology. He is believed to have been the master mind behind the World Trade Center bombing in February 1993, the Riyadh bombing of a Saudi-American training facility in November 1995, and the Dhahran, Al-Khobar bombing of U.S. Air Force housing in June 1998. Yet, the evidence for bin Laden's role in these bombings, as well as in the later bombings of American embassies in Kenya and Tanzania, is sketchy and indirect. He is assumed to have been in command of the operations resulting in the September 11, 2001 World Trade Center and Pentagon atrocities.

Al Qaeda, meaning "the base," refers to the organization that bin Laden employs in carrying out his program. It is described as a supple spider-net of tiny enclaves located in many different countries. It began as an organization to provide information to concerned family members about their sons who were in the Mujahideen. Later this organization was converted into a Jihad action organization. Until fall 2001, its central command apparatus was in Afghanistan, and under the protection of the Taliban.

The Taliban, (the students), are a radical Islamic militia primarily recruited from the refugees to Pakistan from Afghanistan during the Soviet occupation. In Pakistan these young men were educated in the religious schools (hence the "students"). In September 2001 they controlled two-thirds of Afghanistan and provided the cover for Al Qaeda, but they were then dislodged by U.S. and allied forces.

Source: (Emergency Response and Research Institute) from www.emergency.com. November, 2001.

---

and critics of government brutality. But religious beliefs can also be more directly woven into the fabric of government. Iran and Afghanistan are examples of theocratic regimes, in which religious authorities directly governed and religious law was (or still is) part of the country's legal code. Iran has been moderating its theocratic regime, while the Taliban, a radical Muslim movement that had taken over Afghanistan and was serving as a base for the terrorist organization Al Qaeda, was ousted from power by a U.S.-led alliance of forces in late 2001. (See Box 1.5.)

Christianity is the largest and most widely spread religion, with about 2 billion believers worldwide, whereas the Muslims, the next most numerous group, muster a little more than half that number (see Table 1.3). There are about 800 million Hindus. The Christians are in turn divided into three major groups—Roman Catholics, Protestants (of many denominations), and Orthodox (e.g., Greek and Russian). The Catholics are dominant in Europe and Latin America; there is a more

T A B L E 1 . 3 Adherents of All Religions by Six Continental Areas (mid-1999, in millions)*

Religion	Africa	Asia	Europe	Latin America	North America	Oceania	Total	Percentage
Christian	351.3	306.4	559.2	473.7	258.8	24.8	1974.2	33.0
Muslims	310.5	807.0	31.2	1.6	4.4	.3	1155.1	19.3
Nonreligious and Atheists	5.3	724.5	130.6	18.5	29.8	3.7	912.3	15.3
Hindus	2.3	792.9	1.4	.8	1.3	.3	799.0	13.4
Buddhists	.1	351.0	1.5	.6	2.6	.3	356.3	6.0
Folk and Ethnic	94.6	507.6	1.6	1.5	1.2	.4	607.0	10.2
Sikhs	.1	22.0	.2	0	.5	.0	22.8	.4
Jews	.2	4.3	2.5	1.1	6.0	.1	14.3	.2
Other	2.5	118.6	.7	13.5	2.6	.8	137.4	2.2
Total	766.6	3634.3	728.9	511.3	307.2	30.0	5978.4	100

*Adherents as defined in *World Christian Encyclopedia* (1982).

equal distribution of Catholics and Protestants elsewhere. While the traditional Protestant denominations have been on the decline in North America, Pentecostalism and Evangelical Protestantism have been on the rise. The Muslims are the most rapidly growing religion, primarily concentrated in Asia and Africa, though they are present in substantial numbers as well in Europe and North America, and becoming revitalized in the Asian successor states of the Soviet Union. Muslims have been particularly successful in missionary activities in Sub-Saharan Africa.

Religious beliefs can be a powerful motivation for political involvement in causes ranging from the abolition of slavery, through efforts to bring about world peace, to the banning of secular textbooks in schools. Such beliefs can be a source of intense antagonism since they often form deep personal convictions on which it is difficult or impossible to compromise. Religious groups are often embattled over such issues as education, marriage, divorce, childrearing, freedom of speech and press, sexual morality, abortion and euthanasia, the emancipation of women, and the regulation of religious observances such as the Sabbath. Religious communities commonly take a special interest in education in order to transmit their ideas of nature and humankind. On such issues and others religious groups may clash with one another as well as with more secular groups. Although religious groups can coexist peacefully, indeed are often the source of exemplary acts of pacifism, compassion and reconciliation, they may also be the source of acts of violence, cruelty, and terrorism.[8]

Even societies in which most people ostensibly belong to the same community of faith may be riven by conflicts between "fundamentalists" and those who are either more mainstream or secular in their beliefs. **Religious fundamentalism** is a relatively recent development, world wide, but has emerged in some form in all major faiths as they reassert themselves against expressions of modernity. Fundamentalism got its name in the decades before World War I when some Protestant clergymen in the United States banded together to defend the "fundamentals" of religious belief against the secularizing inroads of science, and against biblical scholarship which questioned the divine inspiration and authorship of the Bible. The "fundamentalists" affirmed the inerrancy (the absolute truth) of the Bible and formed enclaves to protect themselves from error and sin. Fundamentalists have frequently been technologically adaptive, even while militantly rejecting some elements of modernity.[9]

Christianity, Judaism, and Islam are all "religions of the book," although not exactly the same book. The Jews believe only in the Old Testament; the Christians add the New Testament; and the Muslims add the Koran to these two. While each religion has experienced serious disagreement over the interpretation of these texts, Christian, Muslim, and Jewish fundamentalists all believe in the inerrancy of their respective sacred books and criticize their own "mainstream" clergy for lukewarm defense of the truth of these sacred texts. There are also Hindu and Buddhist Fundamentalists. The rise of fundamentalism has affected the entire world.

Some extremist wings of fundamentalist movements have employed violence in many forms: from threats and property destruction to assassination and destructive suicide, as among Palestinian protesters in Israel. In most countries with substantial Muslim populations, fundamentalist Islamic movements have appeared, frequently employing violence and terrorism in their efforts to gain power. The September 11, 2001, attack on the World Trade Center and the Pentagon was an act of mega-terrorism, involving not only suicide pilot-hijackers, but aircraft filled with volatile fuel and innocent passengers, converted into immense projectiles. This act of mega-terrorism required three elements—leadership, organization, and cover. Osama bin Laden provided the first; Al Qaeda provided the second; and the Taliban along with other governments and institutions, the third (See Box 1.5). The massive bombings of tourist spots in Bali in October 2002 appear to have been similarly motivated. The terrorism of these acts lies in their enormity. They stagger the imagination and are intended to lame the will.

Cumulative and Cross-Cutting Cleavages

National, ethnic, linguistic, and religious divisions can interact in a variety of ways. When they systematically affect political allegiances and policies, we refer to such divisions as **political cleavages**. When a political system is affected by more than one such cleavage, it matters whether the different cleavages are *cumulative* or *cross-cutting*. If cleavages are cumulative, it means that they pit the same people against each other on many different issues. If, on the other hand, cleavages crosscut, it means that groups that share a common interest on one issue are likely to be on opposite sides of a different issue. Consider the cases of Northern Ireland and the Netherlands. Both countries have traditionally had class divisions, and both are divided between Catholics and Protestants. The interaction between these cleavages is different, though. In Northern Ireland, class and religion are cumulative cleavages. If you are Catholic, you are also more likely to be poor, and you may have suffered a history of discrimination. In the Netherlands, on the other hand, class and religion tend to cross-cut. Catholics and Protestants are about equally likely to be poor or rich, and discrimination against Catholics is a thing of the past. Where the cleavage lines within a country are cumulative, and especially where they coincide with economic inequalities, they often fuel violence and intractable political struggles (as, for example, in Lebanon). Political conflicts and divisions based on language, ethnicity, and religion once were thought to have been subordinated or even eliminated by "modern" differences between social classes, interests, and ideologies. In the post—Cold War world though, ideological differences have often been overshadowed by ethnic and religious ones.

FOSTERING DEVELOPMENT

As important as the task of building community is, political systems cannot generally expect to satisfy their citizens unless they can foster social and economic development. Thus, as significant as nation building may be, such factors as the availability of natural resources, the level of economic and social development, and the rate of economic growth and social change are of equal, if not greater, importance. Economic development implies that citizens can enjoy new resources. On the other hand, it can often have a devastating impact on nature. For better or worse, the social changes that result from economic development transform the politics of developing countries.

Rich and Poor Countries

Figure 1.2 gives the per capita **gross national product (GNP)**—the total economic output per person—for our twelve nations. There are two ways to compare the economies of countries that use different currencies. The standard measure is computed according to the exchange rates of the national currencies. An alternative and newer measure instead uses **purchasing power parity (PPP),** which takes into account differences in price levels from one country to another. Figure 1.2 shows that the income of developing countries turns out to be substantially higher in purchasing power parity than when we use currency exchange rates. Thus, in U.S. dollar equivalents, Mexican per capita PPP is almost twice its per capita GNP, whereas China's and India's are about five times as high. At the opposite extreme, the Japanese economy is less impressive in actual purchasing power. Thus the gap in economic wealth between the rich and the poor countries is not as great if we take into account what money actually buys. In per capita output, the Brazilian economy is more than one-fourth that of the Japanese economy according to purchasing powers, as opposed to one-tenth according to exchange rates. The Chinese per capita product turns out to be about one-seventh that of Japan, instead of less than one-fortieth.

Traditional official statistics have exaggerated the income inequality among nations in other respects, too. Our statistics tend to underestimate goods and services produced and consumed in subsistence agriculture, or in household production for family use. Similarly, national product estimates are not corrected for differences in the "cost of living" under different environmental conditions. As the World Develop-

F I G U R E   1 . 2   Per Capita GNP and PPP in Selected Nations, 2000 (in U.S. Dollars)

Source: World Bank, *World Development Report: 2002*. (New York, Oxford University Press), 2002, table 1, pp. 232–33.

ment Report points out, "GNP is higher in colder countries, where people spend more money on heating and warm clothing, than in balmy climates, where people are comfortable wearing light clothing in the open air."[10]

Figure 1.3 compares the percentages of the economically active populations employed in agriculture. In comparing Figures 1.2 and 1.3 we see that the smaller the per capita GNP (or PPP), the larger is the proportion of the labor force in agriculture. The five advanced industrial countries all have agricultural labor forces in the single digits, with the United States and Britain at 2 percent each. The three poorest countries—China, India, and Nigeria—have more than two-thirds of their labor forces employed in agriculture. The middle-income countries—Mexico and Brazil—have around a third to a fifth of their labor forces in agriculture. Thus, the economies of the rich countries are predominantly industrial, commercial, and professional, while those of the poor countries are predominantly agricultural. Countries that are rich and industrialized, with a large professional service sector, also tend to have healthy, literate, and educated populations. In highly industrialized countries, practically everyone over the age of 15 can read and write. In India, Nigeria, and Egypt, on the other hand, almost one-half the adult population is illiterate. Moreover, the countries with the fewest literate citizens also have the fewest radios and television sets—devices that do not require literacy.

Industrialization, education, and exposure to the communications media are associated with better nutrition and medical care. In the economically advanced countries, fewer children die in infancy, and the average citizen has a life expectancy at

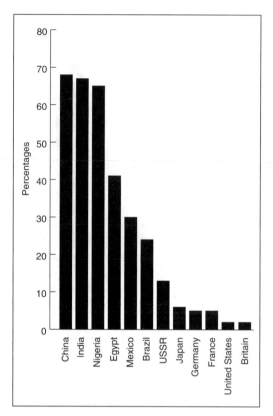

F I G U R E   1 . 3   Percentage of Economically Active Population in Agriculture for Selected Nations (1990)

Source: FAO, United Nations, *FAO Production Yearbook 1990* (Rome: UN, 1991), table 3.

birth of more than 75 years (81 in Japan). The average Mexican has a life expectancy of 72 years; the Egyptian, 67 years; the Indian, 63 years; and the Nigerian only 47 years. Material productivity, education, exposure to communications media, and longer and healthier lives are closely interconnected. Only economically productive countries can afford good education, communications media, and good nutrition and health care. In order to become more productive, a country needs to develop a skilled and healthy labor force and build its infrastructure, but doing so requires significant resources. Preindustrial nations face urgent issues of economic development: how to improve the immediate welfare of their citizens yet also build and invest for the future. Typically, these are newer nations that also face the challenges of building community and effective political institutions.

Economic Inequality

It may be misleading to refer to states only on the basis of average economic measures such as per capita income, gross national product, and so on. Wealth, in-

T A B L E   1 . 4   Income Distribution for Selected Nations

Country	Year	Wealthiest 10%	Poorest 40%	Per Capita GNP (1998)
Japan	1979	22.4	21.9	32,380
United States	1994	28.5	15.3	29,340
Germany	1989	22.6	22.5	25,850
France	1989	24.9	19.9	24,940
Britain	1986	24.7	19.9	21,400
Brazil	1995	47.9	8.2	4,570
Mexico	1992	39.2	11.9	3,970
Russia	1993	22.2	20.0	2,300
Egypt	1991	26.7	21.2	1,290
China	1995	30.9	15.3	750
India	1994	25.0	22.2	430
Nigeria	1992	31.4	12.9	300

Source: World Bank, *World Development Report, 1999–2000* (New York: Oxford University Press, 2000), table 5, pp. 238–39.

come, and opportunity are not evenly distributed domestically, and such inequalities are among the most serious causes of political conflict. A large gross national product may conceal significant differences in the distribution of economic and social amenities and opportunities. A high rate of national growth may benefit only particular regions or social groups, leaving large parts of the population even less well off than before. The "inner cities" of the United States; the older parts of such Indian cities as Delhi and Calcutta; the peripheral ramshackle settlements around the cities of Latin America; such regions as Appalachia in the United States, the Mezzogiorno (south) of Italy, and the arid northeast of Brazil—all suffer from poverty and hopelessness, while other parts of their countries experience growth and improved welfare.

A country's politics may be sharply affected by internal divisions of income, wealth, and other resources. Table 1.4 compares income distribution for our 12 countries. Clearly, there is a positive association between economic development and equality of income, at least past a certain stage of economic growth. Wealthy nations like Japan, the United States, or Germany tend to have more egalitarian income distributions than middle-income countries such as Brazil and Mexico. In Japan, the rich receive a little over four times the income going to the poor. In Mexico, a middle-income country, the ratio is closer to 10 to 1; and in Brazil it is more than 20 to 1. Yet the table also suggests that ideological and political characteristics make a difference. Particularly surprising is the inequality of income in China, the only Communist nation, where the poorest 40 percent get less of the total (15.3 percent), than the poorest 40 percent in Japan (21.9 percent).

Industrialization and high productivity have historically gone along with more equal distribution of income. This tends to be true today, too. Yet, the first stages of industrialization and modernization may actually increase income inequality by creating a dual economy—a rural sector and an urban industrial and commercial sector, both with inequalities of their own. This pattern is apparent if we contrast inequality in India with the even greater inequalities in the somewhat richer countries of Mexico and Brazil. These inequalities tend to increase as education and communication spread. This pattern helps explain the political instability of many developing countries, since income inequality grows at the same time that awareness of it is increasing. Even though inequality may tend to diminish in later stages of development, this trend cannot be taken for granted. In Brazil, income inequality has increased for decades, even as the economy developed. Nor does inequality disappear in the most economically advanced nations. In the United States, income inequality increased substantially from the 1970s to the mid-1990s as a consequence of changes in economic structure, the increase in single-parent families, immigration, and a lowering of income taxes in the 1980s. Similar trends are evident in Britain and in many other advanced states, driven by the same factors as well as by high unemployment, and rapid salary gains among highly educated people. These developments are most dramatic in Russia and other post-communist societies. Inequality is an issue that all nations must face.

Economic inequality has a very important international side. A series of studies sponsored by the World Bank in the 1970s and 1980s, with the title "Redistribution with Growth," proposed a variety of policy solutions to mitigate the hardships economic inequality causes in developing societies and specifically to avoid the extreme cases of "unequal development," such as in Brazil and Mexico.[11] Instead, the economists involved in these studies pointed to Taiwan and South Korea, which had combined rapid economic growth with greater social equality. In these countries early land reforms had equalized opportunity at the outset of the developmental process. Investment in education, in agricultural inputs and rural infrastructure (principally roads and water), and in labor-intensive industries, and an emphasis on export-oriented growth, produced remarkable results for several decades. Their comparative advantage in cheap and skilled labor enabled these countries to compete effectively in international markets. Thus it is possible to identify growth policies with lesser inequalities, but it can be very difficult to put them into practice, especially where substantial inequalities already exist.

Population Growth, Economic Development, and the Environment

While the goal of economic growth for the world's lower-income economies is generally accepted and fostered by such international agencies as the UN, the World Bank, and the International Monetary Fund, as well as the by the foreign aid programs of advanced industrial nations, it has an ominous "downside." The advanced economies have only begun to pay for the environmental costs of their industrial development. Despoiled forests, depleted soils and fisheries, polluted air and water, nuclear waste, endangered species, and a threatened ozone layer now burden their legislative dockets. Some of these environmental problems—for example, deforestation—are even more acute in developing countries. With in-

T A B L E 1 . 5 Population by Economic Development Level in 1992 and Projected to 2025 (in millions US $)

Economic Development Level	*In 1992*		*Projected to 2025*	
	Number	Percentage	Number	Percentage
Low-income economies	3,191	59	5,062	62
Middle-income economies	1,416	26	2,139	27
High-income economies	828	15	922	11
Total	5,437	100	8,123	100

Source: World Bank, World Development Report 1994 (New York: Oxford University Press, 1994), tables 1 and 25.

creasing industrialization and urbanization in the developing world, many environmental problems could get dramatically worse.

Thus economic development can impose serious environmental costs. The book *The Population Explosion* drew attention to the great environmental burden that had resulted from the population growth and industrial development of the nineteenth and twentieth centuries.[12] Our arable soil, our forests, the quality of our air and water, the welfare of our plant and animal life, and the continuity of our climate have been seriously damaged by the combination of economic and demographic growth. In addition to the challenge of combining economic growth with equity, we must now find a way to counteract the environmental degradation caused by the combined growth of the economy and the population.

Table 1.5 puts the second dilemma in sharp relief. The table divides world population into three strata: low-income economies, middle-income economies, and high-income economies. In 1992 the low-income countries had a population total of more than 3 billion, or 60 percent of the total world population; the middle-income group had roughly one-fourth of the total population, and the high-income population had 15 percent. Projections are that world population in 2025 will increase to 8 billion and that the poorer countries will still see a more rapid growth of population. Rapid economic growth in the developing world would result in great burdens on the environment indeed.

These frightening prospects have produced a mixed literature of both light and heat. Economist Amartya Sen warns of a "danger that in the confrontation between apocalyptic pessimism on one hand, and a dismissive smugness, on the other, a genuine understanding of the nature of the population problem may be lost."[13] The first impact of "modernization" on population is to increase it rapidly, as new sanitation measures and modern pharmaceuticals reduce the death rate. As an economy develops, however, public policies and changing incentives tend to reduce fertility. With improved education (particularly of women), health, and welfare, the advantages of lower fertility become clear, and population growth declines. This happened in Europe and North America as they underwent industrialization and appears to be taking place in the developing world. Thus annual population growth in the world has in the last two decades declined from 2.2 percent to 1.4 percent. The rate of population growth in India, for example, rose to 2.2 percent in the 1970s and has since declined. Latin America peaked at a higher rate and then came down sharply. The great problem area is Sub-Saharan Africa with an average growth rate of more than 2.7 percent each year during the 1990s.[14] Tragically, the fertility rate in Africa has most potently been counteracted by a rising death rate from the epidemic spread of AIDS.

But while the trend is in the desired direction, population growth is still a very serious problem. China has confronted this problem with a coercive policy of abortion and contraception, which in urban areas has produced dramatic results at great costs. India and other countries have had some success with what Sen calls a "collaborative" approach, involving governmental intervention in influencing family choices, as well as counting on the market and education to affect family choices.[15] Kerala in southern India is a dramatic example of what can be accomplished by this approach. Expanding education, particularly among women, and otherwise improving living conditions, has reduced fertility more than in China, or even Sweden, the United States, or Canada. To avoid the irreversible catastrophes prophesied by the "apocalyptic pessimists," however, requires sacrifices and foresight.

SECURING DEMOCRACY, HUMAN RIGHTS, AND CIVIL LIBERTIES

Democracy is the form of government to which most contemporary states, more or less sincerely and successfully, aspire. A **democracy**, briefly defined, is a political system in which citizens enjoy a number of basic civil and political rights, and in which their most important political leaders are elected in free and fair elections and accountable under a rule of law. Democracy literally means "government by the people." In small political systems, such as local communities, it may be possible for "the people" to share directly in debating, deciding, and implementing public policy. In large political systems, such as contemporary states, democracy must be achieved largely through indirect participation in policymaking. Elections, competitive political parties, free mass media, and representative assemblies make some degree of democracy, "government by the people," possible. This indirect, or representative, democracy is not complete or ideal. But the more citizens are involved and the more influential their choices, the more democratic the system.

The most important general distinction in classifying political systems is between democratic systems and others. Nondemocracies, which we usually speak of as *authoritarian*, lack one or several of the defining features of democracy. In democracies, competitive elections give citizens the chance to shape the entire policymaking process through their selection and rejection of key policymakers. In authoritarian systems the policymakers are typically chosen by military councils, hereditary families, or dominant political parties. Citizens are either ignored or pressed into symbolic assent to the government's choices. In **oligarchies**, literally "rule by the few," important political rights are withheld from the majority of the population. South Africa until the abolition of apartheid in the early 1990s was a good example. In **totalitarian** systems, such as Nazi Germany or the Soviet Union under Stalin, the government constricts the rights and privacy of its citizens in a particularly severe and intrusive manner. All totalitarian systems are authoritarian, but most authoritarian systems are not totalitarian.

Democracy is not an all-or-nothing question. No democracy is perfect, and we can speak of shades or gradations of democracy. Nor does democracy typically come about overnight. It often takes time to establish democratic institutions and to have citizens recognize them and comply with the rules of the democratic process. One of the most hopeful developments of the past couple of decades is the large number of countries that have undergone or are undergoing a transition to democracy. Transitions toward democracy have been a major feature of world politics in the last 20 or 30 years. Many transitions have been relatively peaceful, as authoritarian rulers have negotiated a solution in response to citizen pressures. Military forces have frequently stood aside or even supported the citizens against the dictators. Authoritarian regimes have lost legitimacy everywhere, especially since the model (and support) of the Soviet Union has collapsed.

As political systems become more complex, richer, and more technologically advanced, the probability of citizen involvement increases. At the same time this participation may become less freely chosen. In the past century most Western states have been transformed from authoritarian regimes, or oligarchies with limited voting rights, to democracies. And during the past century, the power of the state has increasingly been used to meet popular needs and demands. Yet, in a modern society the government can try to control and manipulate the flow of information and communication, the formation of attitudes and culture, and the choices—if any—offered to citizens. Thus more developed political systems, especially in industrial societies, have greater potential for authoritarian control of citizens on a mass scale. On the other hand, independent social and political groups and organizations can exert autonomous political influence. High levels of education and information can contribute to a participant political culture.

Samuel P. Huntington speaks of the recent move toward democracy as a "Third Wave" of worldwide **democratization.** The first of these waves began in the nineteenth century and culminated with the establishment of many new democracies after World War I. But this wave reversed itself in the next 20 years, when many democracies collapsed or were conquered by authoritarian states. After World War II a second democratic wave, which lasted from 1943 until the early 1960s, saw both newly independent states (such as India and Nigeria) and defeated authoritarian powers (such as Germany and Japan) set up the formal institutions of democracy. While quite a number of countries became formally democratic in these years, most quickly lapsed into authoritarianism. Many of these would-be democracies failed in their first decade; another "reverse wave" in the 1960s and early 1970s swept away some older democracies (Chile, Greece, and Uruguay, for example) as well. The third wave of democratization, beginning in 1974, has involved Southern Europe, East Asia, Latin America, and recently Eastern Europe, the successor states to the Soviet Union, and a number of African states.

It can be difficult to consolidate democracies, especially in less economically developed societies. Not all of the newly democratizing countries are succeeding beyond the first few years. In some, democratic processes fail to produce stable institutions and effective public policies and give way to some form of authoritarianism. In Nigeria, a democratic-leaning regime installed in 1979 was overthrown by a military coup in 1983, and a precarious civilian regime was only reestablished in 1999. Nigeria is by no means unique. Transition can move in either direction, toward or away from democracy. While today's Third Wave of democratization is supported by the more favorable environments of more modernized societies and the very fact that there are now more democracies in the world, we cannot be sure how long the democratic gains will last.

Even when states democratize, there is no guarantee that they will grant human rights and civil liberties to all their people. In some countries, majority rule turns into a "tyranny of the majority" against ethnic or religious minorities. Therefore, democracies always have to find a balance between respecting the will of the majority and protecting the rights of the minority. But even when political rulers sincerely try to promote human rights and civil liberties (which is by no means always the case), they do not always agree what those rights should be. Although the United Nations has tried to secure agreement on a range of rights and liberties that all individuals should enjoy, different governments and cultures seriously disagree about the implementation of such protections. Some societies believe that freedom of speech should not be protected when it is used for blasphemy, or to denigrate particular social groups. Governments in Western industrial societies tend to want gender equality policies that are sometimes considered religiously unacceptable in Muslim countries. In most developing societies and most states in the United States, capital punishment is considered an acceptable penalty for particularly heinous crimes. Most Western European societies, however, do not permit such punishment and consider it inhumane.

Community-building, development, and democratization cannot be dealt with in isolation from one another. On the contrary, progress in one of these areas can create new opportunities, but also new problems, in another. Economic development, for example, can reinforce (but also ameliorate) ethnic strife and destabilize political institutions. While development has obvious positive consequences for productivity and welfare, it can disrupt social life. The growth of technology and the service economy coupled with the spread of market economies results in growing wealth and income inequality. This trend has in recent decades become quite noticeable in advanced industrial societies, and it tends to affect the developing economies even more sharply. Increasing inequality of income and wealth can sharpen class antagonisms and partisanship.

The political effects of these developments vary from country to country, depending on economic resources, demography, geography, historical experience, and the like. Environmental deterioration, growing economic inequality, economic dislocation, and migration as well as ethnic and religious mobilization can cause political fragmentation and polarization and make it more difficult to form stable governments. A more affluent and information-driven citizenry impairs the effectiveness of political parties, interest groups, parliaments, and political executives. It is more difficult to structure political alternatives when party and interest group leaders can no longer effectively muster and discipline their followers, and when political leaders are losing control of the political agenda to such new forces as the electronic media. In subsequent chapters, we examine in more detail the ways in which these challenges affect the political choices of citizens and policymakers.

KEY TERMS

anarchists

civil liberties

democracy

democratization

ethnicity

European Union (EU)

externalities

governments

gross national product
(GNP)

human rights

income and wealth
inequality

libertarians

nations

nation-states

night watchman state

oligarchies

police state

political cleavages

political cultures

political system

public goods

purchasing power parity
(PPP)

regulatory state

religious fundamentalism

rent seeking

sovereignty

state

state of nature

totalitarian systems

United Nations (UN)

welfare state

SUGGESTED READINGS

Chenery, Hollis, et al. *Redistribution with Growth.* New York: Oxford University Press, 1981.

Cornelius, Wayne, et al., eds. *Controlling Immigration: A Global Perspective.* Stanford, CA: Stanford University Press, 1995.

Dahl, Robert A. *Democracy and Its Critics.* New Haven: Yale University Press, 1989.

Diamond, Larry, ed. *Developing Democracy: Towards Consolidation.* Baltimore: Johns Hopkins, 1999.

Ehrlich, Paul and Anne Ehrlich. *The Population Explosion.* New York: Simon and Schuster, 1990.

Hoffman, Stanley and Robert Keohane, eds. *The New European Community.* Boulder, CO: Westview, 1991.

Horowitz, Donald. *Ethnic Groups in Conflict.* Berkeley: University of California Press, 1985.

Huntington, Samuel. *The Third Wave: Democratization in the Late Twentieth Century.* Norman, OK: University of Oklahoma Press, 1991.

Lijphart, Arend. *Patterns of Democracy.* New Haven: Yale University Press, 1999.

Linz, Juan and Alfred Stepan, eds. *Problems of Democratic Transitions and Consolidation.* Baltimore: Johns Hopkins, 1996.

Marty, Martin and Scott Appleby. *Fundamentalism Observed.* Chicago: University of Chicago Press, 1991.

Putnam, Robert. *Making Democracy Work: Civic Traditions in Modern Italy.* Princeton, NJ: Princeton University Press, 1993.

Weiner, Myron. *The Global Migration Crisis: Challenge to States and to Human Rights.* New York: HarperCollins, 1995.

World Bank. *World Development Report.* New York: Oxford University Press, annual editions.

ENDNOTES

1. Thomas Hobbes, *Leviathan,* ed. C. B. Macpherson (New York: Penguin, 1968, p. 186).

2. J. J. Rousseau, *Second Discourse On Inequality, The First And Second Discourses* (New York: St. Martin's, 1964), pp.109–10.

3. The Vatican is not a member but maintains a permanent observer mission at the UN headquarters. Taiwan was expelled from the UN in 1971 to accommodate mainland China (the People's Republic).

4. More detailed discussions of the politics of each of these 12 countries are found in chapters 8–19 of Gabriel A. Almond, G. Bingham Powell, Jr., Kaare Strøm, and Russell J. Dalton, *Comparative Politics Today: A World View,* 8th edition, New York: Longman, 2003.

5. Max Weber, *Economy and Society*, ed. Guenther Roth and Claus Wittich (Berkeley: University of California Press, 1978), p. 389.

6. Stephen Castles and Mark J. Miller, *The Age of Migration: International Population Movements in The Modern World* (New York: Guilford, 1994).

7. Erik V. Gunnemark, *Countries, Peoples, and Their Languages: The Geolinguistic Handbook* (Gothenburg, Sweden: Lanstryckeriet, 1991).

8. A recent book dealing with this theme bears the title *The Ambivalence of the Sacred* by R. Scott Appleby, (Rowman & Littlefield, 2000).

9. See, among others, Martin Marty and Scott Appleby, *Fundamentalism Observed* (Chicago, IL: University of Chicago Press, 1991).

10. World Bank, *World Development Report* (New York: Oxford University Press, 1994), p. 230.

11. Hollis Chenery et al., *Redistribution with Growth* (New York: Oxford University Press, 1981).

12. Paul and Anne Ehrlich, *The Population Explosion* (New York: Simon and Schuster, 1990).

13. Amartya Sen, "Population: Delusion and Reality," *New York Review of Books,* Sept. 22, 1994, pp. 62ff.

14. World Bank, *World Development Report, 1998–1999* (New York: Oxford University Press, 1999).

15. Sen, "Population: Delusion and Reality."

Comparing Political Systems

WHY WE COMPARE

The great French interpreter of American democracy, Alexis de Tocqueville, while on his travels in America in the 1830s, wrote to a friend about how his ideas about French institutions and culture entered into the writing of *Democracy in America*. Tocqueville wrote "Although I very rarely spoke of France in my book, I did not write one page of it without having her, so to speak, before my eyes."[1] On a more general note about the comparative method, he offered this comment: "Without comparisons to make, the mind does not know how to proceed."[2]

Tocqueville was telling us that comparison is fundamental to all human thought. We add that it is the methodological core of the humanistic and scientific methods as well. It is the only way we can fully understand our own political system. Comparing the past and present of our nation and comparing our experience with that of other nations deepen our understanding of our own institutions. Examining politics in other societies permits us to see a wider range of political alternatives and illuminates the virtues and shortcomings of our own political life. By taking us beyond our familiar arrangements and assumptions, comparative analysis helps expand our awareness of the possibilities of politics.

Comparison is the methodological core of the scientific study of politics. Comparative analysis helps us develop explanations and test theories of the ways in which political processes work and in which political change occurs. Here the logic and the intention of the comparative methods used by political scientists are similar to those used in more exact sciences. Political scientists cannot normally design experiments to control and manipulate political arrangements and observe the consequences, especially when dealing with large-scale events that drastically affect many people. For example, researchers cannot and would not want to start a social revolution to see its effects. Nor would they want to initiate military escalation to see if it leads to war. It is possible, however, to use the comparative method to describe and explain the different combinations of political events and institutions found in different societies. More than two thousand years ago, Aristotle in his *Politics*

BOX 2.1   Aristotle's Library

There is historical evidence that Aristotle had accumulated a library of more than 150 studies of the political systems of the Mediterranean world of 400–300 B.C. Many of these had probably been researched and written by his disciples.

While only the Athenian constitution survives of this library of Aristotelian polities, it is evident from the references to such studies that do survive, that Aristotle was concerned with sampling the variety of political systems then in existence, including the "barbarian" (Third World?) countries such as Libya, Etruria, and Rome: "the references in ancient authorities give us the names of some 70 or more of the states described in the compilation of 'polities.' They range from Sinope, on the Black Sea, to Cyrene in North Africa; they extend from Marseilles in the Western Mediterranean to Crete, Rhodes, and Cyprus in the East. Aristotle thus included colonial constitutions as well as those of metropolitan states. His descriptions embraced states on the Aegean, Ionian, and the Tyrrhenian Seas, and the three continents of Europe, Asia, and Africa."

Source: Ernest Barker, ed., *The Politics of Aristotle* (London: Oxford University Press, 1977), p. 386.

---

contrasted the economies and social structures of the many Greek city-states in an effort to determine how the social and economic environment affected political institutions and policies. (See Box 2.1.)

A contemporary political scientist, Robert Dahl, in his studies of democracy, compares the economic characteristics, cultures, and historical experiences of many contemporary nations in an effort to discover the combinations of conditions and characteristics that are associated with that form of government.[3] Other theorists, in their attempt to explain differences between the processes and performance of political systems, have compared constitutional regimes with tyrannies, two-party democracies with multiparty democracies, parliamentary with presidential regimes, and stable governments with unstable ones.

The end of the Cold War left a world engaged in vast experiments in different approaches to economic growth, different strategies for transition to democracy, differing ways of controlling and using the powers of government. Governments today are grappling with new issues of preserving our environment, old issues of opportunity and economic security for citizens, and ancient issues of conflicts of ethnic identities and religious beliefs. In a world made ever smaller by instantaneous communication and interdependent economies, these problems and achievements spill across national boundaries. Comparative analysis is a powerful and versatile tool. It enhances our ability to describe and understand political processes and political change in any country by offering concepts and reference points from a broader perspective. The comparative approach also stimulates us to form general theories of political relationships. It encourages and enables us to test our political theories by confronting them with the experience of many institutions and settings. A primary goal of this book is to provide access to this powerful tool for thought and analysis.

HOW WE COMPARE

We study politics in several different ways: we describe it; we seek to explain it; and sometimes we try to predict it. These are all parts of the scientific process, and in each of them we may use the comparative method. The first stage in the study of politics is description. If we cannot describe a political process or event, we cannot really hope to understand or explain, much less predict what might happen next, or in similar situations. In order to describe politics, we need a set of concepts that are clearly defined and well understood. We speak of this as a conceptual framework. The easier this set of concepts is to understand, and the more generally it can be applied, the more helpful it is to the study of politics. Conceptual frameworks are not generally right or wrong, but they may be more or less useful to the task at hand.

Once we are able to describe politics with the help of the conceptual framework that we choose, the next task is to explain it. What we mean by explaining political phenomena is seeking to identify relationships between them. For example, we might be interested in the relationship between democracy and international peace (Box 2.2). Are democratic states more peaceful than others? If so, are they peaceful because they are democratic, are they democratic because they are peaceful, or are they perhaps both peaceful and democratic because they are more prosperous than other states?

These questions show that we often want explanations to go beyond associating one thing with another. Ideally we want to put many political relationships in causal terms, so that we can say that one political feature is the cause of another, and the latter is the effect of the former. For example, a theory may state that countries are peaceful because they are democratic. There are different kinds of causal statements that we can make about this relationship between war and form of government. One such statement might be "only authoritarian governments start wars"; in other words, authoritarianism is necessary to starting wars. Another statement might be, "all democracies are peaceful"; in other words, democracy is sufficient to guarantee peacefulness. A third statement might express only a tendency or probability, such as "authoritarian governments tend to be more warlike than democracies."

Theories are statements about causal relationships between general classes of events—for example, about what causes democracy, war, or political development. Theories are always tentative; they are always subject to modification or falsification as our knowledge improves. And theories need to be testable. A good theory is one that holds up after continued trials and experiments, that can be confirmed or modified as we test the theory again and again. The number of cases that political scientists have to generalize about varies from problem to problem. Similarly, the number of cases that are examined when we test theories can vary dramatically.

Researchers in political science distinguish between studies based on large numbers (large "n") and small numbers (small "n"). Large "n" studies are usually referred to as *statistical studies*, small "n" as *case studies*. Large "n" studies have a sufficient number and variety of cases to enable the researcher to examine the relation among the variables (variables being the dimensions or the parameters on which our cases differ—for example, "form of government: democracy or dictatorship," or "income per capita"). Small "n" studies permit investigators to go deeply

BOX 2.2   Statistical Methods

A popular contemporary research program known as *democratic peace research* illustrates the pros and cons of statistical and case study research. It has been of primary interest to international relations scholars, who took the diplomatic history of the Cold War period and asked whether democratic countries are more peaceful in their foreign policy than authoritarian and nondemocratic ones. Many scholars in the democratic peace research group took the statistical route. They counted each year of interaction between two states as one case, and with roughly half a century of diplomatic history involving a state system of 100 countries or more, they had a very large number of cases, even after eliminating the many irrelevant cases of countries that never, or rarely, had any relations with one another. Political scientists Andrew Bennett and Alexander George drew these conclusions after surveying the statistical research:

> Statistical methods achieved important advances on the issue of whether a nonspurious inter-democratic peace exists. A fairly strong though not unanimous consensus emerged that: (1) democracies are not less war-prone in general; (2) they have very rarely if ever fought one another; (3) this pattern of an inter-democratic peace applies to both war and conflicts short of war; (4) states in transition to democracy are more war prone than established democracies; and (5) these correlations were not spuriously brought about by the most obvious alternative explanations.

There is a consensus now that statistical studies are not as good as are case studies at answering "why" questions. Case studies make clinical depth possible, revealing causal interconnections in individual cases. Careful repetition of these causal tracings from case to case strengthens confidence in these relationships. Thus Bennett and George concluded that the best research strategy to follow is to use statistical and case study methods together, with each one of the methods having its own strengths.

Source: Andrew Bennett and Alexander George, "An Alliance of Statistical and Case Study Methods: Research on the Interdemocratic Peace," APSA-CP: *Newsletter of the APSA Organized Section in Comparative Politics* 9, no. 1: 6.

into a case, identify the particularities of it, get the clinical details, and examine each link in the causal process. In this manner, political scientists may come to know not only whether democracies are more peaceful than dictatorships, but more precisely why democratic leaders behave in the way that they do.

It is now generally recognized that these methods are complementary. Large "n" statistical studies allow us to be more certain and precise in our explanations. On the other hand, we need the depth that case studies provide in order to formulate insightful hypotheses for statistical testing in the first place. Also, case study methods can be used to examine in detail some aspects of cause-and-effect relations better than large "n" studies.

An example may suggest how you might go about theorizing in comparative politics, going beyond "just mastering the facts." It is well known that rich countries are more likely to be democracies than are poor countries; democracy and economic development are strongly associated. But there are many possible reasons for this association. Some have suggested that comes about because democracy encourages education and economic development. Others have argued that as countries develop economically, their new middle classes or better organized working class are more likely to demand democratization. Yet others have seen that both democracy and economic development are commonly found in some regions of the world, such as Western Europe, while both tend to be scarce in the Middle East and Africa, suggesting that certain cultures may encourage or discourage both of them. We want to understand the causal nature of this association, for reasons of both science and policy. The recent work of Przeworski and his associates examines the full experience of democracies, nondemocracies, and transitions between them in all parts of the world between 1950 and 1990.[4] Their statistical analysis leads them to conclude that the explanation for the association does not lie in regional effects or superior economic growth in democracy. Moreover, nations at any level of development seem able to introduce democracy. The key to the relationship lies rather in the consistently greater fragility of democracies in societies at lower levels of economic development; democracy can easily be introduced in poor societies with less educated populations, but in these social conditions it is relatively more likely to be replaced by some kind of dictatorship. We still need to understand just why democracy is more precarious in less developed societies, but we have made progress in understanding the causal element in the relationship.

We can also generate and test hypotheses about the causes and consequences of political change by comparing countries at different historical periods, just as we can compare the institutions of different countries in our search for political theories. Tocqueville's study of the French Revolution contributed to a general theory of revolution by comparing pre- and post-revolutionary France.[5] Theda Skocpol based her theories of the causes of revolution on a comparison of the "old regimes" of France, Russia, and China with their revolutionary and post-revolutionary regimes.[6]

SYSTEMS: ENVIRONMENT AND INTERDEPENDENCE

Comparative Politics Today suggests that we approach the comparison of political systems with a structural-functional system framework. To do so, we need to discuss in some detail these three general concepts that we use throughout this book: (1) system, (2) structure, and (3) function. **System,** as we defined it in Chapter 1, suggests an object having moving parts, interacting with a setting or an **environment.** The **political system** is a set of institutions and agencies concerned with formulating and implementing the collective goals of a society or of groups within it. **Governments** or **states** are the policymaking parts of political systems. The decisions of governments are normally backed up by legitimate coercion, and obedience may be compelled. We discuss legitimacy at greater length in Chapter 3.

Figure 2.1 tells us that a political system exists in both a domestic and an international environment, molding these environments and being molded by them.

FIGURE 2.1 The Political System and Its Environments

The system receives **inputs** from these environments and attempts to shape them through its outputs. In the figure, which is quite schematic and simple, we use the United States as the central actor, and we include some other countries as our environmental examples—Russia, China, Britain, Germany, Japan, Mexico, and Egypt. Exchanges among countries may vary in many ways. For example, they may be "dense" or "sparse"; United States–Canadian relations exemplify the dense end of the continuum, while United States–Nepalese relations would be at the sparse end. Relationships between political systems may be of many different kinds. The United States has substantial trade relations with some nations and relatively little trade with others. Some countries have an excess of imports over exports, whereas others have an excess of exports over imports. With such countries as the NATO nations, Japan, South Korea, Israel, and Saudi Arabia, military exchanges and support have been of great importance to the United States. The interdependence of nations—the volume and value of imports and exports, transfers of capital, the extent of foreign travel and international communication—has increased enormously in the last decades. We might represent this process as a thickening of the input and output arrows between the United States and other countries in Figure 2.1. Fluctuations in this flow of international transactions and traffic attributable to depression, inflation, protective tariffs, international terror-ism, war, and the like may wreak havoc with the economies of the nations affected.

The interaction of the political system with its domestic environment—the economic and social systems and the culture of its citizens—may be illustrated in the American case by the rise of the "high-tech information-based economy." The composition of the American labor force, and consequently its citizenry, has changed dramatically in the last century. Agriculture has declined to under 3 per-cent of the gainfully employed. Employment in heavy extractive and manufactur-ing industries has decreased substantially, and the newer, high-technology occupa-tions, the professions, and the service occupations have increased sharply as a proportion of the labor force. The last half-century has also witnessed significant improvements in the educational level of the American population, although the quality of education particularly at the primary and secondary levels has come in for very serious criticism in recent years. These and other changes in American so-cial structure have transformed the social bases of the party system. There are now as many independents among American voters as loyal Democrats and Republi-cans. Workers of the older, primarily European, ethnic stocks have ceased being a solid support for the Democratic Party; they now tend to divide their votes almost equally between the two parties. On the whole, these changes in the labor force have been associated with a more conservative trend in economic policy and with efforts to cut back welfare and other expenditures. A more educated and cultur-ally sophisticated society has become more concerned with the quality of life, the beauty and healthfulness of the environment, and similar issues. In input-output terms, socioeconomic changes have transformed the political demands of the elec-torate and the kinds of policies that it supports.

Thus a new pattern of society results in different policy outputs, different kinds and levels of taxation, changes in regulatory patterns, and changes in welfare expenditures. The advantage of the system-environment approach is that it directs our attention to the **interdependence** of what happens within and between nations, and it provides us with a vocabulary to describe, compare, and explain these inter-acting events. If we are to make sound judgments in politics, we need to be able to place political systems in their domestic and international environments, recogniz-ing how these environments both set limits on and provide opportunities for politi-cal choices. This approach keeps us from reaching quick and biased political judg-ments. If a country is poor in natural resources and lacks the skills necessary to exploit what it has, we cannot fault it for having a low industrial output or poor ed-ucational and social services. Similarly, a country dominated and exploited by an-other country with a conservative policy cannot be condemned for failing to intro-duce social reforms.

The policies that leaders and political activists can follow are limited by the in-terdependence of the system and its institutions, as well as by the environment. However, in this era of rapid change, if the goals of the leadership and the political activists change, one set of political institutions may quickly be replaced by another. One of the most dramatic illustrations of such an institutional transformation was the breakdown of control by the Communist parties in Eastern Europe, and their replacement by multiparty systems when the leadership of the Soviet Union lost its confidence in the Soviet system and the future of socialism. Once the Soviet leadership lost confidence in the legitimacy of the Soviet Communist Party, it had no choice but to adopt a permissive and conciliatory policy toward its former satellites.

The notion of interdependence goes even further than this relationship between policy and institutions. The various structural parts of a political system are also interdependent. If a government is based on popularly elected representatives in legislative bodies, then a system of election must be instituted. If many people enjoy the right to vote, then the politicians seeking office will have to mobilize the electorate and organize political parties to carry on election campaigns. As the policymaking agencies of the political system enact laws, they will need administrators and civil servants to implement these laws, and they will need judges to determine whether the laws have been violated and to decide what punishments to impose on the violators.

STRUCTURES AND FUNCTIONS

Governments do many things—from establishing and operating school systems, to maintaining public order, to fighting wars. In order to carry on these many activities, governments have specialized agencies, or **structures,** such as parliaments, bureaucracies, administrative agencies, and courts, which perform **functions,** which in turn enable the government to formulate, implement, and enforce its policies. The policies reflect the goals; the agencies provide the means.

Figure 2.2 locates within the political system six types of political structures—political parties, interest groups, legislatures, executives, bureaucracies,

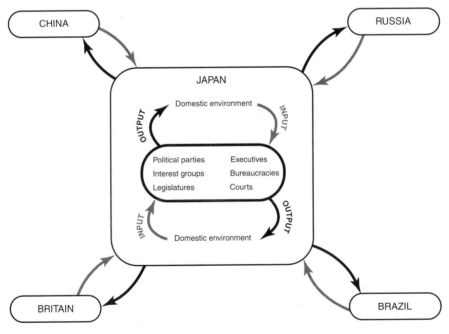

FIGURE   2.2   The Political System and Its Structures

and courts. Such structures are found in almost all modern political systems. One might therefore think that if we understand how such structures work in one political system, we can apply this insight to any other system. Unfortunately that is not always the case, and this sixfold classification will not carry us very far in comparing political systems with each other. The problem is that similar structures may have very different functions across political systems. Britain and China have all six types of political institutions, at least in name; however, these institutions are organized differently in the two countries, and they function in dramatically different ways. Britain has a monarch—currently Elizabeth II—who performs ceremonial functions, like opening Parliament and conferring knighthoods and other honors. China does not have a specialized ceremonial executive. There is, however, a president, elected by the National People's Congress, who performs the ceremonial functions as well as some political functions. The political executive in Britain consists of the prime minister, the ministers assigned to the Cabinet, and the larger ministry, which consists of all the heads of departments and agencies. All these officials are usually selected from Parliament. There is a similar structure in China, called the State Council, headed by a premier and consisting of the various ministers and ministerial commissions. But while the British prime minister and Cabinet have substantial policymaking power, the State Council in China is closely supervised by the general secretary of the Communist Party, the Politburo, and the Central Committee of the party. Both Britain and China have legislative bodies—the House of Commons in Britain and the National People's Congress in China. But while the House of Commons is a key institution in the policymaking process, the Chinese Congress meets for only brief periods, ratifying decisions made mainly by the Communist Party authorities.

There are even larger differences between political parties in the two countries. Britain has a competitive party system. The majority in the House of Commons and the Cabinet are constantly confronted by an opposition party or parties, competing for public support and looking forward to the next election when they may unseat the incumbent majority, as happened most recently in 1997, when the Labour Party replaced the Conservatives in government. In China the Communist Party controls the whole political process. There are no other political parties. The principal decisions are taken in the Politburo and to some extent in the Central Committee of the Communist Party. The governmental agencies implement the policies, which have to be initiated and/or approved by the top Communist Party leaders.

British interest groups are autonomous organizations that play important roles in the polity and the economy. Chinese trade unions and other professional organizations have to be viewed as parts of the official apparatus, dominated by the Communist Party, that perform mobilizing, socializing, and facilitating functions. Thus an institution-by-institution comparison of British and Chinese politics that did not spell out functions in detail would not bring us far toward understanding the important differences in the politics of these countries.

Figure 2.3 shows how we relate structure to function and process to policy and performance. (The functions and processes shown in the figure are discussed in greater detail in Chapter 3 through Chapter 6.) In the center of Figure 2.3 under the heading "Process functions" are listed the distinctive activities necessary

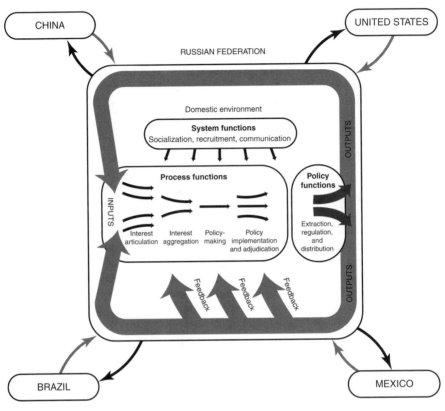

F I G U R E   2 . 3   The Political System and Its Functions

for policy to be made and implemented in any kind of political system: interest articulation, interest aggregation, policymaking, and policy implementation and adjudication. We call these process functions because they play a direct and necessary role in the process of making policy. Before policy can be decided, some individuals and groups in the government or the society must decide what they want and hope to get from politics. The political process begins as these interests are expressed or articulated. The many arrows on the left of the figure show these initial expressions.

To be effective, however, these demands must be combined (aggregated) into policy alternatives—such as higher or lower taxes or more or less social security benefits—for which substantial political support can be mobilized. Thus the arrows on the left are consolidated as the process moves from interest articulation to interest aggregation. Alternative policies are then considered. Whoever controls the government backs one of them, and authoritative policymaking takes place. The policy must be enforced and implemented, and if it is challenged or violated, there must be some process of adjudication. Each policy may affect several different aspects of a society, as reflected in the many arrows for the implementation phase.

These process functions that we have been describing are performed by such political structures as parties, legislatures, political executives, bureaucracies, and courts. The structural-functional approach stresses the point that while a particular institution such as a legislature may have a special relationship to a particular function such as law-making or rule-making, it does not have a monopoly on this function. Presidents and governors may share in the legislative function (veto powers), as do the higher courts (judicial review of statutes for their constitutionality).

The three functions listed at the top of the figure—socialization, recruitment, and communication—are not directly involved in making and implementing public policy but are of fundamental importance to the political system. We refer to these three functions as **system functions,** because they determine whether or not the system will be maintained or changed—for example—whether policymaking will continue to be dominated by a single authoritarian party or military council, or whether competitive parties and a legislature will replace them. The arrows leading from these three functions to all parts of the political process suggest their crucial role in underpinning and permeating the political process. **Political socialization** involves families, schools, communications media, churches, and all the various political structures that develop, reinforce, and transform attitudes of political significance in the society. **Political recruitment** refers to the selection of people for political activity and government offices. **Political communication** refers to the flow of information through the society and through the various structures that make up the political system. Understanding the performance of the system functions is essential to understanding how political systems respond to the great contemporary challenges of building community, fostering economic development and securing democracy that we discussed in Chapter 1.

The third set of functions, listed at the right of the figure, treats the **outputs**—the implementations of the political process. We call these the **policy functions,** the substantive impacts on the society, the economy, and the culture. These functions include the various forms of **regulation** of behavior, **extractions** of resources in the form of taxes and the like, and **distribution** of benefits and services to various groups in the population. The **outcomes** of all these political activities, in a cyclical fashion, result in new inputs, in new demands for legislation or for administrative action, and in increases or decreases in the amount of support given to the political system and incumbent officeholders. These functional concepts describe the activities carried on in any society regardless of how its political system is organized, or what kinds of policies it produces. Using these functional categories, we can determine how institutions in different countries combine in making and implementing different kinds of public policy. The term **political regime** is often used to describe the structural-functional-policy configuration governments take on at different times.

Some writers have argued that structural functionalism is an approach to politics that is conservative in its methodology, that it is biased in favor of the status quo, since it describes a set of institutions at a particular time. However, to describe political institutions precisely and comprehensively at some particular time is not to praise or defend them but to try to comprehend them. We would use the structural-functional approach to compare Nazi Germany, which we reject with horror, with democratic, peaceful, and prosperous states such as Sweden and Switzerland, which many of us may admire. Moreover, we recognize the need to supplement the structural-functional approach with a dynamic developmental approach, since we want to know not only how a political system functions, but why as well. A structural-functional approach does not in itself tell us why Germany or France developed as they did in the 1930s and 1940s. It tells us what changes occurred in these regimes. The explanation of why they changed requires that we bring in the economic, social, cultural, and international context in a historical way. We may speak of the structural-functional mapping of government and politics that we do in the theoretical chapters that follow, as a "comparative statics," a way to understand how different political processes interact at any one time, and of the analysis of political development and change as a "political dynamics."

AN ILLUSTRATIVE COMPARISON: RUSSIA IN 1985 AND 2002[7]

Figures 2.4 and 2.5 offer a simplified graphic comparison of structures and functions in Russia before and after the breakdown of communist rule in the Soviet Union. They illustrate the use of the comparative method to assess the way a political regime changed significantly in a short period of time. The point

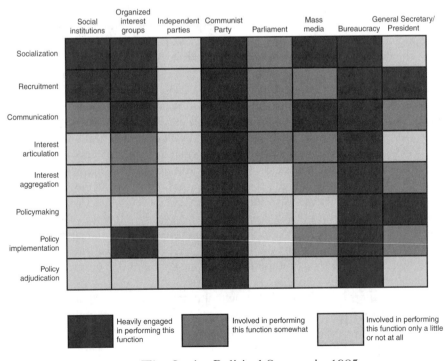

FIGURE 2.4   The Soviet Political System in 1985

here is to illustrate how we can use the tools of political analysis, rather than provide the details of the Russian case. The figures depict the changes in the functioning of the major structures of the political system brought about by the collapse of communism. These include two revolutionary changes: the end of the single-party political system dominated by the Communist Party of the Soviet Union, which held together the vast, multinational Soviet state, and the dissolution of the Soviet Union itself as a state into its 15 member republics. As a result of these two remarkable events, Russia, the republic that was the core republic of the old union, became an independent noncommunist state.

In June 1991, Boris Yeltsin, a bitter rival to the Soviet president, Mikhail Gorbachev, was elected President of Russia. Six months later, the Soviet Union collapsed and Gorbachev gave up his office. In December 1993, Russian voters were called upon to ratify a new Constitution, which provided for a powerful executive presidency and at the same time elected a new parliament dominated by a diverse range of political parties.

In the new Russia, democratic tendencies competed with pressures for authoritarian rule. Overall the system was a mixture of pluralism with vestiges of the old, bureaucratically run, state socialist order. The major political parties were represented in Parliament and were developing national political bases of support

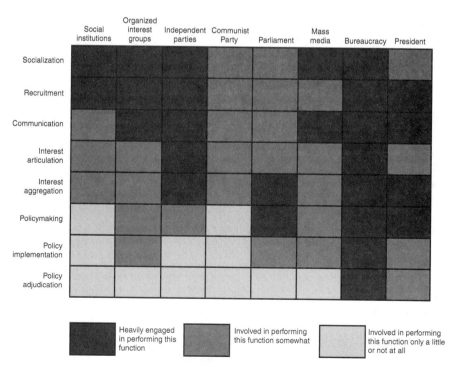

FIGURE   2.5   The Russian Political System in 2002

for the next elections, while the reborn Communist Party—called the Communist Party of the Russian Federation—regularly denounced Yeltsin and called for the restoration of a strong state and more social protection. Parliament, now called the Federal Assembly, had become a meaningful site for policy debate and decision making. The mass media were no longer tightly controlled by the Communist Party. New organized interest groups, such as business associations and labor unions, were actively involved in policymaking. The bureaucracy remained a powerful central player in the political process, however, with substantial continued control over the economy.

These and subsequent changes are reflected in the differences between the two figures. In 1985 (the year that the reform leader Mikhail Gorbachev came to power), the Soviet Union was a communist regime. Its Communist Party ruled the country. The top leader of the country was the General Secretary of the Communist Party. Although the country had the formal trappings of democracy, power actually flowed downward from the decisionmakers at the top to government and society. Figure 2.4 therefore shows how the basic functions of the political system were performed in 1985, when the Communist Party was the dominant political institution of the country, overseeing schools and media, the arts and public organizations, the economy and the courts. For this reason, all the cells of the chart in the column marked "Communist Party" are shaded dark, as are the cells under the column marked "Bureaucracy." Although social institutions such as the family, workplace, arts, and hobby groups exercised some influence over such system-level functions as socialization, recruitment, and communication, it was the Communist Party and state bureaucracy that dominated process-level functions. Under their tutelage, the mass media in 1985 were a key agent of communist political socialization and communication, while Parliament was a compliant instrument for ratifying decisions made by the party and bureaucracy. No other parties could exist beside the Communist Party, and the only organized interest groups were those authorized by the party. The party's General Secretary was the most powerful official in the country, since there was no state presidency.

By 2002 the political system had undergone fundamental change, as shown in Figure 2.5. Many more structures played a role in the political process, as is immediately evident by the larger number of cells that are heavily shaded. In particular, Parliament, independent political parties, and regional governments all acquired important new powers in policymaking. The freedom enjoyed by ordinary citizens to articulate their interests and to organize to advance them had expanded enormously. The Communist Party, no longer an official or monopolistic party, had declined substantially in power and was playing by the rules of the parliamentary game. The state bureaucracy remained an important element in the political system, although adapting itself to the new trend of movement toward a market economy by adopting quasi-commercial forms. The presidency, now occupied by Vladimar Putin, was a dominant policymaking institution. The Parliament, although fairly representative of the diversity of opinion in the country, was frustrated in its policymaking and oversight roles by the inertia of the vast state bureaucracy, its inability to compel compliance with its laws, its weak links with the electorate, and by the president's power to make policy by decree. Nevertheless, it played a crucial role in aggregating interests and making policy.

The brief comparisons presented here are meant to illustrate the use of the structural-functional approach, an approach that enables us to examine how the same functions are performed in different countries, or in the same country, at two different points in time. Similarly, we may examine changes in the functions performed by the same structures over time or across different political systems. In a country undergoing as rapid and dramatic transition as Russia in the 1990s, this framework helps us to analyze changes in the distribution of power among the major institutions making up the political system. Neither the analysis of structures nor that of functions is complete without the other. A structural analysis tells us the number of political parties, or the organization of the legislature, and how the executive branch, the courts, the bureaucracy, the mass media, interest groups, and other elements of the political system are set up and by what rules or standards they operate. A functional analysis tells us how these institutions and organizations interact to produce and implement policies. In Part 2 of this book we deal more specifically with the functions of the various political institutions, with the variety of interest groups and their functions, and with the structural-functional properties of party systems, legislatures, executives, and cabinets. Here we have only illustrated the method and its advantages.

THE POLICY LEVEL: PERFORMANCE, OUTCOME, AND EVALUATION

The important question is what these differences in structure and function do for the interests, needs, and aspirations of people. Looking again at Figures 2.1 and 2.3, we see a reflection of the relationship between what happens in politics and in the society, and between what happens in the society and the international environment. The structural-functional differences determine the give-and-take between politics and environment, and the importance of that give-and-take for such goals and objectives as welfare, justice, freedom, equality, peace, and prosperity. At the left of Figure 2.3 are arrows signifying inputs of demands and supports from the society and the international system and inputs from the independent initiatives of political leaders and bureaucrats. At the right are arrows signifying outputs and outcomes, the end products of the political process, the things a government does for and to its people.

We have to distinguish between the efforts—the things a government does— and the actual outcome of these efforts. Governments may spend equal amounts on education and health, or defense, but with different consequences. Not only government efficiency or corruption but the underlying cultural, economic, and technological level, as well as changes in its environment, play a role in the effectiveness of politics. Americans spend more per capita on education than any other people in the world, but their children perform less well in important subjects such as mathematics than do children in some other countries that spend substantially less. The United States and the Soviet Union spent enormous sums on defense in the 1970s and 1980s, and yet both countries were held at bay by small countries resolved to resist at all costs, and because of these failed efforts, they were weakened internally. The outcome of public policy is never wholly in the hands of the people and their leaders in the various nations of the world. Conditions in the internal environment, conditions and events in the larger external world, and simple chance may frustrate the most thoughtfully crafted programs and plans. We call the outputs of a political system—its extractions, distributions, regulations, and symbolic acts—its performance.

Finally, we must step even further back to consider the whole situation of political system, process, and policy, and the environment, to evaluate what political systems are doing. Evaluation is complex because people value different things and put different emphasis on what they value. We will refer to the different things people may value as political "goods." In Chapter 7 we discuss goods associated with the system level, such as the stability or adaptability of political institutions; goods associated with the process level, such as citizen participation in politics; and goods associated with the policy level, such as welfare, security, and liberty. To evaluate what a political system is doing, we must look at each of these areas and assess performance and outcomes. We must also be aware of how outcomes affect individuals and subgroups in the society, of specific changes that may often be overlooked in presenting averages, and of the continuing problem of building for the future as well as living today. This last problem affects both poor nations, which wish to survive and alleviate suffering today but also to improve their children's lot tomorrow, and rich nations, which must deal with the costs to their children of polluted and depleted natural resources as the result of the thoughtless environmental policies of the past.

KEY TERMS

adjudication	interest articulation	political system
communication	outcomes	process functions
distribution	outputs	regime
environment	policy functions	regulation
extraction	policymaking	states
functions	political communication	structural functional
government	political performance	approach
implementation	political recruitment	structures
inputs	political regime	system
interdependence	political socialization	system functions
interest aggregation		

SUGGESTED READINGS

Collier, David. "The Comparative Method," in Ada W. Finifter, ed., *Political Science: The State of the Discipline II.* Washington: American Political Science Association, 1993.

Dogan, Mattei and Dominique Pelassy. *How to Compare Nations: Strategies in Comparative Politics.* Chatham, NJ: Chatham House, 1990.

Goodin, Robert E. and Hans-Dieter Klingemann. *A New Handbook of Political Science.* New York: Oxford University Press, 1996, chs. 2 and 3, and part 4.

King, Gary, Robert O. Keohane, and Sidney Verba. *Scientific Inference in Qualitative Research.* New York: Cambridge University Press, 1993.

Lichbach, Mark and Alan Zuckerman. *Comparing Nations: Rationality, Culture, and Structure.* New York: Cambridge University Press, 1997.

Przeworski, Adam and Henry Teune. *The Logic of Comparative Social Inquiry.* New York: Wiley, 1970.

ENDNOTES

1. Alexis de Tocqueville to Ernest de Chabrol, October 7, 1831, and Louis de Kergolay, October 18, 1847, in *Alexis de Tocqueville: Selected Letters on Politics and Society*, ed. Roger Boesche (Berkeley: University of California Press, 1985), pp. 59 and 191.

2. See also George Wilson Pierson, *Tocqueville and Beaumont in America* (New York: Oxford University Press, 1938).

3. Robert A. Dahl, *Polyarchy: Participation and Opposition* (New Haven, Ct.: Yale University Press, 1971); Robert A. Dahl, *Democracy and Its Critics* (New Haven, Ct.: Yale University Press, 1989.)

4. Adam Przeworski, Michael E. Alvarez, Jose Antonio Cheibub, Fernando Limongi, *Democracy and Development* (Cambridge: Cambridge University Press, 2000).

5. Alexis de Tocqueville, *The Old Regime and the French Revolution,* trans. Stuart Gilbert (New York: Doubleday, 1955).

6. Theda Skocpol, *States and Social Revolutions* (New York: Cambridge University Press, 1979).

7. Figures 2.4 and 2.5 and the text of "An Illustrative Comparison: Russia in 1985 and 2002" were contributed by Thomas Remington.

CHAPTER 3

Political Culture and Political Socialization

POLITICAL CULTURE

Americans' strong feelings of patriotism, the Japanese deference toward political elites, and French proclivity toward protest are all examples of how cultural norms shape politics. Our attitudes and values inevitably affect how we act, and it is the same with politics. The functioning of political institutions at least partially reflects the attitudes, norms, and expectations of the citizenry. Thus the English use their constitutional arrangements to sustain their liberty, while the same institutions were once used as instruments of repression in South Africa and Northern Ireland. In times of systemic change a supportive public can facilitate the development of a new political system, while the lack of public support may erode the foundations of a political system. To understand the tendencies for present and future behavior in a nation, we must begin with public attitudes toward politics and their role within the political system—what we call a nation's **political culture.**

Political culture does not explain everything about politics. Even people with similar values and skills will behave differently when they face different opportunities or problems. Nor is political culture unchangeable. New experiences can alter the attitudes of individuals; for example, peasants who migrate to the city learn new ways of urban life. But cultural norms typically change slowly and reflect enduring patterns of political action. This means that political culture is a critical element in understanding politics across countries or across time. If we do not take it into account, we will not understand how politics really functions.

This chapter begins by mapping the important parts of political culture. Then, we discuss **political socialization:** how individuals form their political attitudes and thus, collectively, how citizens form their political culture. We conclude with observations about the trends in political culture in world politics today.

T A B L E   3 . 1   The Aspects of Political Culture

Aspects of Political Culture	Examples
System	Pride in nation
	National identity
	Legitimacy of government
Process	Role of citizens
	Perceptions of political rights
Policy	Role of government
	Government policy priorities

MAPPING THE THREE LEVELS OF POLITICAL CULTURE

A nation's political culture includes its citizens' orientations toward three levels: the political system, the political and policymaking process, and policy outputs and outcomes (Table 3.1). The *system* level involves the citizens' and leaders' views of the values and organizations that comprise the political system. Do citizens identify with the nation and accept the general system of government? The *process* level includes expectations of how politics should function, and individuals' relationship to the political process. The *policy* level deals with citizens' and leaders' policy expectations from the government. What are the government's policy goals and how are they to be achieved?

The System Level

Orientations toward the political system are important because they tap basic commitments to the polity and the nation. Feelings of national pride are a revealing example of this aspect of the political culture (Figure 3.1). National pride seems strongest in nations with a long history that has emphasized feelings of patriotism—the United States is a prime example. Such a common sense of identity and national history is often what binds a people together in times of political strain. The figure indicates that high levels of pride exist in nations with much different political and economic systems, such as the United States and Poland. In contrast, national pride is low in Japan and Germany, two nations that have avoided nationalist sentiments in reaction to the pre–World War II regimes and their excesses. In other cases, ethnicity, language, or history divide the public, which may strain national identities and ultimately lead to conflict and division.

The **legitimacy** of the political system also provides a foundation for a successful political process. When citizens believe that they ought to obey the laws, then legitimacy is high. If they see no reason to obey, or if they comply only from fear, then legitimacy is low. Because it is much easier for government to function when

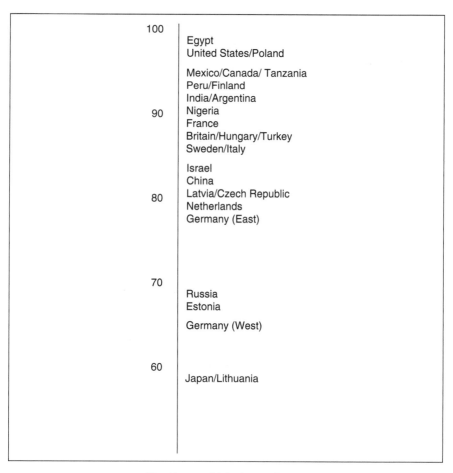

100	
	Egypt
	United States/Poland
	Mexico/Canada/ Tanzania
	Peru/Finland
	India/Argentina
90	Nigeria
	France
	Britain/Hungary/Turkey
	Sweden/Italy
	Israel
	China
80	Latvia/Czech Republic
	Netherlands
	Germany (East)
70	
	Russia
	Estonia
	Germany (West)
60	
	Japan/Lithuania

FIGURE   3 . 1   Feelings of National Pride (in percent)

Source: Selected nations from the 2000–2002 *World Values Survey* and the 1999 *European Values Survey*. Figure entries are the percent "proud" and "very proud"; missing data are excluded from the calculation of percentages.

citizens believe in the legitimacy of the political system, virtually all governments, even the most brutal and coercive, try to make their citizens believe that the laws ought to be obeyed. A political system and a government with high legitimacy will be more effective in making and carrying out policies and more likely to overcome hardships and reversals.

Citizens may grant legitimacy to a government for different reasons. In a traditional society, legitimacy may depend on the ruler's inheriting the throne or on the ruler's obedience to religious customs, such as making sacrifices and performing rituals. In a modern democracy, the legitimacy of the authorities will depend on their selection by voters in competitive elections and on their following constitutional procedures in their actions. In other political cultures, the leaders may base their claim to legitimacy on their special grace, wisdom, or ideology, which they claim will transform citizens' lives for the better, even though the government does not respond to specific demands or follow prescribed procedures.[1]

Whether legitimacy is based on tradition, ideology, citizen participation, or specific policies, the basis of legitimacy defines the fundamental understanding between citizens and political authorities. Citizens obey the laws—and in return the government meets the obligations set by the terms of its legitimacy. As long as the government meets its obligations, the public is supposed to comply, be supportive, and act appropriately. If legitimacy is violated—the line of succession is broken, the constitution is subverted, or the ruling ideology is ignored—then the government may expect resistance and perhaps rebellion.

In systems with low legitimacy or where the claimed bases for legitimacy are not accepted, people often resort to violence to solve political disagreement. Legitimacy may be undermined where the public disputes the boundaries of the political system (as in Northern Ireland or East Timor) rejects the current arrangements for recruiting leaders and making policies (as when Filipinos took to the streets and demanded the ouster of Ferdinand Marcos and free elections) or loses confidence that the leaders are fulfilling their part of the political bargain in making the right kinds of laws or following the right procedures (as when Indonesians protested deteriorating living conditions under Sukarno).

The Soviet Union disintegrated in the early 1990s because all three kinds of legitimacy problems appeared. After Communist ideology failed as a legitimizing force, there was no basis for a national political community in the absence of common language or ethnicity. Similarly, the general loss of confidence in the Communist Party as the dominating political structure led many people to call for new arrangements. Finally, shortages of food and consumer goods caused people to lose faith in the government's short-term economic and political policies. Soviet President Mikhail Gorbachev failed in his efforts to deal with all three problems at the same time.

Another systemic orientation involves regime norms. In the early twentieth century a variety of political systems divided the world. Fascism was on the rise in Europe, communism was establishing itself in the Soviet Union, colonial administrations governed large parts of the world, monarchical or authoritarian governments ruled other parts of the world, and Western Europe and North America strained to maintain democracy in this sea of conflicting currents.

Today, many of these forms of governance are no longer widely accepted. Communism still has strongholds in China and Cuba, but it has lost its image as a progressive force for global change. Some nations of the world still accept autocratic or religiously based systems of government. However, the global wave of democratization in the 1990s has raised democratic principles to a position of prominence. Most of the people in the world today seem to favor democratic principles even if they differ in how those principles should be applied.[2]

The Process Level

The second level of the political culture involves what the public expects of the political process. If you are English or Nigerian, what do you think about the institutions of your political system and what is expected of you as a citizen?

Broadly speaking, three different patterns describe the citizens' role in the political process.[3] **Participants** are involved as actual or potential participants in the political process. They are informed about politics and make demands on the polity, granting their support to political leaders based on performance. **Subjects** passively obey government officials and the law, but they do not vote or actively involve themselves in politics. **Parochials** are hardly aware of government and politics. They may be illiterates, rural people living in remote areas, or simply people who ignore politics and its impact on their lives.

As shown in Figure 3.2, in a hypothetical modern industrial democracy a sizable proportion (for instance, 60 percent) are participants, another third are simply subjects, and a small group are parochials. Such a distribution provides enough political activists to ensure competition between political parties and sizable voter turnout, as well as critical audiences for debate on public issues by parties, candidates, and pressure groups. At the same time, not all citizens feel the need to be active or concerned about the political system.

The second column in Figure 3.2 depicts the pattern we expect in a industrialized authoritarian society, such as the former communist nations of Eastern Europe. A small minority of citizens are involved in a one-party system, which penetrates and oversees the society, as well as decides government policies. Most other citizens are mobilized as subjects by political institutions: political parties, the bureaucracy, and government-controlled mass media. People are encouraged and even forced to

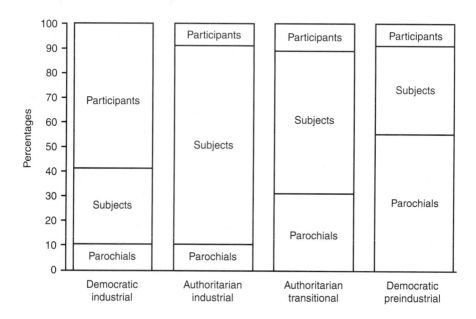

F I G U R E   3 . 2   Models of Political Culture: Orientations Toward Involvement in the Political Process

cast a symbolic vote of support in elections and to pay taxes, obey regulations, and accept assigned jobs. Because of the effectiveness of modern social organization and mass communications and the efforts of the authoritarian power structure, few citizens are unaware of the government and its influence on their lives. If such a society suddenly attempts to democratize its politics, many citizens must learn to become participants as well as democrats.

The third column shows an authoritarian society that is partly traditional and partly modern, such as in Egypt or China. In spite of an authoritarian political organization, some participants—students and intellectuals, for example—oppose the system and try to change it by persuasion or more aggressive acts of protest. Favored groups, like business people and landowners, discuss public issues and engage in lobbying. Most people in such systems are passive subjects, aware of government and complying with the law but not otherwise involved in public affairs. The parochials—poor and illiterate urban dwellers, peasants, or farm laborers—have little conscious contact with the political system.

Our fourth example is the democratic preindustrial system, perhaps one like India, which has a predominantly rural, illiterate population. In such a country there are few political participants, chiefly educated professionals, business people, and landowners. A much larger number of employees, workers, and perhaps independent farmers are directly affected by government taxation and other official policies. The largest group of citizens are illiterate farmworkers and peasants, whose knowledge of and involvement with national politics is minimal. In such a society it is a great challenge to create a more aware citizenry that can participate meaningfully and shape public policies through democratic means.

In summary, the distribution of these cultural patterns is related to the type of political process that citizens expect and support. For instance, we normally identify democracy with a more participatory political culture. Authoritarian states are more likely to endure when the public is characterized by subjects and parochials—although authoritarian states can come in many forms, ranging from communism, to dictatorships, to religion-based regimes.

Another critical feature of the process culture involves beliefs about other groups and oneself as a group member. Do individuals trust their fellow citizens? Do they see the society as divided into social classes, regional groups, or ethnic communities? Do they identify themselves with particular factions or parties? How do they feel about groups of which they are not members? When people trust others they will be more willing to work together for political goals, and group leaders may be more willing to form coalitions.[4] Governing a large nation requires forming large coalitions, and there must be substantial amounts of trust in other leaders to keep bargains and ensure honesty in negotiations.

The opposite of trust is hostility, which can destroy intergroup and interpersonal relations. The tragic examples of ethnic, religious, and ideological conflict in many nations—such as the conflicts in Rwanda, Lebanon, Northern Ireland, and Chechnya—show how easily hostility can be converted into violence and aggressive action. Respect for human life and dignity is sometimes in too short supply in the contemporary world.

The Policy Level

The politics of a country are also influenced by public images of what constitutes the good society and how to achieve it. At one level, the political culture includes expectations of the government's overall involvement in society and the economy. Should government manage the economy, or should private property rights and market forces guide economic activity? Should the state be interventionist in addressing societal issues, or follow a minimalist strategy? The ongoing debates over "big government" versus "small government" in democratic states, and between socialist and market-based economies reflect these different images of the scope of government (see Chapter 1).

Figure 3.3 illustrates the extent of cross-national differences in public expectations about whether it is the government's role to ensure that everyone is provided for. The range in opinions is considerable, from around three-quarters believing this is a government responsibility in Israel and Nigeria, to only a quarter of the French. In general, such sentiments are more common in developing nations and in the formerly communist nations in Eastern Europe—reflecting both the socioeconomic context and political ideologies. There are some Western nations, such as Sweden and Finland, where traditions also include a large role for the government. In general, however, it appears that public support for government action decreases as national affluence increases.[5] When the public expects a larger role for government, it is likely that the policies of the government will grow to meet the public's expectations.

Policy expectations also involve specific policy demands.[6] Some policy goals, such as material welfare, are valued by nearly everyone. Concern about other policy goals may vary widely across nations because of the nation's circumstances and because of cultural traditions. People in developing countries are more likely to focus on the government's provision of basic services to ensure public well-being. Advanced industrial societies provide for basic needs, and in these nations people may be more concerned with quality of life goals, such as preservation of nature and even government support for the arts. One of the basic measures of government performance is its ability to meet the policy expectations of its citizens.

Another set of expectations involves the functioning of government. Some cultures put more weight on the policy outputs of government, such as providing welfare and security. Other cultures also emphasize how the process functions, which involves values such as the rule of law and procedural justice. Among Germans, for example, the rule of law is given great importance; in many developing nations political relations are personally based, and there is less willingness to rely on legalistic frameworks.

Cultural Congruence

At the heart of our discussion of political culture is the belief that political structures and political cultures are mutually reinforcing in stable political systems. It is difficult to sustain democracy in a nation lacking participatory democrats, just as it is difficult to sustain an authoritarian state if the citizens are politically sophisticated

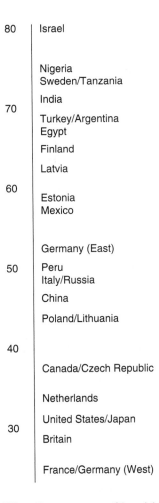

80 │ Israel

│
│ Nigeria
│ Sweden/Tanzania
│ India
70 │
│ Turkey/Argentina
│ Egypt
│ Finland
│
│ Latvia
│
60 │
│ Estonia
│ Mexico
│
│
│ Germany (East)
50 │ Peru
│ Italy/Russia
│
│ China
│
│ Poland/Lithuania
│
40 │
│
│ Canada/Czech Republic
│
│ Netherlands
│
│ United States/Japan
30 │
│ Britain
│
│
│ France/Germany (West)

F I G U R E   3 . 3   The Government Should Ensure Everyone
Is Provided For (percent agreeing)

Source: Selected nations from the 2000–2002 *World Values Survey* and 1999 *European Values Survey;* missing data are
excluded from the calculation of percentages.

and want to participate. Indeed, one of the major political issues in the world today
is whether the democratic transitions in Eastern Europe, Latin America, and East
Asia that began in the 1990s can be sustained. The political culture in these nations
will provide a significant part of the answer.

Figure 3.4 illustrates the relationship between history and political culture.
The figure displays public satisfaction with the functioning of democracy for three
groups of nations; each oval in the figure represents a separate nation. One can
readily see that satisfaction with democracy is higher in the first group of stable
and very democratic nations; these are largely the established democracies of
Western Europe and North America. Political satisfaction is lower in the second

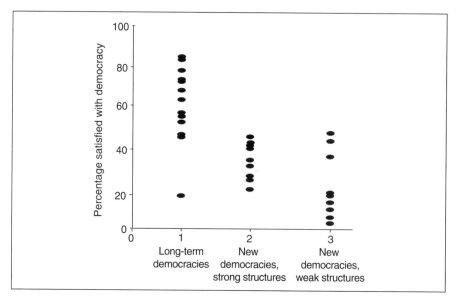

FIGURE 3.4   The Relationship Between Democratic Experience and Political Support

Source: Calculated from data on system age from Ted Gurr, *Polity III* dataset; the 1996 democracy rating from the Freedom House; satisfaction with the functioning of democracy is from Hans-Dieter Klingemann, "Mapping Political Support in the 1990s: A Global Analysis," in Pippa Norris, ed. *Critical Citizens: Global Support for Democratic Government* (Oxford, England: Oxford University Press, 1999), table 2.10.

group of nations that have recently developed strong democratic structures—several Latin American and East European nations fall into this category. Finally, political satisfaction is lowest in the third group—nations with new political systems having weak democratic structures, such as the states of the former Soviet Union. Structure and culture do overlap in these nations.[7]

One may ask whether democracies create a satisfied and democratic public, or whether such a political culture leads to a democratic political system. Obviously it works both ways. For example, immediately after World War II Germans were less supportive of democracy, but the political culture was transformed by political institutions and political experiences over the generation.[8] At the same time, democracy endured in Britain during the strains of the Great Depression and World War II at least in part because the British public was supportive of the democratic process. The important conclusion is that there is normally a relationship between political culture and political structures.

Consensual or Conflictual Political Cultures

We have described political culture as a characteristic of a nation, but values and beliefs also vary within nations. Political cultures may be consensual or conflictual on issues of public policy and, more fundamentally, on views of legitimate governmental and political arrangements. In a **consensual political culture,** citizens tend to agree on the appropriate means of making political decisions and to agree on the major problems facing the society and how to solve them. In a **conflictual political culture,** the citizens are sharply divided, often on both the legitimacy of the regime and solutions to major problems.

When a country is deeply divided in political attitudes and these differences persist over time, distinctive **political subcultures** may develop. The citizens in these subcultures may have sharply different points of view on at least some critical political matters, such as the boundaries of the nation, the nature of the regime, or the correct ideology. Typically, they affiliate with different political parties and interest groups, read different newspapers, and even have separate social clubs and sporting groups. Thus they are exposed to quite distinctive patterns of learning about politics. Such organized differences characterize the publics in India, Nigeria, and Russia today.

Where political subcultures coincide with ethnic, national, or religious differences, as in Northern Ireland, Bosnia, and Lebanon, the divisions can be enduring and threatening. The fragmentation of the Soviet empire, the breakup of Yugoslavia, and the impulses toward autonomy and secession among ethnically distinct regions (such as in Scotland or separatist movements in Africa) all reflect the lasting power of language, culture, and historical memory to create and sustain the sense of ethnic and national identity among parts of contemporary states. Samuel Huntington has predicted that the places in the world where the major traditional cultures collide will be major sources of political conflict in the next century.[9]

POLITICAL SOCIALIZATION

Political cultures are sustained or changed as people acquire their attitudes and values. We use the term *socialization* to refer to the way in which political values are formed and the political culture is transmitted from one generation to the next. Most children acquire their basic political orientations and behavior patterns at a relatively early age.[10] Some of these attitudes will evolve and change through life, but others may remain part of the political self throughout life.

At any specific time, an individual's political self will be a combination of several feelings and attitudes. At the deepest level, there are general identifications and beliefs such as nationalism, ethnic or class self-images, religious and ideological commitments, and a fundamental sense of rights and duties in the society. Divisions between ethnic or religious groups often generate such attachments because they are based on such self-images. At an intermediate level, individuals acquire less intense emotional attitudes toward politics and governmental institutions. Finally, there are more immediate views of current events, policies, issues, and personalities. All these attitudes can change, but those in the first group usually were acquired earliest, have been most frequently reinforced, and tend to be the most durable.

Three general points about political socialization and learning need to be emphasized. First, there can be either **direct** or **indirect socialization.** Socialization is direct when it involves the explicit communication of information, values, or feelings toward politics. Civics courses in public schools are direct political socialization, as are the efforts of Islamic fundamentalist movements to indoctrinate children in such countries as Iran and Pakistan. Communist political systems also heavily use indoctrination programs. Political socialization is indirect when political views are inadvertently molded by our experiences. Such indirect political socialization may have particular force in a child's early years. For example, the child's relationships to parents, teachers, and friends are likely to affect the adult's posture toward political leaders and fellow citizens in later life. Or, growing up in a time of deprivation and hardship may leave the future adult more concerned about economic well-being.

Second, socialization continues throughout an individual's life. Early family influences can create an individual's initial values, but subsequent life experiences—becoming involved in new social groups and roles, moving from one part of the country to another, shifting up or down the social ladder, becoming a parent, finding or losing a job—may change one's political perspectives. More dramatic experiences, such as immigration to a new country or suffering through an economic depression or a war, can alter even quite basic political attitudes. Such events seem to have their greatest impact on young people just becoming involved in politics, such as first-time voters, but most people are affected to some degree.

Third, patterns of socialization in a society can either be *unifying* or *divisive*. Some events, such as international conflict or the loss of a popular public figure, can affect nearly the entire nation similarly. In contrast, subcultures in a society can have their own distinctive patterns of socialization. Social groups that provide their members with their own newspapers, their own neighborhood groups, and perhaps their own schools can create distinctive subcultural attitudes. Divisive patterns of socialization can lead to civil strife or social hostility within a nation.

AGENTS OF POLITICAL SOCIALIZATION

Individuals in all societies are affected by **agents of political socialization:** institutions and organizations that influence political attitudes. Some, like civics courses in schools, are direct and deliberate sources of political learning. Others, like play and work groups, are likely to affect political socialization indirectly.

The Family

The direct and indirect influences of the family—the first socialization source that an individual encounters—are powerful and lasting. The family has distinctive influences on attitudes toward authority. Participation in family decision making can increase a child's sense of political competence, providing skills for political interaction and encouraging active participation in the political system as an adult. By the same token, unquestioning obedience to parental decisions may predispose the child to a role as a political subject. The family also shapes future political attitudes by locating the individual in a vast social world; establishing ethnic, linguistic, class, and religious ties, affirming cultural values, and directing occupational and economic aspirations.

The family is also changing in some societies. A revolution in women's resources and expectations in recent decades has profoundly affected the advanced industrial nations. Greater gender equality in education, occupation, and profession has transformed the structure of the family. The lessening of gender differences in self-images, in parental roles, and in relations to the economy and the political system is significantly affecting patterns of political recruitment, political participation, and public policy. A more open family, equality of parenting, and the early exposure of children to child care and preschool group experiences have modified the impact of the family in the socialization process in ways that are still being assessed. Especially in the developing world, the changing role of women may have profound influences in modernizing the society.[11]

Schools

Schools provide children and adolescents with knowledge about the political world and their role in it and with more concrete information on political institutions and relationships. Schools also transmit the values and attitudes of the society. They can play an important role in shaping attitudes about the unwritten rules of the political game, instilling the values of public duty, and developing informal political relations. Schools can reinforce affection for the political system and provide common symbols, such as the flag and pledge of allegiance, that encourage emotional attachments to the system. When a new nation comes into being, or a

BOX 3.1   Socializing Values

Communist East Germany had a special ceremony for eighth graders that marked their passage to adulthood. The heart of the ceremony was the endorsement of the following four pledges:

- As young citizens of our German Democratic Republic, are you prepared to work and fight loyally for the great and honorable goals of socialism, and to honor the revolutionary inheritance of the people?

- As sons and daughters of the worker-and-peasant state, are you prepared to pursue higher education, to cultivate your mind, to become a master of your trade, to learn permanently, and to use your knowledge to pursue our great humanist ideals?

- As honorable members of the socialist community, are you ready to cooperate as comrades, to respect and support each other, and to always merge the pursuit of your personal happiness with the happiness of all the people?

- As true patriots, are you ready to deepen the friendship with the Soviet Union, to strengthen our brotherhood with socialist countries, to struggle in the spirit of proletarian internationalism, to protect peace and to defend socialism against every imperialist aggression?

revolutionary regime comes to power in an old nation, it usually turns immediately to the schools as a means to supplant "outdated" values and symbols with new ones more congruent with the new ideology.

In some nations educational systems do not provide unifying political socialization but send starkly different messages to different groups. For instance, some Muslim states segregate girls and boys within the school system. Even if educational experiences are intended to be equivalent, such segregation begins to create different experiences and expectations. And often the content of education differs between boys and girls. Perhaps the worst example occurred under the Taliban in Afghanistan, where for several years young girls were prohibited from attending school. Such treatment of young girls severely limits their life changes, and ensures they will have limited roles in society and the economy—which was the intent of the Taliban system. One of the new programs of the post-Taliban government was to reverse this policy, and now young Afghani girls are being included in the education system, and their future life prospects are improving as a result.

Education also affects the political skills and resources of the public. Educated persons are more aware of the impact of government on their lives and pay more attention to politics. The better-educated have mental skills that improve their ability to interpret and act on new information. They also have more information about political processes and undertake a wider range of political activities. These effects of education appear in studies of political attitudes in many nations.[12]

Religious Institutions

The religions of the world are carriers of cultural and moral values, which often have political implications. The great religious leaders have seen themselves as teachers, and their followers have usually attempted to shape the socialization of children through schooling, preaching, and religious services. In contrast to the pattern in the United States, in most nations there are formal ties between the dominant religion and the government. In these instances, religious values and public policy inevitably overlap. Catholic nations, for instance, are less likely to have liberal abortion policies, just as Islamic governments enforce strict moral codes.

Where the churches systematically teach values that may be at odds with the controlling political system—as in the conflict between Islamic fundamentalists and secular governments in Algeria and Egypt, or in the efforts of American fundamentalists to introduce prayer in the schools—the struggle over socialization can be of the greatest significance in the society. In these nations religious subcultures may oppose the policies of the state, or even the state itself.

The emergence of aggressive religious fundamentalism in recent decades has had a major impact on the society and politics of countries as diverse as the United States, India, Israel, Lebanon, Iran, Pakistan, Algeria, and Nigeria. Such fundamentalism is often a defensive reaction against the spread of scientific views of nature and human behavior, and the libertarian values and attitudes that accompany these views. Fundamentalism usually defines a world in which believers must engage in the great struggle between the forces of spiritual goodness and evil.[13] While the influence of fundamentalism has been most visible in the Middle East and among Muslim countries, it is important in Christian countries as well. There are both Protestant and Catholic versions of fundamentalism in the United States, Europe, and Latin America. Versions of fundamentalism are also to be found, combined with ethnic and nationalist tendencies, among the Confucian, Buddhist, and Hindu countries of Asia. Broadly speaking, fundamentalism seeks to raise conservative social, moral, and religious issues to the top of the contemporary policy agenda.

Of course, religious institutions of many kinds offer valuable moral and ethical guidance that individuals often need to make choices in complex societies. Religious affiliations are often important sources of partisan preferences and can guide people in making other political choices. Thus even though the frequency of church attendance is declining in many nations, the political relevance of religion continues.

Peer Groups

Peer groups are important social units that shape political attitudes. They include childhood play groups, friendship cliques, school and college fraternities, and small work groups, in which members share relatively equal status and close ties. They can be as varied as a group of Russian mothers who meet regularly at the park, a street gang in Brazil, or a group of Wall Street executives who are members of a social club.

A peer group socializes its members by motivating or pressuring them to conform to the attitudes or behavior accepted by the group. Individuals often adopt the views of their peers because they like or respect them or because they want to be like them. An individual may become interested in politics or attend a political demonstration because close friends do so.[14] In such cases, the individual modifies his or her interests and behavior to reflect those of the group in an effort to be accepted by its members. The international youth culture symbolized by rock music, T-shirts, and blue jeans may have played a major role in the failure of communist officials to mold Soviet and Eastern European youth to the "socialist personality" that was the Marxist-Leninist ideal. Likewise, the "skinheads" groups that have sprouted up among lower-class youth in many Western countries have adopted political views that are based on peer interactions.

Social Class and Gender

Most societies have significant social divisions based on class or occupation. Individuals live in different social worlds defined by their class position. For instance, industrialization created a working class in Britain that was concentrated in particular neighborhoods and developed its own forms of speech, dress, recreation, and entertainment and its own organizations, including trade unions and political parties. Similarly, in many less-developed nations the life experience of the rural peasantry is radically different from urban dwellers. In many instances these social divisions are politically relevant: identifying oneself as a member of the working class or the peasantry leads to distinct political views about what issues are important and which political groups best represent one's interest.

Gender is another important pattern of social and political learning. From birth, nature and society ascribe different patterns of behavior to males and females. Traditionally these social divisions have carried over to politics, defining politics as a male activity and focusing the interests of women on social and family issues. In many less-developed nations these gender roles still exist today. In many industrial nations, however, gender roles are changing.[15] The rise of the women's movement and self-help groups have encouraged women to become active and provided social cues about how women should relate to politics.

Mass Media

Much of the world has become a single audience, exposed to the same information and moved by the same events. There is virtually no part so remote that its inhabitants lack the means to be informed almost simultaneously about events elsewhere: mass-produced and inexpensive transistor radios are omnipresent, even in Third World villages far removed from political power centers. The mass media— newspapers, radio, television, magazines—play an important part in internationalizing attitudes and values around the globe.

Television, enlisting the senses of both sight and sound, can have a powerful emotional impact on large public audiences. Watching war on television—such as the live broadcasts provided by CNN during the war in Iraq—gives a reality to the news, just as people's feelings were touched by media coverage of Princess Diana's death in 1997. The mass media can also transcend national boundaries and ideological divides. The movements for democracy throughout Eastern Europe were partially created by the image of another way of life that came through the international media. As these democratic revolutions spread in the late 1980s, they fed on the knowledge of the tactics and successes of others, given extra impact through newspapers, television, and radio newly free to report these exciting events. Today the internet is providing a new source of news for those who live in closed societies.

In addition to providing specific and immediate information about political events, the mass media also convey, directly or indirectly, the major values on which a society agrees. The media can portray certain events as symbolizing the nation—for example, national holidays or traditional government activities—and the events take on a specific emotional color. Mass media controlled by an authoritarian government can shape political beliefs. However, citizens eventually will ignore reports that are inconsistent with their personal experiences, and word-of-mouth transmission of inconsistent attitudes is often a powerful antidote to the effectiveness of government-controlled mass media.

Interest Groups

Interest groups, associations, economic groups, and similar organizations also shape political attitudes. Among economic groups, trade unions may have had the most important consequences for politics. In most industrial countries, the rise of trade unions transformed political culture and politics, created new political parties, and ushered in new social benefit programs. Other occupational and professional associations, such as groups of peasants and farmers, manufacturers, wholesalers and retailers, medical societies, and lawyers can also influence political attitudes in modern and modernizing societies. These groups ensure the loyalty of their members by defending their economic and professional interests. They can also provide valuable political cues to nonmembers, who might identify with a group's interests or political ideology.

Also important in political socialization are the public groups that define a civil society; this might include ethnic organizations, fraternal associations, civic associations (such as parent-teacher associations), and policy groups (such as taxpayers' associations, women's groups, or environmental groups). Such groups provide valuable political cues to their members and try to reinforce distinct social and political orientations. In addition, these groups—using the media and other sources—send out large quantities of information on political, social, and economic issues to the public and elites.

Political Parties

As specialized political structures that exist in democratic and nondemocratic systems, political parties play an important role in political socialization. Political parties attempt to mold issue preferences, arouse the apathetic, and find new issues to mobilize support. Party leaders and party spokespersons provide the public with a steady flow of information on the political issues of the day. Party organizations regularly contact voters by mail or phone, and in many nations party activists visit voters at home. And every few years there is an election in democratic systems, in which parties present their past accomplishments and discuss the nation's political future. Elections can serve as national civics lessons, and parties are the teachers.

In competitive party systems, partisan socialization can be also a divisive force. In their efforts to gain support, leaders may appeal to class, language, religion, and ethnic divisions and make citizens more aware of these differences. The Labour and Conservative parties in Britain, for example, draw heavily on traditional symbols of class to attract supporters. Similarly, the Congress Party in India tries to develop a national program and appeal, but other parties emphasize the ethnic and religious divisions. Leaders of preindustrial nations often oppose competitive parties because they fear such divisiveness. Although this is sometimes a sincere concern, it is also self-serving to government leaders, and is becoming increasingly difficult to justify against widespread contemporary demands for multiparty systems.

Authoritarian governments often use a single party to attempt to inculcate common attitudes of national unity, support for the government, and ideological agreement. The combination of a single party and controlled mass media is potent: The media present a single point of view, and the party activities reinforce that perspective by directly involving the citizen. Yet, as demonstrated in Eastern Europe in 1989, years of directed socialization by media and the government cannot compete with citizens' personal experiences in shaping basic attitudes.

Direct Contact with Governmental Structures

In modern societies, the wide scope of governmental activities brings citizens into frequent contact with various bureaucratic agencies. One study found that 72 percent of adult Americans had interacted with at least one government agency in the preceding year; about a third had interacted with more. The most frequent contacts were with tax authorities, school officials, and the police.[16] The degree of government intervention in daily life, and hence the necessity for contacts with government, is greater in many Western European nations than in the United States, and it is greater yet in the remaining communist countries.

These personal experiences are powerful agents of socialization, strengthening or undercutting the images presented by other agents. No matter how positive the view of the political system that has been taught in school, citizens who face a different reality in everyday life are likely to change their early-learned views. Indeed, the contradictions between ideology and reality proved to be one of the weaknesses of the communist systems in Eastern Europe.

In their study of citizen attitudes in five nations, Almond and Verba found marked differences across countries in the expectations that citizens had of their treatment by police and bureaucrats.[17] Italians, and particularly Mexicans, had quite dismal expectations as to equality and responsiveness of treatment. African Americans also reported quite negative expectations in these 1960 interviews. It is likely that these expectations were in large measure a response to actual patterns of treatment by government.

TRENDS IN CONTEMPORARY POLITICAL CULTURES

A political culture exists uniquely in its own time and place. Citizens' attitudes and beliefs are shaped by personal experiences and by the agents of political socialization. Yet, in any historical period there may be trends that change the culture in many nations. The major social trends of our time—modernity and secularism, postmaterial values, fundamentalism and ethnic awareness, democratization, and marketization—reflect both general societal developments and specific historic events.

The major cultural trend that has transformed the world and public values has been **modernization.** For almost two centuries now, the secularizing influences of science and control over nature have altered economic and social systems and shaped political cultures, first in the West and increasingly throughout the world. This trend toward cultural modernization continues to have powerful effects as it penetrates societies (or parts of societies) that have been shielded from it. Exposure to modernity through work, education, and the media shapes an individual's personal experiences and sends messages about modernity in other societies. It encourages citizen participation, a sense of individual equality, the desire for improved living standards and increased life expectancy, and government legitimacy based on policy performance. It also frequently disrupts familiar ways of life, traditional bases of legitimacy, and political arrangements that depend on citizens remaining predominantly parochials or subjects. Alex Inkeles and David Smith's study of the development of modern attitudes emphasized how factory experience can create an awareness of the possibilities of organization, change, and control over nature (see Box 3.2).

A by-product of socioeconomic modernization appears in the nations of North America, Western Europe, and Japan that have developed the characteristics of a postindustrial society. Younger generations who grew up under con-

BOX 3.2   Becoming Modern

Inkeles and Smith report how one Nigerian worker replied to a question about how his new job in a factory made him feel. "Sometimes like 9 feet tall with arms a yard wide. Here in the factory I alone with my machine can twist any way I want a piece of steel that all the men in my home village together could not begin to bend at all." Such experiences, and the parallel changes in educational levels and access to information can create a more modern political culture.

Source: Alex Inkeles and David Smith, *Becoming Modern* (Cambridge, MA: Harvard University Press, 1974), p. 158.

ditions of economic prosperity and international peace are now less concerned with material well-being and personal security than their parents.[18] Instead, the young are more likely to emphasize **postmaterial values:** social equality, environmental protection, cultural pluralism, and self-expression. Postmaterial values have spawned new citizen groups, such as the environmental movement, the women's movement, and other public interest associations. These changing values have also reshaped the policy agenda of industrial democracies; more citizens are asking government to restore the environment, expand social and political freedoms, and emphasize policies to ensure social equality. Politicians in these democracies are struggling to balance these new policy demands against the continuing policy needs of the past.

A much different response to modernization has been the resurgence of **ethnicity,** or ethnic identities, in many parts of the world.[19] As citizen skills and self-confidence have increased, formerly suppressed ethnic groups are expressing their identities and demanding equal treatment. Development of education and communication skills may encourage a flourishing of literature in a local language whose previous tradition has been informal and oral. This development can further intensify awareness of common symbols and history. While resurgence of distinctive local cultures enriches the global society, clashes between cultures and subcultures can also be particularly deadly bases of political conflict. Moreover, the migration of peoples into new areas, made possible by easier transportation and encouraged by wars, political conflicts, and the desire for economic betterment, can seem to threaten the way of life of the host society. The exposure to values from other cultures may intensify one's own self-image, which may increase cultural tensions. Although such exposure may eventually lead to greater tolerance, there is no guarantee of this outcome.

In the last decade the major new development is the trend toward democracy in Eastern Europe, East Asia, and other parts of the developing world. This **democratization** trend reflects long-term responses to modernity as well as immediate reactions to current events. Modernization gradually eroded the legitimacy of nondemocratic ideologies, while the development of citizens' skills and political resources made their claim to equal participation in policymaking (at least indirectly) more plausible. Thus many studies of political culture in Eastern Europe and the former Soviet Union uncovered surprising support for democratic norms and processes among the citizenry as the new democratic system formed.[20]

Ironically, as democratic values have begun to take root in Eastern Europe, citizens in many Western democracies have become increasingly skeptical about politicians and political institutions. In 1964, three-quarters of Americans said they trusted the government; today only a third of the public say as much—and the malaise is spreading to Western Europe and Japan.[21] Recent research shows that citizen support for democratic norms has not waned; in fact, democratic norms and values have strengthened over time as democracy has developed in the West. Instead, people are critical about how democracy functions. Western citizens expect democracy to fulfill its ideals and are critical of politicians and political parties when they fall short of these ideals. Although this cynicism is a strain on democratic politicians, it presses democracy to continue to improve and adapt, which is ultimately democracy's greatest strength.

Another cultural trend in recent years has been a shift toward **marketization**—that is, a greater public acceptance of free markets and private profit incentives, rather than a government-managed economy. The movement appeared in the United States and many Western European nations in the 1980s, where economies had experienced serious problems of inefficiency and economic stagnation. Margaret Thatcher in Britain and Ronald Reagan in the United States rode to power on waves of public support for reducing the scale of government. Public opinion surveys show that people in these nations feel that government had grown too large (see again Figure 3.3). The political victories of Reagan and Thatcher gave further prestige to efforts to roll back government involvement.

Just as Western Europeans began to question the government's role in the economy, the political changes in Eastern Europe and the Soviet Union added a new feature to the discussion. The command economies of Eastern Europe were almost exclusively controlled by state corporations and government agencies. The government set both wages and prices and directed the economy. Today, the collapse of these systems raises new questions about public support for marketization. Public opinion surveys generally find that Eastern Europeans support a capitalist market system.[22]

Support for market economies has also apparently grown in the developing world. In the past decade, many developing nations had difficulties in modernizing their economies through government-controlled economic development; this made freer markets a plausible alternative. The successes of the Asian "tigers" of South Korea, Taiwan, and Singapore in achieving rapid economic growth encouraged this movement, which has even affected policy directions in the People's Republic of China. It is difficult to disentangle the fundamental political economy issues here from the effects of contemporary events. The trend toward marketization is a response to a long period of increased government intervention in economies. At the moment, no particular mixture of free market and government intervention seems ideal. We expect much further experimentation; the current trend to marketization may also encounter reversals or countertrends in the future.

Clearly, political culture is not a static phenomenon. Our understanding of political culture must be dynamic. It must encompass how the agents of political socialization communicate and interpret historic events and traditional values. It must juxtapose these with the exposure of citizens and leaders to new experiences and new ideas. We must understand also that the gradual change of generations means continuing modification of the political culture as new groups of citizens have different experiences on which to draw.

KEY TERMS

agents of political
 socialization
conflictual political culture
consensual political
 culture
democratization
direct and indirect
 socialization

ethnicity
fundamentalism
legitimacy
marketization
modernization
parochials

participants
political culture
political socialization
political subcultures
postmaterial values
subjects

SUGGESTED READINGS

Aberbach, Joel D., Robert D. Putnam, and Bert A. Rockman. *Bureaucrats and Politicians in Western Democracies.* Cambridge, MA: Harvard University Press, 1981.

Abramson, Paul and Ronald Inglehart. *Value Change in Global Perspective.* Ann Arbor: University of Michigan Press, 1995.

Almond, Gabriel A. and Sidney Verba. *The Civic Culture.* Princeton, NJ: Princeton University Press, 1963.

————, eds. *The Civic Culture Revisited.* Boston: Little Brown, 1980.

Barnes, Samuel and Janos Simon, eds. *The Postcommunist Citizen.* Budapest: Erasmus Foundation, 1998.

Eckstein, Harry. "A Culturalist Theory of Political Change." *American Political Science Review* 82 (Sept. 1988): 789–804.

Harrison, Lawrence and Samuel P. Huntington, eds. *Culture Matters: How Values Shape Human Progress.* New York: Basic Books, 2000.

Horowitz, Donald. *Ethnic Groups in Conflict.* Berkeley: University of California Press, 1985.

Huntington, Samuel. *The Clash of Civilizations and the Remaking of World Order.* New York: Simon & Schuster, 1996.

Inglehart, R. *Modernization and Postmodernization: Cultural, Economic and Political Change in 43 Societies.* Princeton, NJ: Princeton University Press, 1997.

Inkeles, Alex and David H. Smith. *Becoming Modern.* Cambridge, MA: Harvard University Press, 1974.

Jennings, M. Kent and Richard Niemi. *Generations and Politics: A Panel Study of Young Adults and their Parents.* Princeton, NJ: Princeton University Press, 1981.

Klingemann, Hans Dieter and Dieter Fuchs. *Citizens and the State.* Oxford, England: Oxford University Press, 1995.

Norris, Pippa, ed. *Critical Citizens: Global Support for Democratic Government.* Oxford, England: Oxford University Press, 1999.

Norris, Pippa and Ronald Inglehart. *Rising Tide: Gender Equality and Cultural Change around the World.* New York: Cambridge University Press, 2003.

Pharr, Susan and Robert Putnam. *Disaffected Democracies: What's Troubling the Trilateral Democracies.* Princeton: Princeton University Press, 2000.

Putnam, Robert. *The Beliefs of Politicians.* New Haven, CT: Yale University Press, 1973.

———. *Making Democracy Work: Civic Traditions in Modern Italy.* Princeton, NJ: Princeton University Press, 1993.

Pye, Lucian W. and Sidney Verba, eds. *Political Culture and Political Development.* Princeton, NJ: Princeton University Press, 1965.

Rochon, Thomas. *Culture Moves: Ideas, Activism and Changing Values.* Princeton, NJ: Princeton University Press, 1998.

Rose, Richard, Christian Haerpfer, and William Mishler. *Testing the Churchill Hypothesis: Democracy and its Alternatives in Post-communist Societies.* Cambridge, UK: Polity/Baltimore: Johns Hopkins University Press, 2000.

Sears, David O. "Political Socialization." In F. I. Greenstein and N. W. Polsby, *Handbook of Political Science,* vol. 2, ch. 2. Reading, MA: Addison-Wesley, 1975.

ENDNOTES

1. This concept of legitimacy and its bases in different societies draws upon the work of Max Weber. For example, see Max Weber, *Basic Concepts in Sociology,* trans. H. P. Secher (New York: Citadel Press, 1964), chs. 5–7.

2. Pippa Norris, ed., *Critical Citizens: Global Support for Democratic Government* (Oxford, England: Oxford University Press, 1999).

3. These terms were developed in Gabriel A. Almond and Sidney Verba, *The Civic Culture: Political Attitudes and Democracy in Five Nations* (Princeton, NJ: Princeton University Press, 1963).

4. On the importance of trust, see Almond and Verba, *Civic Culture,* ch. 10; Ronald Inglehart, *Culture Shift in Advanced Industrial Society* (Princeton, NJ: Princeton University Press, 1990), ch. 1; and Robert D. Putnam, *Making Democracy Work: Civic Traditions in Modern Italy* (Princeton, NJ: Princeton University Press, 1993), especially chs. 4 and 6.

5. Ronald Inglehart, *Modernization and Postmodernization* (Princeton: Princeton University Press, 1997), chs. 6–7.

6. Ole Borre and Elinor Scarbrough, eds., *The Scope of Government* (Oxford, England: Oxford University Press, 1995).

7. Also see, Putnam, *Making Democracy Work.*

8. Kendall Baker, Russell Dalton, and Kai Hildebrandt, *Germany Transformed* (Cambridge, MA: Harvard University Press, 1981).

9. Samuel P. Huntington, *The Clash of Civilizations and the Remaking of World Order* (New York: Simon and Schuster, 1996).

10. See Almond and Verba, *Civic Culture,* ch. 12; M. Kent Jennings, Klaus R. Allerbeck, and Leopold Rosenmayr, "Generations and Families," in Samuel H. Barnes, Max Kaase, et al., *Political Action* (Beverly Hills, CA: Sage, 1979), chs. 15 and 16.

11. Martha Nussbaum and Jonathan Glover, eds., *Women, Culture, and Development: A Study of Human Capabilities* (New York: Oxford University Press, 1995).

12. For example, see Sidney Verba, Norman H. Nie, and Jae-on Kim, *Participation and Political Equality: A Seven-Nation Study* (New York: Cambridge University Press, 1978); Barnes, Kaase, et al., *Political Action,* ch. 4.

13. See, among others, Martin Marty and Scott Appleby, *Fundamentalism Observed* (Chicago: University of Chicago Press, 1991).

14. Richard E. Dawson, Kenneth Prewitt, and Karen Dawson, *Political Socialization,* 2nd ed. (Boston: Little, Brown, 1977), ch. 9.

15. Pippa Norris and Ronald Inglehart, *Rising Tide: Gender Equality and Cultural Change around the World* (New York: Cambridge University Press, 2003).

16. Robert G. Lehnen, *American Institutions: Political Opinion and Public Policy* (Hinsdale, IL: Holt, Rinehart, and Winston, 1976), p. 183; see also Charles Goodsell, *The Case for Bureaucracy,* 3rd ed. (Chatham, NJ: Chatham House, 1994), ch. 2.

17. Almond and Verba, *Civic Culture,* pp. 108–09.

18. Ronald Inglehart, *Culture Shift in Advanced Industrial Society*; Ronald Inglehart, *The Silent Revolution: Changing Values and Political Styles among Western Publics* (Princeton, NJ: Princeton University Press, 1977).

19. Donald Horowitz, *Ethnic Groups in Conflict* (Berkeley: University of California Press, 1985).

20. Arthur Miller, William Reisinger, and Vicki Hesli, eds., *Public Opinion and Regime Change* (Boulder, CO: Westview Press, 1993); William Mishler and Richard Rose, "Trajectories of Fear and Hope: Support for Democracy in Post-communist Europe," *Comparative Political Studies* 28 (1995): 553–81. Compare to Robert Rohrschneider, "Institutional Learning Versus Value Diffusion," *Journal of Politics* 58 (1996): 442–66.

21. Norris, *Critical Citizens*; Russell Dalton, *Democratic Challenges, Democratic Choices* (Oxford: Oxford University Press, 2003).

22. See William Zimmerman, *The Russian People and Foreign Policy: Russian Elite and Mass Perspectives* (Princeton: Princeton University Press, 2002), ch. 2; Raymond Duch, "Tolerating Economic Reform," *American Political Science Review* 87 (1993): 590–608. Russian support for marketization noticeably lags behind that of most Eastern Europeans.

4

Interest Articulation

Every political system has some way for citizens and social groups to express their needs and demands to the government. This process of **interest articulation** can take many forms. The most basic might be an individual making a request to a city council member or other government official, or, in a more traditional system, to the village head or tribal chieftain. Collective action by groups of citizens is also an essential part of the articulation process. In larger political systems, individuals working together as a formal interest group are a prime tool in promoting political interests.

During the last hundred years or so, as societies have become internally more complex and the scope of government activity has widened, the quantity and variety of different forms of interest articulation have grown proportionately. Citizens work together to address local and national needs, ranging from the provision of clean water in a village to the passage of national clean water standards. Social movements involve the public in issues as diverse as protecting the rights of indigenous people in the Amazon to debating nuclear power. Interest group headquarters, in large numbers, are found in capitals like London, Washington, Tokyo, and Rome. Some of these headquarters are in buildings as imposing as those housing major governmental agencies. In countries with powerful local governments, interest groups are active at the provincial or local level as well.

This chapter considers the multiple ways that political interests might be expressed and represented in political systems. We discuss both the informal and direct forms of citizen action, as well as more institutionalized forms of articulation. For example, in most countries that allow them, labor unions, manufacturers' associations, farm groups, and associations of doctors, lawyers, engineers, and teachers form to represent these interests. And in the end, most political systems rely on all of these forms of interest articulation to determine what the public and social groups desire of their government.

CITIZEN ACTION

Before political institutions and political processes come into play, we are first members of a society. We interact with family and friends throughout our lives, we express our interests and needs, and we work with others to achieve our goals. These human patterns of social interaction carry over to politics.

In interest articulation, individual citizens can use a variety of methods to make requests, demands, and pleas for policies (Table 4.1). The most common form of citizen participation is voting in an election—something found even in many authoritarian political systems. Elections provide a basis for the public to express their interests and to make a collective choice about the government's past progress and the future policies for the nation. Even though elections select political elites, they often have a blunt policy impact because elections involve many different issues, and between elections officeholders may stray from the voters' preferences.

Another form of interest articulation occurs when people work with others in their community to address common social or political needs, as when parents work to better the local schools or residents express a concern about how the community is developing. These activities tend to be very policy focused and to exert direct pressure on decision-makers. Such group activity can be found in democratic and authoritarian systems, although nondemocracies may limit the methods of expression to ones that do not openly confront authorities.

Some interest articulation involves only an individual and his or her family, as when a veteran writes to his legislator for help in getting benefits approved, or when a homeowner asks the local party precinct leader to get her driveway snowplowed regularly. These are **personal interest contacts,** and they are universal in all kinds of political systems including the authoritarian ones. However, the interests being expressed tend to be limited to those of a specific individual or a small group of people.

The expression of interests and political demands also may extend beyond the bounds of conventional politics to involve protests or other forms of direct action. The spontaneous gathering of outraged ghetto dwellers, the public **protests** that overthrew the communist governments of Eastern Europe, and the environmental protests of Greenpeace are all examples of how political protest can focus political interests and influence. Protests and other direct actions tend to be high-pressure activities that can both mobilize the public and directly pressure elites; these activities can also be very focused in their political content.

T A B L E   4 . 1   Forms of Citizen Interest Articulation

Form	Scope of Interests	Degree of Pressure on Elites
Voting, participation in elections	Broad, collective decision on government leaders and their programs	Modest pressure, but unfocused
Informal group, social movement	Collective action focused on a common interest	High pressure
Personal interest contact	Normally deals with specific, personal problem	Low pressure
Protest activity	Highly expressive support for specific interests	High pressure

In summary, citizens have many routes available to them in expressing their political interests, and each of these routes has particular characteristics associated with it.

How Citizens Participate

The amount of citizen participation in politics varies greatly according to the type of activity and the type of political system. Table 4.2 shows some examples of different types of citizen participation in several nations examined in this book. The table reveals that common forms of political participation revolve around elections: turning out to vote, trying to convince others how to vote, or working with political parties. Because elections are the most common form of public involvement in the political process, they are important in the interest articulation process. During elections, citizens speak their minds on current issues through conversations, attending meetings, contributing to campaigns, and even expressing their opinions to pollsters. Ultimately, individuals decide their preferences in their ballot choices. At the same time, however, elections perform many other functions: the aggregation of political interests (see Chapter 5), the recruitment of political elites, and even the socialization of political values and preferences through the campaign process.

Democracies are remarkable in that competitive elections offer important political resources to all citizens. Among the democracies, the United States stands out for its rather low levels of national voting participation: both West Europeans (with their long democratic experience) and Russians (who are new to democratic elections) vote more frequently than Americans. However, as the table shows,

TABLE 4 . 2   Citizen Participation in Eight Nations (percentage)

Type of Participation	United States	Britain	France	Germany	Japan	Russia	Mexico	Nigeria
Voter turnout in most recent national elections	49%	59%	72%	82%	63%	62%	64%	41%
Discussed politics with others	74	46	65	84	64	75	58	74
Participated in political party activities	18	3	2	3	4	1	5	—
Participated in citizen interest group	36	7	6	7	9	2	11	—
Signed a petition	81	81	68	52	63	12	19	7
Participated in lawful protest demonstration	21	13	39	28	13	24	4	17

Sources: Election turnout data for most recent national election from Elections in the World, downloaded Oct. 30, 2002 from www.electionworld.org; 2000–2002 *World Values Survey* and the 1999 *European Values Survey* for other participation statistics. We would like to thank Ronald Inglehart for granting access to these data.

Americans' low level of election turnout does not simply reflect apathy. Americans are much more likely to try to discuss politics with others than are their British counterparts, and they are much more likely to work for a party or candidate than either Britons or Germans.

Public efforts to express political interests and influence public policy extend beyond elections. Grassroots politics, people working together to address a common problem, represents a very direct method for articulating political interests and attempting policy influence. Alexis de Tocqueville considered such grassroots community action as the foundation of democratic politics. Today such activities are often identified with middle-class participation in affluent societies—PTA groups, community associations, public interest groups—but group activity can be a form of political participation in any nation.[1] Indian villagers working together to build a communal latrine or to develop rural electricity, or indigenous people protecting their land rights are other examples of community action.

Table 4.2 also indicates that group activity has become a frequent form of political expression in the advanced industrial democracies. Nearly a third of Americans are members of a citizen interest group, and significant numbers are active in European polities as well.[2] Such activity is high in Mexico, perhaps because this survey overlaps with the politicization of Vincente Fox's election. However, surveys from the developing world suggests that these activities are regularly used, albeit less frequently than in more developed nations.

Perhaps the most expressive and visible form of citizen action involves participation in protests, demonstrations, or other direct actions. What better way to articulate one's interest in preventing pollution than to hang an environmental banner from a polluting smokestack, stage a mass demonstration outside of parliament, or boycott polluters? Participation in political protests can arise for quite different reasons. On the one hand, protest and direct action is often used by individuals and groups that feel they lack access to legitimate political channels. The mass demonstrations in Eastern Europe in the late 1980s and the public rallies and marches of black South Africans against apartheid illustrate protests as the last resort of the disadvantaged. On the other hand, peaceful protests are also increasingly used by the young and better-educated citizens in Western democracies. To many democratic citizens, protest is the continuation of "normal" politics by other means.

A majority in most nations have signed a petition, a form of political action that has become so common that it no longer can be described as unconventional (see again Table 4.2). Roughly a fifth of Americans and Germans have at some time participated in a legal demonstration. Protests are now used by many sectors of society.[3] The French have far more protest involvement than the other established democracies, with nearly two-fifths of the population reporting participation at some point. These numbers reflect both French traditions of popular protest and the difficulties citizens often find in getting the attention of government. The Russian patterns are also striking, in 1990 only 4 percent of citizens reported participating in a protest, reflecting the communist government's repression of such activities. A decade later, nearly a quarter of Russians now say they have participated in a

---

B O X   4 . 1   The Velvet Revolution

On November 17, 1989, a large group of students staged a sit-in in the center of Prague to urge democratic reform. They placed lighted candles on the ground, and sang the Czech version of "We Shall Overcome." Confronted by this civil disobedience, the police beat the students and several bystanders. This was the spark that set the Czech democracy movement on fire. The students went on strike and called for a general strike by the workforce. The public demonstrations grew day by day, and the government entered into negotiations with Vaclav Havel and representatives of the Civic Forum reform movement. By November 25, half a million protestors assembled in a demonstration against the regime, and the government was struggling under the weight of the general strike. A television broadcast showing tapes of the November 17 protest mobilized further support for the reformers. By mid-December the regime capitulated: communism had come to an end, its demise marked by large celebrations in the city center. In less than a month, people had seized power in order to establish democracy in Czechoslovakia.

Source: Timothy Garton Ash, *The Magic Lantern: The Revolution of 1989* (New York: Random House, 1990), ch. 5.

---

legal demonstration—they are learning to express their grievances in a more democratic setting. The table also indicates that challenging activities are relatively less frequent in developing societies such as Mexico and Nigeria.

Citizen participation thus reflects the way that people with various participant attitudes utilize the opportunities existing within a political system. In nations with active political parties and competitive elections, many citizens may be mobilized to participate in the electoral process; in nations where such activities are limited, people may turn to group-based activity or protest in order to express their preferences.

Cross-national research shows that the better-educated and higher social status individuals are more likely to use the various opportunities for participation. These individuals tend to develop attitudes that encourage participation, such as feelings of efficacy and a sense of civic duty,[4] and they possess the personal resources and skills that are easily converted into political involvement when duty calls or need arises. Skill and confidence are especially important in complicated activities like organizing new groups or becoming a leader in an organization. This pattern is less pronounced for easier activities, such as voting participation and personal contacting. The tendency for the better-off to dominate in the arenas of participation is also more evident in societies, such as the United States, with weak party organizations, weak working-class groups (such as labor unions), and a lack of parties appealing distinctively to the interests of the lower classes. In nations with stronger working-class parties and labor unions, organizational networks encourage the relative awareness and participation of less affluent citizens.

INTEREST GROUPS

A more institutionalized form of interest articulation occurs through the activities of social or political groups that represent the interests of their constituents. In contrast to individual citizen action, interest groups normally have an enduring organizational base, and they often have professional staffs to provide the group with expertise and representation. In addition, interest groups often participate within the political process, serving on government advisory bodies and testifying at parliamentary hearings. Interest groups vary in structure, style, financing, and support base, and these differences may influence a nation's politics, its economics, and its social life.

Anomic Groups

Anomic groups are generally spontaneous groups that form suddenly when many individuals respond similarly to frustration, disappointment, or other strong emotions. They are flash affairs, rising and subsiding suddenly. Without previous organization or planning, frustrated individuals may suddenly take to the streets to vent their anger as news of a government action touches deep emotions or as a rumor of new injustice sweeps the community. Their actions may lead to violence, although not necessarily. Particularly where organized groups are absent or where they have failed to obtain adequate representation in the political system, smoldering discontent may be sparked by an incident or by the emergence of a leader. It may then suddenly explode in relatively unpredictable and uncontrollable ways.

Some political systems, including those of the United States, France, Italy, India, and some Arab nations, report a rather high frequency of violent and spontaneous anomic behavior.[5] This often involves spontaneous public demonstrations or acts of violence, rather than the planned and orchestrated protests of institutionalized political groups. Other countries are notable for the infrequency of such disturbances. Traditions and models of anomic behavior help turn frustration into action.

In France, for example, protests have become part of the tradition of politics (see Table 4.2). In the late 1960s, the French government nearly collapsed as the result of protests that began when university students were not allowed to have members of the opposite sex visit their dorm rooms. Soon other disenchanted French men and women joined the students' protest. In a typical year Paris might experience protests by students, shopkeepers, farmers, housewives, government employees, environmentalists, women's groups, and a host of other interests. Protest is almost a national political sport in France.

Anger over the assassination of a popular political leader or other catastrophic event can also stimulate a public outburst. For instance, one commonly sees relatively spontaneous public demonstrations when one nation makes a hostile action toward another nation. Wildcat strikes (spontaneous strike actions by local workers, not organized actions by national unions), long a feature of the British trade union scene, also occur frequently in such European countries as France, Italy, and Sweden.

Sometimes anomic groups are a subset of autonomous individuals drawn from a larger social grouping, such as a racial or ethnic group. For instance, in 1992 there was rioting and looting by some residents in minority neighborhoods of Los Angeles following the acquittal of police officers accused of excessive violence in the beating of an African-American suspect. Similarly, in 1992, riots broke out in Algeria when some Muslim fundamentalists protested the government's invalidation of the recent election. We treat these as anomic group actions because there is no structure or planning to the event, and the individuals involved disperse after the protest ends.

We must be cautious, however, about characterizing as anomic political behavior what is really the result of detailed planning by organized groups. For instance, the demonstrations against the World Trade Organization in Seattle and Geneva have owed much to indignation but little to spontaneity.

Nonassociational Groups

Like anomic groups, **nonassociational groups** rarely are well organized, and their activity is episodic. They differ from anomic groups because they are based on common interests and identities of ethnicity, region, religion, occupation, or perhaps kinship. Because of these continuing economic or cultural ties, nonassociational groups have more continuity than anomic groups. Subgroups within a large nonassociational group (such as blacks or workers) may act as an anomic group, as in the 1992 Los Angeles riots or the riots in East Timor in the late 1990s. Throughout the world, ethnicity and religion, like occupation, are powerful identities that can be a basis for collective activity.

There are two especially interesting kinds of nonassociational groups. One is the very large group that has not become formally organized, although its members perceive, perhaps dimly, their common interests. Many ethnic, regional, and occupational groups fit into this category. It can be very difficult to organize such groups. Members may share a common problem, but none of them may find it sufficiently rewarding to commit the effort and time needed to organize other group members. Moreover, if large collective benefits—for example, ending discriminatory legislation or cleaning up water pollution—are achieved, they will be shared even by those who did not work to achieve them, the so-called "free riders." Thus many may prefer to wait for the rewards without sharing the cost or risk of action. The study of such **collective action problems** is valuable in understanding why some groups (including governments and revolutionary challengers) become organized and others do not, and why and under what circumstances the obstacles to collective action can be overcome.[6]

A second type of nonassociational group is the small village or economic or ethnic subgroup whose members know each other personally. The small, face-to-face group has some important advantages and may be highly effective in some political situations. If its members are well connected or its goals unpopular or illegal, the group may prefer to remain informal or even inconspicuous. Examples of the action of such groups include work stoppages and petitions demanding better support and training by students, requests made by large landowners asking a bureaucrat to continue a grain tariff, and the appeal by relatives of a government tax collector for favored treatment for the family business. As the last two examples suggest, personal interest articulation may often have more legitimacy and be put on a more permanent basis by invoking group ties and interests.

Institutional Groups

Political parties, business corporations, legislatures, armies, bureaucracies, and churches often support separate political groups or have members with special responsibility for representing a group's interests. **Institutional groups** are formal and have other political or social functions in addition to interest articulation. Either as corporate bodies or as smaller groups within these bodies (legislative blocs, officer cliques, groups in the clergy, or ideological cliques in bureaucracies), such groups express their own interests or represent the interest of other groups in the society. The influence of institutional interest groups is usually derived from the strength of their primary organizational base—for instance, the size of their membership or their income. A group based on a governmental institution has direct access to policymakers.

In industrial democracies, bureaucratic and corporate interests use their resources and special information to affect policy. In the United States the military-industrial complex consists of the combination of personnel in the Defense Department and defense industries who join in support of military expenditures. Similarly, the farm lobby and the Department of Agriculture often unite in advocating agricultural policies. Political parties represent one of the most active institutional participants in the policy process of most democracies. And as in most societies, government bureaucracies do not simply react to pressures from the outside; in the absence of political directives they often act as independent forces of interest representation.

Nonpolitical institutional groups can also become involved in the political process. In Italy, for example, the Roman Catholic Church has been an institutional interest group with great influence in Italian politics. A major form of intervention has been religious education. In electoral politics, the Church used to admonish Catholics to use their votes to defeat the Communists. Less overtly, the Church seeks influence by having members of the clergy call on officeholders to express opinions on matters of concern to the Church. In Islamic countries fundamentalist clergy pursue a similar role, prescribing what morals public policy should follow, actively lobbying governmental officials, and sometimes participating in the governing process.

In authoritarian regimes, which prohibit or at least control explicit political groups, institutional groups can still play a large role. Educational officials, party officials, jurists, factory managers, officers in the military services, and government bodies representing other social units had significant roles in interest articulation in Communist regimes.[7] In preindustrial societies, which usually have fewer associational groups and where such groups usually fail to mobilize much support, military groups, corporations, party factions, and bureaucrats often play prominent political roles. Even where the military does not seize power directly, the possibility of such action often forces close government attention to military requests.

Associational Groups

Associational groups are formed explicitly to represent the interests of a particular group. This includes trade unions, chambers of commerce and manufacturers' associations, ethnic associations, and religious associations. These organizations have orderly procedures for formulating interests and demands, and they usually employ a full-time professional staff. Associational groups are often very active in representing the interests of their members in the policy process. For instance, in recurring debates about health care in the United States there is an enormous mobilization of pressure groups and lobbyists—from representatives of doctors and health insurance organizations to consumer groups and the like—in efforts to influence legislation.

Associational interest groups—where they are allowed to flourish—affect the development of other types of groups. Their organizational base gives them an advantage over nonassociational groups, and their tactics and goals are often recognized as legitimate in society. Labor unions, for example, are often central political actors because they represent the mass of the working class; in the same way, business associations often speak for the corporate interests of the nation. By representing a broad range of interests, these groups may limit the influence of anomic, nonassociational, and institutional groups.

A special subset of associational group is composed of citizens who are united not by a common economic or individual self-interest but by a common belief in a political ideology or a policy goal.[8] The environmental movement, many women's groups, and other civic groups are examples of this kind of associational group. In some of these issue groups the members may seldom interact directly and not even share common social characteristics (such as employment or ethnicity), but are bound together by their support of a political organization, such as Greenpeace or Amnesty International. On the organizational side, many of these new social groups have more fluid and dynamic organizations, with frequent turnover in both leadership and membership. On the tactical side, they use a wide range of approaches, often discounting the value of partisan campaigning and conventional lobbying in favor of unconventional protests and direct actions.

Civic associations represent another way for citizens to directly and explicitly articulate their policy goals by supporting groups that advocate their preferred policy positions. Such groups have proliferated in most advanced industrial democracies in the past generation, and they are now spreading to the developing world.

In summary, a social interest can manifest itself in many different groups. We can illustrate this point with examples of different groups that might involve members of the working class:

Anomic group: a spontaneous group of working-class individuals living in the same neighborhood

Nonassociational group: the working class as a collective

Institutional group: the labor department within the government

Associational group: a labor union

Civil Society

In recent years there has been increasing attention to whether an extensive network of interest groups and public participation in these groups creates a **civil society**—a society in which people are involved in social and political interactions free of state control or regulation. Community groups, voluntary associations, and even religious groups, as well as access to free communication and information through the mass media and (now) the Internet, are important parts of a civil society.[9] Participation in associational and institutional groups socializes individuals into the types of political skills and cooperative relations that are part of a well-functioning society. People learn how to organize, how to express their interests, and how to work with others to achieve common goals. They also learn the important lesson that the political process itself is as important as the immediate results. Thus a system of active associational groups can lessen the development of anomic or nonassociational activity. Group involvement can also be an important route into politics for citizens with fewer individual resources. Group activity can help citizens to develop and clarify their own preferences, provide important information about political events, and articulate the interests of citizens more clearly and precisely than parties and elections.[10] Thus, an active public involved in a diversity of interest groups provides a fertile ground for the development of democratic politics.

As political and economic conditions become interdependent across nations, there is also increasing attention directed toward the development of a global civil society to parallel these political and economic developments. Individuals and groups in one nation are connected to groups with similar concerns in other nations, and jointly reinforce their individual efforts. Environmental groups in the developed democracies, for example, assist environmental groups in developing nations with the expertise and organizational resources to address the issues facing their country. National groups meet at international conferences and policy forums, and the network of social relations, as well as Internet connections, extends across national borders.[11] This is another sign of how the international context of domestic politics is growing throughout the world.

One of the problems faced by the nations of Eastern Europe and other newly democratizing nations is building a rich associational group life in societies where organized groups have long been suppressed or controlled. The Communist Party and the government bureaucracy dominated these nations for over 40 years, and the government controlled associational life to pursue its goals. The process of building new, independent associational groups to articulate the specialized interests of different citizens is underway and will be important to the democratic process. Similarly, many less economically developed nations face an urgent need to develop a civil society of associational groups to involve citizens in the political process and represent their interests if democratization is to have a chance for success.

Interest Group Systems

Another characteristic of politics is the systematic connection between interest groups and government policymaking institutions. Differences in the types of connections create different interest group systems. All modern societies have large numbers of interest groups, but the patterns of relationships differ. Interest group systems are classified into three major groupings: (1) pluralist, (2) democratic corporatist, and (3) controlled.[12]

Pluralist interest group systems are characterized by several features that involve both how interests are organized and how they participate in the political process:

- Multiple groups may represent a single societal interest.
- Group membership is voluntary and limited.
- Groups often have a loose or decentralized organizational structure.
- There is a clear separation between interest groups and the government.

For instance, not only are there different groups for different social sectors, such as labor business, and professional interests, but there may be many multiple labor unions or business associations within each sector. These groups compete among themselves for membership and influence, and all simultaneously press their demands on policymakers and the bureaucracies. The United States is the best-known example of a strongly pluralist interest group system; Canada and New Zealand are also typically cited as examples. Despite its greater labor union membership and somewhat greater coordination of economic associations, Britain tends to fall on the pluralist side in most analyses, as do France and Japan.

Democratic corporatist interest group systems are characterized by a much more organized representation of interests:

- A single peak association normally represents each societal interest.
- Membership in the peak association is often compulsory and nearly universal.
- Peak associations are centrally organized and direct the actions of their members.
- Groups are often systematically involved in making and implementing policy.

For instance, in a corporatist system there may be a single peak association that represents all the major business or industrial interests; a pluralist system may have a wide diversity of business groups that act autonomously. Equally important, interest groups in corporatist systems often regularly and legitimately work with the government agencies and/or political parties as partners in negotiating solutions to policy problems. The best-studied democratic corporatist arrangements have been in the area of economic problems. Countries with large and unified peak associations of business and labor that negotiate with each other and the government have better records than more pluralist countries in sustaining employment, restraining inflation, and increasing social spending.[13] The most thoroughly corporatist interest group systems are in Austria, the Netherlands, Norway, and Sweden. Substantial democratic corporatist tendencies are also found in Germany and Denmark. Some developing nations also follow a corporatist pattern.

Because different sectors of a society may vary in their organized interest groups and in their government relations, we must be cautious about generalizing too much about interest group systems. Figure 4.1, however, describes the striking differences in organization of the labor movements in some industrial-

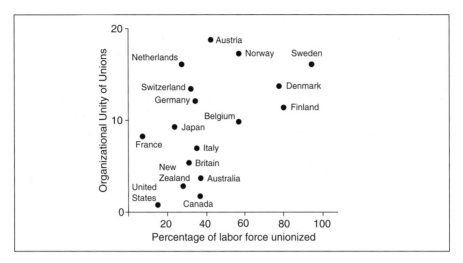

F I G U R E   4 . 1   Interest Group Systems of Labor Unions

Sources: Data for the percentage of the labor force unionized is from Organization for Economic Cooperation and Development, *Employment Outlook, July 1997* (Paris: OECD, 1997), p. 71; the unity of unions is from Arend Lijphart and Marcus Crepaz, "Corporatism and Consensus Democracy in Eighteen Countries," *British Journal of Political Science* 21 (1991): pp. 235–56.

ized societies. The countries are arrayed along the horizontal axis in terms of the percentage of the total labor force that belongs to a labor union. The vertical axis displays the degree or organizational unity within the labor union movement.

In Sweden, for example, about 90 percent of the nonagricultural workforce is organized into unions, and the movement is highly centralized and united on most labor-related issues. This is an example of a highly corporatist system of labor union interests.

Examples of more pluralist systems can be seen in Britain and the United States. Less than half the British labor force is unionized, but these unions are not as highly coordinated as those in corporatist countries. The member unions in the British Trades Union Congress have strong traditions of individual autonomy and are themselves relatively decentralized. Moreover, the influence of the labor unions on government policymakers has waned over the past two decades. The Thatcher government moved away from direct negotiation with labor, and thus away from corporatism in the 1980s, and even the Labour Party distanced itself from the labor unions in the 1990s. The United States is the polar opposite to Sweden; only about a sixth of the labor force is unionized, and the unions maintain a great deal of independence.

Figure 4.1 also shows that union membership in Japan and France is relatively low, with only about one worker in four or fewer belonging to a union. Moreover, the union movements themselves are relatively fragmented and decentralized. In these countries there are few traditions of "social partnership" between government, unions, and employer associations. In the area of labor policy, at least, these are highly pluralist, not corporatist, interest group systems. However, corporatist-type arrangements among individual industries, trade associations, and governmental bureaucracies (without organized labor involvement) exist in Japan.

In some democratic systems—for example, in Latin America—some interest groups such as trade unions and peasant associations are controlled by political parties or religious interests. Usually, these groups mobilize support for the political parties or social institutions that dominate them. This lack of autonomy can have serious consequences for politics. Restricting the independent expression of interest groups may lead to outbreaks of violence, and the subordination of interest group interests may limit the adaptability of the political process.

Finally, the pattern of interest groups is completely different in **controlled interest group systems:**

- There is a single group for each social sector.
- Membership is often compulsory.
- Each group is normally hierarchically organized.
- Groups are controlled by the government or its agents in order to mobilize support for government policy.

The most important factor is the last: Groups exist to facilitate government control of society. The best examples are the traditional Communist systems in which the dominating party organizations penetrate all levels of society and exercise close control over all the associational groups that are permitted to exist. Unions and youth associations, for example, are completely subordinated to the Communist Party, and they are only rarely permitted to articulate the interests of their members. This control was exercised in the Soviet Union and Eastern Europe; it continues today in North Korea, Vietnam, and Cuba. The political systems of several non-Communist nations, such as Brazil and Mexico, also encourage highly controlled interest groups. These nations limit interest articulation to leaders of institutional groups, who can use their positions in political institutions as a base for expressing their demands. As we have already noted, numerous institutional interest groups do emerge in these societies, especially from parts of the party and bureaucracy, such as the military, as do informal nonassociational groups.

ACCESS TO THE INFLUENTIAL

To be effective, interest groups must be able to reach key policymakers through **channels of political access.** Groups may express the interests of their members and yet fail to have an impact on policymakers. Political systems vary in the ways they respond to political interests. Interest groups vary in the tactics used to gain access to policy makers. Their tactics are shaped in part by the opportunities offered by the structure of policymaking, as well as by their own values and preferences.

It is useful to distinguish between legitimate and constitutional channels of political access (such as the mass media, parties, and legislatures) and illegitimate, coercive access channels. These channels correspond to the two major types of political resources that can be used to influence elites. The first type is established by the legitimate structures of the government, which designate the resources to be used in policymaking. In a democratic political system, an appropriate resource may be votes in the national assembly. Various groups may attempt to control legislative votes by influencing the parties that win elections, or the voters who choose them, or through bargaining, persuasion, or promises of support to incumbents. However, direct action remains as a second type of resource, a coercive channel of influence for individuals and groups who feel that they are otherwise ineffective.

If only one major legitimate channel of political access is available, as in a political system dominated by a single party, it is difficult for all groups to have access. Demands transmitted through that channel may be distorted as they work their way to key decision-makers. The leadership thus may not get information about the needs and demands of important groups. Over the long run, such misperceptions can easily lead to miscalculations by the leadership and to unrest among the dissatisfied groups, who may turn to violence. Thus a system with multiple channels of access is often more efficient in responding to societal interests.

Legitimate Access Channels

An important means of reaching political elites in all societies is through personal connections—the use of family, school, local, or other social ties. An excellent example is the information network among the British elite based on old school ties originating at Eton, Harrow, or other "public" schools, or in the colleges at Oxford and Cambridge universities. Similarly, in Japan many alumni of the University of Tokyo Law School hold top positions among the political and bureaucratic elites who interact because of these personal ties. Although personal connections are commonly used by nonassociational groups representing family or regional interests, they serve other groups as well. Face-to-face contact is one of the most effective means of shaping attitudes and conveying messages. Demands communicated by a friend or neighbor carry much more weight than a formal letter from a stranger. In modern nations personal connections are usually cultivated with special care. In Washington, the business of advising interest groups and individuals on access to politicians has become an increasingly lucrative profession (and, increasingly a target of government regulation). These activities are often carried on by former officeholders who use their personal governmental contacts for their lobbyist clients.

The **mass media**—television, radio, newspapers, and magazines—are another important access channel in democratic societies. The mass media can also mobilize support for interest group efforts, leading to donations of time and money, as well as stimulating similar demands from sympathizers. Many interest groups thus spend a great deal of effort hiring skillful public relations specialists, purchasing direct advertising, trying to see that their interests receive favorable attention in the media. Interest groups, such as senior citizens organizations, encourage media reports on their needs as well as coverage of their views on specific policies. When a cause receives national media attention, the message to policymakers carries added weight because they know that millions of voters have been sensitized to the issue. Moreover, groups believe that in an open society, "objective" news coverage has more credibility than sponsored messages. However, the confusion created by multiple messages and by their lack of specific focus can limit the effectiveness of the mass media for many less important groups.

The loosening of government control from the media in the communist regimes of Eastern Europe and the former Soviet Union gave a huge boost to democracy movements. When asked what caused the democratic revolution in Poland in the 1990s, Lech Walesa pointed to a television and said "that did." Media reports on the failures in communist government policy and the lifestyles in the West undermined the legitimacy of the regimes. As democratic protests spread across Eastern Europe in 1989 and 1990, stories of successful protests in other parts of the country, or in other countries, enhanced the confidence of demonstrators. Citizen protest encouraged by mass media reports helped convince the ruling groups that their support had vanished.

Political parties are another important legitimate channel of access. Democratic political parties often rely on interest groups for financial and voter support, and serve as institutional representatives of these interests within government. In a nation like Germany, the various components of the party organization, particularly parliamentary committees, are important channels for transmitting demands to the cabinet and the party in power. In some cases, other factors may limit the role of parties as interest representatives. For instance, highly ideological parties with a hierarchical structure, such as most Communist parties, are more likely to control affiliated interest groups than to communicate the interest groups' demands. Decentralized party organizations, like those in the United States, whether inside or outside the legislative organization, may be less helpful than individual legislators in providing access.

Legislatures are another common target of interest group activities. Standard lobbying tactics include appearances before legislative committees, providing information to individual legislators, and similar activities. In the United States political action committees raise campaign contributions for individual members of Congress and can usually be sure of some political attention in exchange. In Britain and France the strong party discipline in the legislature lessens the importance of individual members of Parliament (MPs) as access channels for interest groups. In Germany and many other European democracies, the presence of strong committees and/or power divided among multiple parties encourage interest groups to use them as access channels. The combination of loose party discipline and decentralized committees as a source of much legislation makes the members of the U.S. Congress major targets of group efforts.

Government bureaucracies are major access channels in most political systems. Contacts with the bureaucratic agencies may be particularly important where the bureaucracy has been delegated policymaking authority, or where interests are narrow and directly involve few citizens. A bureaucrat sympathetic to a group may try to respond to its demands without leaving bureaucratic channels, by exercising administrative discretion. A government official may also help to gain consideration of a problem, or may help to frame an issue in a way more likely to receive a sympathetic hearing by policymakers. Thus a study of access channels used by groups in Birmingham, England, showed that on broad issues involving class, ethnic, or consumer groups, interest groups tended to work through the political parties. On narrower issues, involving few other groups and less political conflict, the groups tended to turn to the appropriate administrative department.[14]

Protest demonstrations, strikes, and other forms of dramatic and direct pressure on government may be regarded by authorities as legitimate or illegitimate tactics, depending on the political system. Demonstrations may be either spontaneous actions of an anomic group or a planned use of unconventional channels by an organized group. In democratic societies, demonstrations may attempt to mobilize popular support—eventually electoral support—for the group's cause. The gay rights and environmental demonstrations in the United States are examples of such activity, as are the continuing pro-life and pro-choice rallies on the Mall in Washington. In nondemocratic societies, such demonstrations are more hazardous and represent perhaps more extreme dissatisfaction with alternative channels.

Lawful protest can be a tactic of society's powerless, those who do not have access or resources to influence policymakers through conventional channels. As a tactic of the powerless, protest activity is especially attractive to young people and minority groups, who are not among the elite. Protests have also been a favored tactic of groups whose ideological commitments focus on challenging the established social and political order.[15] Yet, since the 1970s protest demonstrations have increasingly been used as a channel for interest articulation by organized and accepted interests who feel that disciplined parties and bureaucratic agencies are deaf to their complaints. Protests can supplement other channels, especially in gaining the attention of the mass media in an age when television comes to every household. Thus we find doctors in Paris, civil servants in Sweden, and "gray panthers" (the elderly) in Germany using a tactic once limited to the poor and minorities.

Coercive Access Channels and Tactics

Most scholars see acts of collective violence as closely associated with the character of a society and the circumstances that prevail there. In his studies of civil strife, Ted Robert Gurr developed the concept of relative deprivation to explain the frustration or discontent that motivates people to act aggressively. Gurr defines relative deprivation as a "discrepancy between people's expectations about the goods and conditions of life to which they are entitled, on the one hand, and, on the other, their value capabilities—the degree to which they think they can attain these goods and conditions."[16] The sense of relative deprivation leads to frustration and anger; aggressive violence releases those feelings.

Feelings of relative deprivation are a source of frustration, discontent, and anger. The more such discontent and anger persist, the greater the chance of collective violence. Other conditions are important as well. People will tend to turn to violence if they believe it is justified and if they believe it will lead to success. If they think that their government is illegitimate and that the cause of their discontent is justified, they will more readily turn to political violence if there are no other means of bringing about change. To this end, it is the responsibility of the government and its institutions to provide peaceful alternatives to violence as a means of change.

This general analysis of violence should not blind us to the differences between types of violent political activity. A riot, for example, involves the spontaneous expression of collective anger and dissatisfaction by a group of citizens. Though riots have long been dismissed as aberrant and irrational action by social riffraff, modern studies have shown that rioters vary greatly in their motivation, behavior, and social background.[17] Most riots in fact seem to follow some fairly clear-cut patterns, such as confining destruction or violence to particular areas or targets. Relative deprivation seems to be a major cause of riots, but the release of the frustrations is not as aimless as is often supposed.

In the 1992 riots in Los Angeles, although the destruction began within hours of the acquittal of Rodney King's assailants, there was consensus among those involved that the trial outcome was only a proximate cause, a "spark" that ignited already volatile ingredients. Violence against the property of Korean shopowners during the riots reflected widely felt ethnic hostility unrelated to Rodney King. At least a few individuals justified looting through comparison with the massive thefts from savings and loans and insider trading in the previous few years. Many more simply felt that society had moved on and left them in poverty and decay; clear examples of relative deprivation abounded. The immediate results made matters worse: more than 50 people dead, mostly African Americans; thousands of businesses destroyed, with a loss of 14,000 jobs; and thousands of people left without access to necessary retail outlets. Although much of the mayhem seems poorly related to effective political action, it was a poignant cry for attention; and the slogan that emerged—"no peace without justice"—was a clear political message.

While deprivation may help fuel the discontent, strikes and obstructions—such as the recent efforts in the United States to block or prevent the blocking of entry into abortion clinics—are typically carried out by well-organized associational or institutional groups. Many violent demonstrations are called "riots" but should not be. For instance, recent violent protests in Seattle and Genoa against the World Trade Organization and "globalization" involved highly organized activities among some of the more radical groups participating in the protests (see Box 4.2).

Historically, labor unions used the general strike to pressure the government or employers on fundamental issues. However, the influence of strikes and obstructions has varied, depending on the legitimacy of the government and coercive pressure from other groups. A massive truckers' strike helped bring down the government in Chile in 1972 and 1973, but student-inspired boycotts in Korea in the 1980s had only a modest impact on the government. Most spectacularly, the strikes, obstructions, and demonstrations in Eastern Europe in 1989 and 1990, like the earlier people's power movement in the Philippines, had massive success against regimes that had lost legitimacy.

Finally, **political terror tactics,** including deliberate assassination, armed attacks on other groups or government officials, and provocation of bloodshed have been used to articulate interests in some societies. The use of terrorism typically reflects the desire of some group to change the rules of the political game. The tragedies in Northern Ireland, the frequent suicide bombings and attacks by groups in the Middle East seeking to dramatize the situation of the Palestinians, and the as-

BOX 4.2   Attacks on Globalization

In July 2001 tens of thousands of protestors arrived in Genoa to demonstrate at the G8 Summit Meeting. Hundreds of different groups came to protest at the meetings, and several of the more radical groups engaged in running battles with the police. Many of the most violent clashes involved what became known as the "Black Block". The Block was comprised of several loosely organized anarchist and radical groups, wearing trademark black clothing, black hoods, and gas masks. Confrontations with police often appeared choreographed in advance, coordinated by cell phones, and videotaped by sympathetic activists—and subsequently distributed through the Internet. Many other protest groups in Genoa were worried that the radical anarchist goals of the Block detracted attention from their policy concerns about the economic and social impacts of globalization. After two days of violent clashes the summit ended. Damage ran into the tens of millions of dollars, 200 protestors were arrested, and one protestor was shot in a clash with police. In the end, the violence in the streets overshadowed both the elected politicians at the summit and the policy goals of the non-violent groups in Genoa.

Source: BBC World News.

---

sassinations carried out by the Sendero Luminoso (Shining Path) guerrillas in Peru in the 1980s demonstrate the use of such tactics.

The use of political terror tactics has seldom been successful without large-scale backing of terrorist groups, the public or an international sponsor. Massive deadly violence may destroy a democratic regime, leading to curtailment of civil rights or even military intervention when many people and leaders feel that any alternative is preferable to more violence. President Fujimori and military leaders in Peru justified their suppression of democratic institutions in April 1992 as necessary to their battle against the Shining Path and cocaine lords. An authoritarian, repressive response often promises quick results against terrorists; however, small-group terrorism usually fails when confronted by united democratic leadership.[18] In a democratic society, violence often forfeits the sympathy that a group needs if its cause is to receive a responsive hearing.

POLICY PERSPECTIVES ON INTEREST ARTICULATION

As we pointed out in Chapter 2, we need to look at the structures performing political functions from both a process and a policy perspective. If we are to understand the formation of policies, we need to know which groups articulate interests, and what policy preferences they express. Many associational interest groups specialize in certain policy areas. The concerns of other interest groups, such as anomic or institutional groups, may be less easily discerned, but they are equally important for the policy process.

Table 4.3 provides examples of interest articulation for different types of interest groups and different policy areas: extractive, distributive, and regulative policies

T A B L E   4 . 3   Process and Policy Perspectives on Interest Articulation

Examples of Interest Articulation in Various Policy Areas

Types of Interest Groups	Domestic Extractive Policy	Domestic Distributive Policy	Domestic Regulative Policy	International Policy
Anomic groups	Nigerian women riot over rumor of taxes (1950s).[a]	Russian workers strike to protest price increases.	Indonesians demonstrate against dictatorship (1997).[a]	Germans demonstrate against war in Iraq.
Nonassociational groups	Mexican business leaders discuss taxes with president.	U.S. Black Caucus Congress calls for minority jobs.	Foreign workers in Germany protest citizenship law.	Saudi royal family faction favor s oil price increase.
Institutional groups	American universities urge that charitable contributions remain tax deductible.	U.S. Department of Agriculture proposes price supports for honey production.	Church leaders ask for an end to apartheid in South Africa.	Chinese politburo faction favors liberal international trade.
Associational groups	French student groups protest government-imposed tuition increases.[b]	British Medical Association negotiates salaries under Health Services.	National Rifle Association lobbies against gun control.	Palestinian Hamas launch terror attacks on Israel.[a]

[a] Use of coercive, unconstitutional access channels and tactics.

[b] Use of coercion by some elements or subgroups.

in the domestic arena, and international policies. The table footnotes indicate when coercive or illegitimate channels were used. Careful examination of each case provides a more precise illustration of the access channels, such as elite representation by African-American members of Congress, Mexican business leaders lobbying their government, Hamas using terror tactics on the West Bank. One can also use this framework to think about how a single interest might pursue their goals through multiple channels, including protests, representation by institutional groups, and lobbying by associational groups. U.S. honeybee farmers, for instance, have lobbied their representatives in Congress to maintain federal price supports, but also used their allies in the Department of Agriculture to lobby in their behalf (will honeybee protests be next?). This table uses examples from many nations in order to suggest the varied possibilities, as well as to fill in all the categories with reasonably obvious cases. If we were studying interest articulation patterns in one nation, of course, we could build a table showing the structures, policies, and channels involved during a particular period.

INTEREST GROUP DEVELOPMENT

One of the consequences of modernization is a widespread belief that the conditions of life can be altered through human action. Modernization normally involves education, urbanization, rapid growth in public communication, and in most cases improvement in the physical conditions of life. These changes are closely related to increases in political awareness, participation, and feelings of political competence. Such participant attitudes encourage more diverse and citizen-based interest articulation.

At the same time that participant attitudes emerge in the political culture of modernizing countries, there is a specialization of labor as people work in many types of jobs—a process that leads to the formation of large numbers of special interests. The interdependence of modern life, the exposure provided by mass communications, and the wide-ranging role of government further multiply political interests. Complex processes organize these interests and attitudes into associational interest groups. The barriers to coordination and cooperation are overcome in many different ways. The emergent interest group systems, pluralist or corporatist, autonomous or controlled, dominated by the better-off or more equally mobilized, are shaped by the history of interest group development during modernization.

Successful democratic development requires that complex interest group systems emerge to express the needs of groups and individuals in the society. Yet, this process is by no means automatic. The problems of organizing large groups for collective action are very large. Societies vary widely in the extent to which people engage in associational activity. One factor explaining participation is the level of trust shared among members of the society. Robert Putnam and his colleagues found that an active associational life in Northern Italian communities was associated with widespread trust in others and that these qualities of political culture were related to economic growth and a participant political life.[19] Ronald Inglehart has shown similar continuity in social trust across nations.[20] Thus modernization may weaken traditional structures in some societies but fail to foster the development of effective associational groups in others because of the inhibition of social attitudes. A nation's ability to achieve either stability or democracy will be hindered as a result.

In other cases, as we have noted, authoritarian parties and bureaucracies may control and penetrate associational groups and choke off the channels of political access. Eastern Europe offers a situation in which 40 years or more of authoritarian domination suppressed autonomous interest groups. Eventually, the processes of economic modernization put great pressure on these authoritarian systems to allow more open organization and expression of political interests. In addition, social change led to an expansion of interest articulation activity and a need for associational groups to provide regular and organized expression for citizens' interests. Associational groups are also needed to counterbalance the demands from institutional groups in the civilian and military bureaucracies.

The recent development of organized interest groups in Eastern Europe should not, however, lead us to conclude that every conceivable group now has equal standing. Using the American experience as an example, the articulation of interests is frequently biased toward the goals of the better-off, who are also often better organized.[21] It is often pointed out that the American Association of Retired Persons (AARP) is an effective group that is not counterbalanced by a "Young Taxpayers Group," and that the traditional labor-management competition leaves consumers under represented.

We might test this notion more broadly by evaluating systems in terms of their inclusiveness: What proportion of the population is represented to what degree in national-level politics? In South Africa under apartheid, we had the extreme case where the majority were prevented outright from forming associational groups. In the Third World competing interests in the capital rarely involve the interests of rural peasants; sometimes peasant organizations are brutally suppressed, while urban middle- and upper-class groups are able to petition authorities. It seems to be no coincidence that the bias in group inclusion appears greatest where the gap in income and education is widest. We have suggested above that, pushed to the extreme, those excluded from the process will engage in anomic activity or resort to violence, a conclusion supported by statistical studies of inequality and violence.[22] Even in less extreme cases, the presence of different levels of political awareness means that every interest group system is somewhat biased. Democratization involves not only the provision of competitive elections but also the reduction of the bias in interest representation.

Another challenge faces the patterns of interest articulation and representation in advanced industrial democracies. Turnout in national elections has gradually declined over the last few decades. In the United States, for example, turnout in presidential elections averaged 61 percent during the 1950s and was only 51 percent in 2000. Fewer citizens in the established democracies attend a campaign rally or display their partisan support during a campaign than participated a generation ago. There is evidence that participation in associational groups is also decreasing in the United States, and perhaps in other established democracies.[23] Some scholars argue that it represents a growing social isolation in developed nations, as people forsake social and political involvement for the comfort of their favorite chair and their favorite TV program. If elections are the celebration of democratic politics, fewer individuals seem to be joining in.

Political analysts worry that decreasing political involvement and group activity signal the erosion in the democratic, participatory spirit in the established democracies. This presents a basic puzzle. Why are citizens in established democracies voting *less often* and participating less frequently in democratic elections? At the same time, other peoples around the world are struggling to win their political freedom and the opportunity to participate in democratic politics.

The one thing that can be certain is that democratic politics rests upon a participatory public that uses individual and group methods to express and represent their interests. Thus the development of an active social and political life is an important standard for measuring the political development of a nation.

KEY TERMS

anomic groups

associational groups

channels of political access

civil society

collective action problems

controlled interest group
  systems

democratic corporatist
  interest group systems

institutional groups

interest articulation

mass media

nonassociational group

personal interest contacts

pluralist interest group
  systems

political terror tactics

protests

SUGGESTED READINGS

Barnes, Samuel H., Max Kaase, et al. *Political Action: Mass Participation in Five Western Democracies.* Beverly Hills, CA: Sage, 1979.

Dahl, Robert A. *Polyarchy: Participation and Opposition.* New Haven, CT: Yale University Press, 1971.

———. *Democracy and Its Critics.* New Haven, CT: Yale University Press, 1989.

Dalton, Russell J. *Citizen Politics: Public Opinion and Political Parties in Advanced Industrial Democracies,* 3rd ed. New York, NY: Chatham House, 2002.

Denardo, James. *Power in Numbers: The Political Strategy of Protest and Rebellion.* Princeton, NJ: Princeton University Press, 1985.

Grant, Wyn, ed. *The Political Economy of Corporatism.* New York: St. Martin's, 1985.

Hirschman, Albert. *Exit, Voice, and Loyalty.* Cambridge, MA: Harvard University Press, 1970.

Keck, Margaret and Kathryn Sikkink. *Activists Beyond Borders: Advocacy Networks in International Politics.* Ithaca: Cornell University Press, 1998.

Lichbach, Mark. *The Rebel's Dilemma.* Ann Arbor: University of Michigan Press, 1994.

Meyer, David and Sidney Tarrow, eds. *The Social Movement Society: Contentious Politics for a New Century.* Lanham, MD: Rowman and Littlefield, 1998.

Norris, Pippa. *Democratic Phoenix: Reinventing Political Activism.* New York: Cambridge University Press, 2003.

Olson, Mancur. *The Logic of Collective Action.* Cambridge, MA: Harvard University Press, 1965.

Putnam, Robert. *Making Democracy Work: Civic Traditions in Modern Italy.* Princeton, NJ: Princeton University Press, 1993.

Putnam, Robert. *Bowling Alone: The Collapse and Revival of American Community.* New York: Simon and Schuster, 2000.

Putnam, Robert D. ed. *Democracies in Flux: The Evolution of Social Capital in Contemporary Society.* Oxford: Oxford University Press, 2002

Richardson, Jeremy J., ed. *Pressure Groups.* New York: Oxford University Press, 1993.

Rootes, Christopher. *Environmental Movements: Local, National, and Global.* London: Frank Cass, 1999.

Shi, Tianjian. *Political Participation in Beijing.* Cambridge, MA: Harvard University Press, 1997.

Thomas, Clive. *Political Parties and Interest Groups: Shaping Democratic Governance.* Boulder, CO: L. Rienner, 2001.

Van Deth, Jan, et al. *Social Capital and European Democracy.* New York: Routledge, 1999.

Verba, Sidney, Norman H. Nie, and Jae-on Kim. *Participation and Political Equality.* Cambridge, England: Cambridge University Press, 1978.

Verba, Sidney, Kay Schlozman, and Henry Brady. *Voice and Equality.* Cambridge, MA: Harvard University Press, 1996.

Wattenberg, Martin. *Where Have all the Voters Gone?* Cambridge, MA: Harvard University Press, 2003.

Wiarda, Howard J. *Corporatism and Comparative Politics: The Other Great "ism."* Armonk, NY: Sharpe, 1997.

ENDNOTES

1. International Studies of Values in Politics Project, *Values and the Active Community: A Cross-national Study of the Influence of Local Leadership* (New York: Free Press, 1971); Sidney Verba, Norman N. Nie, and Jae-on Kim, *Participation and Political Equality* (Cambridge, England: Cambridge University Press, 1978).

2. Citizen interest group activity includes membership in groups working on local community issues, environmental interests, humans rights issues, women's issues, or the peace movement. For additional analyses, see Russell Dalton and Robert Rohrschneider, "Political Action and the Political Context: A Multi-level Model of Environmental Activism," in Dieter Fuchs, et al., eds. *Citizens and Democracy in East and West: Studies in Political Culture and Political Process* (Opladen: Westdeutscher Verlag, 2002).

3. Russell Dalton, *Citizen Politics,* 3rd ed. (Chatham, NJ: Chatham House, 2002), ch. 4; M. Kent Jennings, Jan W. van Deth, et al., *Continuities in Political Action* (New York: de Gruyter, 1990); Richard Topf, "Beyond Electoral Participation," in Hans D. Klingemann and Dieter Fuchs, eds., *Citizens and the State* (Oxford, England: Oxford University Press, 1995), pp. 27–51.

4. See Verba, Nie, and Kim, *Participation and Political Equality;* and Barnes, Kaase, et al., *Political Action.*

5. See the data on riots in Charles Taylor and David Jodice, *World Handbook of Political and Social Indicators,* vol. 1, 3rd ed. (New Haven, CT: Yale University Press, 1983), chs. 2–4.

6. Studies of these problems were stimulated by the now classic work of Mancur Olson, *The Logic of Collective Action* (Cambridge, MA: Harvard University Press, 1965). See also Mark Lichbach, *The Rebel's Dilemma* (Ann Arbor: University of Michigan Press, 1994); Mancur Olson, "Dictatorship, Democracy, and Development" *American Political Science Review* 87, no. 3 (Sept. 1993): 567–76; Todd Sandler, ed., *Collective Action: Theory and Applications* (Ann Arbor: University of Michigan Press, 1992).

7. See G. F. Skilling and F. Griffiths, eds., *Interest Groups in Soviet Politics* (Princeton, NJ: Princeton University Press, 1971); the essays by Frederick C. Barghoorn and Skilling in Robert A. Dahl, *Regimes and Oppositions* (New Haven, CT: Yale University Press, 1973); and Roman Kolkowicz, "Interest Groups in Soviet Politics," *Comparative Politics* 2, no. 3 (April 1970): 445–72.

8. Christopher Rootes, ed. *Environmental Movements: Local, National, and Global.* (London: Frank Cass, 1999); Amrita Basu, ed., *The Challenges of Local Feminism: Women's Movements in Global Perspective* (Boulder, CO: Westview, 1995).

9. Jean Cohen and A. Arato, *Civil Society and Political Theory* (Cambridge, MA: MIT Press, 1992); M. Walzer, ed., *Toward a Global Civil Society* (Oxford, England: Berghahn Books, 1995).

10. Gabriel A. Almond and Sidney Verba, *The Civic Culture* (Princeton, NJ: Princeton University Press, 1963), pp. 300–22; John Pierce et al., *Citizens, Political Communication, and Interest Groups: Environmental Organizations in Canada and the United States* (Westport, CT: Praeger, 1992).

11. Keck, Margaret and Kathryn Sikkink. *Activists Beyond Borders: Advocacy Networks in International Politics.* (Ithaca: Cornell University Press, 1998).

12. Philippe Schmitter, "Interest Intermediation and Regime Governability," in Suzanne Berger, ed., *Organizing Interests in Western Europe* (New York: Cambridge University Press, 1981), ch. 12; Arend Lijphart and Markus Crepaz, "Corporatism and Consensus Democracy in 18 Countries," *British Journal of Political Science* 21, no. 2 (April 1991): 235–46; Wyn Grant, ed., *The Political Economy of Corporatism* (New York: St. Martin's Press, 1985).

13. On the relative success of the corporatist systems in economic performance, see Miriam Golden, "The Dynamics of Trade Unionism and National Economic Performance," *American Political Science Review* 87, no. 2 (June 1993): 439–54; Arend Lijphart, Ronald Rogowski, and R. Kent Weaver, "Separation of Powers and Cleavage Management," in R. Kent Weaver and Bert A. Rockman, *Do Institutions Matter? Government Capabilities in the United States and Abroad* (Washington: Brookings Institution, 1993), pp. 302–44.

14. Kenneth Newton and D. S. Morris, "British Interest Group Theory Reexamined," *Comparative Politics* 7 (July 1975): 577–95.

15. See the essays in Russell J. Dalton and Manfred Kuechler, *Challenging the Political Order: New Social and Political Movements in Western Democracies* (New York: Oxford University Press, 1990).

16. Ted Robert Gurr, "A Comparative Study of Civil Strife," in Hugh David Graham and Ted Robert Gurr, eds., *The History of Violence in America* (New York: Bantam Press, 1969), pp. 462–63.

17. See Mark Baldassare, ed., *The Los Angeles Riots: Lessons for the Urban Future* (Boulder, CO: Westview, 1994); James F. Short and Marvin E. Wolfgang, eds., *Collective Violence* (Chicago: Aldine-Atherton, 1972).

18. On violence and democratic survival, see G. Bingham Powell, Jr., *Contemporary Democracies: Participation, Stability and Violence* (Cambridge, MA: Harvard University Press, 1982), ch. 8; see also the contributions to Juan J. Linz and Alfred Stepan, eds., *The Breakdown of Democratic Regimes* (Baltimore: Johns Hopkins University Press, 1978).

19. Robert D. Putnam, *Making Democracy Work: Civic Traditions in Modern Italy* (Princeton, NJ: Princeton University Press, 1993).

20. Ronald Inglehart, *Culture Shift in Advanced Industrial Societies* (Princeton, NJ: Princeton University Press, 1990), pp. 34–36; see also Almond and Verba, *Civic Culture,* ch. 11.

21. Sidney Verba, Kay Schlozman, and Henry Brady, *Voice and Equality* (Cambridge, MA: Harvard University Press, 1996); Frances Piven and Richard Cloward, *Why Americans Don't Vote* (New York: Pantheon, 1989).

22. Many of these studies are reviewed by Mark I. Lichbach, "An Evaluation of 'Does Economic Inequality Breed Political Conflict' Studies," *World Politics* 41 (1989): 431–70. More recent references and analysis appear in T. Y. Wang, William Dixon, Edward N. Muller, and Mitchell A. Seligson, "Inequality and Political Violence Revisited," *American Political Science Review* 87, no. 4 (Dec. 1993): 979–93.

23. Putnam, Robert. *Bowling Alone: The Collapse and Revival of American Community.* New York: Simon and Schuster, 2000; Eva Cox and Robert D. Putnam, eds. *Democracies in Flux: The Evolution of Social Capital in Contemporary Society.* (Oxford: Oxford University Press, 2002).

Interest Aggregation and Political Parties

Interest aggregation is the activity in which the political demands of individuals and groups are combined into policy programs. For example, farmers' desires for higher crop prices, public preferences for lower taxes, environmentalists' demands for natural resource quality, and the interests of businesses often have to be balanced together in determining an economic policy program. A specific program becomes politically significant when it is backed up by substantial political resources, such as popular votes, commitments of campaign funds, seats in the legislature, positions of executive influence, media access, or even armed force.

How interests are aggregated is a key feature of the political process. The nature of the aggregation process inevitably has major implications for which interests are heard, and what individuals and groups are allowed to participate in the process. Interest aggregation also helps create a balanced government program, as competing policy goals must be compromised to produce a single governing program. The pattern of interest aggregation also is linked to the stability of governments and their ability to function and adapt.

Interest aggregation can occur in many ways. If an influential party leader or military dictator controls substantial political resources, his or her personal impact on interest aggregation may be considerable. Large nations usually develop more specialized organizations for aggregating interests and resources behind a policy. Political parties are just such organizations.

Political parties are important in interest aggregation in democratic and in many nondemocratic systems. Each party (or its candidates) stands for a set of policies and tries to build a coalition of support for this program. In a democratic system two or more parties compete to gain support for their alternative policy programs. In authoritarian systems a single party or institution may try to mobilize citizens' support for its policies. In both systems interest aggregation may take place within a political party; for example, party leaders hear the demands of different groups—unions, consumers, party factions, business organizations—and create policy alternatives. In authoritarian systems the process is frequently covert and controlled, and interests are often mobilized to support the government, rather than the government responding to public interests.

The structural-functional approach highlights the point that political parties may perform many different functions and that different structures may perform the interest aggregation function. For instance, in addition to aggregating interests, parties frequently shape the political culture as they organize thought about political issues and strive to build support for their ideologies, issue positions, and candidates. Parties are involved in political recruitment as they mobilize voters and select would-be officeholders. They articulate interests of their own and transmit the demands of others. Governing parties are also involved in making public policy and even overseeing its implementation and adjudication. The distinctive and defining goal of a political party, its mobilization of support for policies and candidates, is especially related to interest aggregation. In this chapter we compare the role of parties to other structures in interest aggregation.

PERSONAL INTEREST AGGREGATION

One way to bring political interests together in the governing processes is through personal connections. A nearly universal political connection is the **patron-client network**—a structure in which a central officeholder, authority figure, or group provides benefits to supporters in exchange for their loyalty. It was the defining principle of feudalism. The king and his lords, the lord and his knights, the knight and his serfs and tenants—all were bound by ties of personal dependence and loyalty. The American political machines of Boss Tweed of New York or Richard Daley, Sr., of Chicago were similarly bound together by patronage and loyalty. Such networks are not confined to relationships cemented by patronage only. The president of the United States, for instance, usually has a circle of personal confidants, a "brain trust" or "kitchen cabinet," bound to their chief by ideological and policy propensities as well as by ties of friendship.

The patron-client network is so common in politics that it seems to be like the cell in biology or the atom in physics—the primitive structure of all politics, the human interactions out of which larger and more complicated political structures are composed. Students of politics in all countries report such networks.

Contemporary patron-client theory was pioneered in studies of Asian politics, where this structure runs through the political processes of countries such as the Philippines, Indonesia, Thailand, Japan, and India.[1] Once these networks were discussed as part of the political process, parallels were found in Europe, Latin America, and most regions of the world. The political processes in the kingdom of Saudi Arabia or the Brunei Sultanate conform to many aspects of the patron-client model. Patron-client relationships involve the recruitment to political office, interest aggregation, policymaking, and policy implementing. As we see in Table 5.1, the extensive reliance upon patron-client networks as a means of aggregating political interests is confined mainly to the less economically developed countries.

When interest aggregation is predominately performed by patron-client ties, this affects the style of the political process. In such a system it is difficult to mobilize

T A B L E   5 . 1   Structures Performing Interest Aggregation in Selected Contemporary Nations*

| Country | Extensiveness of Interest Aggregation by Actor | | | | |
	Patron-Client Networks	Associational Groups	Competitive Parties	Authoritarian Parties	Military Forces
Britain	Low	High	High		Low
Brazil	Moderate	Moderate	Moderate		Moderate
China	Moderate	Low		High	High
Egypt	High	Low		Moderate	High
France	Low	Moderate	High		Low
Germany	Low	High	High		Low
India	High	Moderate	Moderate		Low
Japan	Moderate	High	High		Low
Mexico	Moderate	Moderate	Moderate		Low
Nigeria	High	Low	Moderate		Moderate
Russia	Moderate	Low	Moderate		Moderate
United States	Low	Moderate	High		Low

*Extensiveness of interest aggregation rated as low, moderate, or high. Rating refers to broad-level performance and may vary in different issue areas and at different times. Blank implies not appropriate.

political resources behind unified policies of social change or to respond to crises, because taking action depends on ever-shifting agreements between many factional leaders (patrons). Patron-client politics thus typically means a static political system.

INSTITUTIONAL INTEREST AGGREGATION

In modern societies, as citizens become aware of larger collective interests and have the resources and skills to work for them, personal networks tend to be regulated, limited, and incorporated within broader organizations.

The subtle dividing line between interest articulation and aggregation can easily be crossed by organizations with powerful resources. **Associational groups** operate to express demands and support political contenders such as political parties. But they can occasionally wield sufficient resources to become contenders in their own right. For instance, the political power of the labor unions within the British Labour Party historically rested on the unions' ability to develop coherent policy positions and mobilize the votes of their members (who were formally represented in the party) to support those positions. As we discussed in Chapter 4, a system of democratic corporatism can effectively aggregate the interests of both labor and business groups into economic policies. These arrangements include continuous political bargaining among organized labor, official representatives of business interests, political parties, and state bureaucracies. Such corporatist systems interconnect organizations that in other political systems play very different, often antagonistic, roles.

Institutional groups like bureaucratic and military factions can also be important interest aggregators. Indeed, the bureaucracy acts as an interest aggregator in most societies. Although established primarily to implement policies set by higher authorities, the bureaucracy may negotiate with various groups to identify their preferences or to mobilize their support. Government agencies may even be "captured" by interest groups and used to support their demands. The desire of bureaucrats to expand their organizations by discovering new problems and policies, as well as increasing their ability to solve problems in their areas of expertise, often leads them to create client support networks.

Military organizations, with their special control of physical force, have great potential power as interest aggregators. If the legitimacy of the government breaks down and all groups feel free to use coercion and violence to shape policies, then a united military can usually be decisive. By one account, around two-fifths of the world's nations have confronted military coup attempts at some time, and these were at least partially successful in changing leaders or policy in about a third of the nations. Less than half of these coup attempts, however, focused on general political issues and public policy. Most coups seemed motivated by grievances and fear that the professional interests of the military would be slighted by civil authorities.[2]

Table 5.1 illustrates how associational groups tend to play a larger role in democratic politics that accept the independence of interest groups and their attempts to influence government policy. Conversely, the military generally plays a role in non-democratic states, often providing the leadership of government or supporting an authoritarian regime.

COMPETITIVE PARTY SYSTEMS AND INTEREST AGGREGATION

In many contemporary political systems, parties are the primary structures of interest aggregation. However, we must keep in mind the critical distinction between **competitive party systems,** which primarily try to build electoral support, and noncompetitive or **authoritarian party systems,** which seek to direct society. This distinction does not depend on the closeness of electoral victory, or even on the number of parties. It depends on the ability of political parties to freely form and to compete for citizen support, and their winning citizen support as a prerequisite for controlling government. Thus a party can win most of the votes in a certain area, or even one national election, but nonetheless still be a competitive party. Its goals involve winning elections, either as a primary objective or as a means for policymaking; its dominance at the polls can be challenged by other parties.

The role of competitive parties in interest aggregation depends not only on the individual party but also the structure of parties, electorates, electoral laws, and policymaking bodies that interact together. Typically, interest aggregation in a competitive party system takes place at several stages: within the individual parties, as the party chooses candidates and adopts policy proposals; through electoral competition, as voters give varying amounts of support to different parties; and through bargaining and coalition building in the legislature or executive.

Competitive Parties and Elections

At the first step, individual parties develop policy positions. Typically, a party believes that its positions are backed by a large or cohesive group of voters. In systems with only two parties, it is important for a party to win a majority, so targeting the "center" of the electorate is often strategically necessary to win the enough votes.[3] In systems with many political parties, where no one group has much chance of winning a majority, parties may seek a distinctive and cohesive electoral base. Party policies may reflect the preferences of specific groups, such as labor unions, business associations, or religious and ethnic groups. Historical issue commitments and ideological traditions also play a role.[4]

In developing their policy proposals parties anticipate the way that election competition brings together party offerings and voter choices. One important element is the election law that determines how voter choices are translated into election outcomes.[5] In the United States, Britain, and many countries once influenced by Britain (such as India, Jamaica, and Canada), the legislative election rules divide the country into many election districts. In each district, the candidate who has more votes than any other—a *plurality*—wins the election in the district. This simple, **single-member district plurality election rule** is often called "first past the post," a horse racing term, because the winner need only finish ahead of the others but not win a majority of the votes. (See Box 5.1: Duverger's Law.) This system seems obvious and natural to Americans, but it is rarely used in the democracies in Europe or in Latin America.

In contrast to the single-member district system, most democracies use some form of **proportional representation.** In these systems the country is divided into a few, large districts (or kept as a single national district). The competing parties offer lists of candidates, rather than a single candidate. The number of legislative representatives a party wins depends on the overall proportion of the votes it receives. If

---

BOX 5.1   Duverger's Law

Duverger's Law is one of the best-known phenomena in political science. It reflects the tendency for plurality single-member district election rules to create "two-party" systems in the legislature, while proportional representation electoral systems generate multiple party systems. In single-member district systems, smaller parties that receive a minority of the vote across many districts receive little or no representation in Parliament. This discourages politicians from forming more parties and greatly underrepresents small parties that do compete. In Britain in the 2001 election, for example, 18 percent of the electorate voted for the Liberal Democratic Party, but it received only 8 percent of the seats in Parliament. Duverger's Law is named after the French political scientist Maurice Duverger, who recognized and analyzed it as a general rule.

Source: Maurice Duverger, *Political Parties: Their Organization and Activity in the Modern State,* [1954] trans. Barbara and Robert North, New York: John Wiley, 1963.

the entire country were a single legislative district, as in the Netherlands and Israel, a party receiving 4 percent of the vote would be awarded 4 percent of the seats in the national legislature. Sometimes parties must achieve a minimum threshold of votes, usually 3–5%, to receive any seats at all. (If so many parties compete that a lot of them fall below the threshold, many voters may be left unrepresented, as happened in Russia in 1995 and in some other early elections in the new Eastern European democracies.)

The procedure that parties use to develop policy positions varies greatly from country to country and from party to party. In the United States the national party conventions held at each presidential election formalize the party's policy positions, both through the development of party platforms and through the selection of candidates committed to certain policies. In other countries, parties have more regular congresses, centralized party organizations issue party programs, and the parties develop manifestos for each national election.[6] Whatever the system, the final party position is usually a mixture of strategic electioneering and the aggregation of interests existing within the party.

The parties then offer their chosen candidates and policies to the electorate. They not only present candidates, but they also attempt to publicize them and mobilize electoral support through rallies, media advertising, door-to-door campaigning, and other activities. The act of voting by the individual citizen is one of the simplest and most frequently performed political actions. The citizen enters a voting booth and indicates support for a political candidate, party, or policy proposal. Elections are one of the few devices where diverse interests can be expressed equally and comprehensively. By casting ballots and aggregating these votes the citizens can make a collective decision about their future leaders and public policies.[7]

Figure 5.1 shows levels of voter turnout in a variety of nations in recent years.[8] In Britain, Germany, and the United States, as in most of the world's democracies, most citizens are eligible to participate, and they may choose between competing political parties and candidates. In Western Europe about three-quarters of the citizens usually vote; in the United States about half the electorate goes to the polls in presidential elections, which was about the same level as in Nigeria in 1999. Voter turnout in Russia, Japan and Mexico fell between these. The lowest turnout in Figure 5.1 appears in Egypt, where government control made elections distinctly noncompetitive.

Despite the simplicity and limitations of the vote, its implications can be profound. The voters' choice between competing parties or candidates is one of the few ways that a nation can make a collective choice on government goals—thus this is a prime method of aggregating specific interests. Electoral outcomes determine who manages the affairs of government and who makes public policy. Shifts in citizen support can bring to power new coalitions committed to new policies. Citizens thus can influence interest aggregation and policymaking through their role in selecting elites.

In other countries, however, elections have other functions. Elections have been used to legitimate the government, even though the electoral outcome was predetermined, as in Egypt, or to select a government, even while excluding many

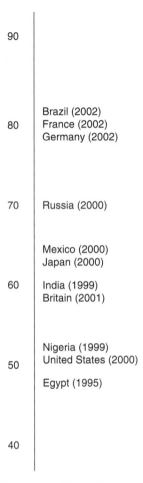

90

80   Brazil (2002)
      France (2002)
      Germany (2002)

70   Russia (2000)

      Mexico (2000)
      Japan (2000)

60   India (1999)
      Britain (2001)

      Nigeria (1999)
50   United States (2000)

      Egypt (1995)

40

F I G U R E   5 . 1   Turnout in Most Recent National Elections

Source: Elections in the World, downloaded October 30, 2002 from www.electionworld.org. Voter turnout is percent of registered voters except in the USA, where it is percent of voting age population. Egypt 2000, not available.

citizens. Nearly all the communist nations of Eastern Europe utilized some form of elections to legitimize their governments. In these nations reported turnout routinely exceeded 98 percent of the electorate. At the same time, the government guaranteed the outcome in advance. Until 1990, voters in the Soviet Union could only vote for one candidate, who was always a nominee of the Communist Party. In some other communist nations, the voters could endorse a government slate of candidates or parties, but the parties had agreed upon the division of seats before the votes were counted. The very high levels of voter participation in these nations reflected government pressure on the public to express their symbolic support for the regime. Elections and voting in these systems, as in national elections in Egypt

B O X   5 . 2   Election Upset!

E lections can often show that the public's preferences are much different from what political leaders expect. After the Khomeini revolution in 1979, Iran was governed by a conservative religious establishment and its political allies. The regime rolled back civil liberties and followed repressive policies in several areas, while claiming popular legitimacy for its actions. In 1997 Iranians went to the polls to select a president. The choices were between the conservative speaker of parliament and a moderate who few thought would do well. In a stunning upset the moderate, Mohammed Katami, won 69 percent of the vote. Katami has attempted to expand the freedoms enjoyed by Iranians, but he is constrained by the strong conservative and religious forces in Iran.

and China today, played a role in socializing and shaping citizens' attitudes, but had little to do with interest articulation or aggregation.[9]

Political scientists have shown that voting choices reflect a mix of motivations.[10] Many citizens evaluate past government policies or the future policy promises of the parties; issue-based voting enables the public to express their policy preferences. For other individuals, elections are a simple referendum on government performance; vote the rascals out if times are bad, and reelect them if times are good. In other cases, the charisma of a strong leader, or the incompetence of a weak one, can dominate an election. In each case, however, elections aggregate these diverse concerns to make a collective decision on the composition of government.

Figure 5.2 offers a comparative "snapshot" of interest aggregation by parties and voters in several democratic countries. It uses the device of the left-right scale, which in many countries acts as a summary of the issues that voters find most important. The figure shows where party supporters in each country placed themselves on a scale of numbers, with 1 identified as Left (or liberal in the United States) and 10 identified as Right (or conservative in the United States) in public opinion surveys in the late 1990s. It's important to realize that the left-right placements reflect the relative positions of party supporters in the national issues within the society; the meaning of the "center" is substantively different in different societies (see Table 3.3 in Chapter 3, for example.) The height of the columns above the scale shows what percentage of the electorate voted for each party.

In the countries at the top of Figure 5.2, especially in the United States, most voters support only a few parties. Moreover, the parties are fairly close to the center of the continuum, where the bulk of voters place themselves. Democrats are somewhat to the left and Republicans somewhat to the right, with a lot of overlap. The left-right "gap" between the average party supporters, although larger than it was 20 years ago, is still fairly small. Thus aggregation implies concentration of political resources behind the fairly "centrist" policies of both parties.

In France, toward the bottom of the figure, many parties received voter support. Leftist voters divided themselves between the Communist, Socialist, and

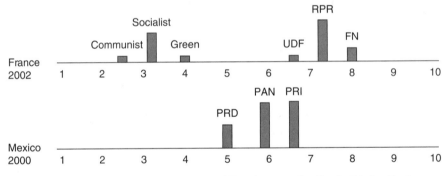

F I G U R E   5 . 2   Placement of Parties on the Left-Right Scale and Their Voter Support in Election

Green parties, (and several other smaller leftist parties not shown.) The rightist vote was split between the Gaullist RPR and the more moderate UDF. In addition, there was significant support for an extreme right-wing party, the National Front. There is a very large distance between the left-most party (the Communists) and right-most party (the National Front), and even between the two largest parties (Socialists and RPR.) The dispersed aggregation of the party-electoral outcomes means that a much more diverse range of ideological interests may be represented in the electoral debates.

Britain and Germany fell between these more extreme cases. Britain looked more like the United States in its pattern of voter support, but the parties were further apart and the smaller Liberal Democratic Party fell between them. The major German political parties were the SPD on the left and the CDU/CSU on the right, a small centrist party between them, an environmentally oriented Green party, and a reformed communist party (the PDS) on the left.

Mexico in 2000 shows the intense competition that emerged between the long-dominant, previously-authoritarian PRI and its challengers as transition to a real democracy took place. In the legislative election the PAN, which competed in an alliance with the Green Party in the Alliance for Change, was neck and neck with the newly democratic PRI, and drew voters from across the left-right spectrum. Cardenas's PRD, competing in a coalition called Alliance for Mexico, posed a left-ist challenge to both major parties. The exciting presidential election was won by PAN's Vincente Fox, who became the first non-PRI president in three-quarters of a century.

Competitive Parties in Government

If a competitive party wins control of the legislature and the executive, it will (if unified) be able to pass and implement its policies. Sometimes this control emerges directly from the electoral process, as a single party wins a majority of the vote. In many countries the election laws are designed to benefit the largest party to help it gain the votes to govern. If these distortions are sufficient, less than 50 percent of the vote may be converted into more than 50 percent of the legislative seats. Such "artificial" legislative majorities have been the rule in countries with "first past the post" electoral systems, such as Britain.[11]

For example, since 1974 none of the legislature majorities won by either the Conservative Party or the Labour Party in Britain were based on support of a majority of voters. Margaret Thatcher's Conservative Party won a solid majority of legislative seats in 1983 and 1987 with the backing of only about 42 percent of the voters. With almost exactly the same level of support in the 1997 and 2001 elections, Tony Blair and the Labour Party won nearly two-thirds of the seats in Parliament. In all these elections, the quarter of the electorate supporting the smaller parties received only a handful of legislative seats.

In other countries, multiparty elections do not yield single-party majorities, but party coalitions formed before the election may still offer the voters a direct choice of future governments. During the election, a group of parties may encourage mutual support from their voters, agree to run candidates in different districts in order to maximize their combined vote, or agree to govern together if they jointly win a majority of legislative seats. Such agreements have appeared in many (but not all) elections in France and Germany. Preelection coalition governments are similar to majoritarian governments because they can provide voters with clear targets if they choose to reward or punish the incumbents of government. Voters thus have the ability to choose the direction of government policy through their party choice.

The aggregation of policy preferences through elections is important because parties generally fulfill their electoral promises when they gain control of government.[12] For example, British parties take pride in carrying out their promises while in office. When Socialist and Social Democratic governments have come to power in Europe, they have tended to expand the size and efforts of the governmental sector; conservative parties have generally retarded the growth of government programs. Republicans and Democrats in the United States also have been fairly responsible in keeping their promises. However, parties that have been out of office a long time or that have developed radical programs often find it difficult to implement their programs when they eventually come to power. After coming to power as part of a coalition government in 1998, the Green Party had to modify its promise to shut down Germany's nuclear power plants immediately, negotiating instead a phase out over many years.

When elections do not create a majority party (or preelection coalition), then a new government is formed by postelection negotiations among political parties and their leaders. This is a common aspect of politics in many party systems, such as those in the Netherlands and Belgium.[13] In these nations interests are not aggregated at the level of elections, because the election does not determine the government. Instead, the aggregation of interests occurs at the governmental level when a coalition is negotiated. (Also see the discussion in Chapter 6, and Figure 6.2.)

The aggregation of interests at the governmental level, rather than the electoral level, can have both costs and benefits. On the one hand, when coalitions formed at the elite level determine government policy, voters may be frustrated and disillusioned, feeling that elections do not directly define government outcomes. In addition, because interest aggregation occurs among political elites this means that new elite coalitions can form on different issues. This can be confusing to citizens (and even informed observers). It is difficult for people to assign clear responsibility for government policy when power is shifting and widely shared. This situation lessens the value of the vote as an instrument to shape future governments or to punish parties held responsible for undesirable policy.[14]

On the other hand, the aggregation of interests at the governmental level can mean that voters for all parties, not just the election winners, are represented in policymaking. Such representation can be especially important for minority interests. All citizens hold minority opinions on some issues, and some are minorities on many issues. If the rules of election and representation are fair, the possibility that their representatives can influence policy between elections is a valuable protection for minority interests. Finally, even elected governments that win a majority of votes typically lack majority support for all of their policy proposals. So a flexible pattern of interest aggregation at the legislative level, if based on fair representation, may benefit the nation as a whole. Bargaining between fairly represented groups may even increase the possibility that policies reflect different majorities on different issues. The role of elections as instruments of representation may increase through a system of aggregating interests within the government, even though the role of elections as instruments of accountability may diminish.[15]

Classifying Competitive Party Systems

Figure 5.3 classifies examples of each type of competitive party system. Majoritarian and multiparty systems are distinguished by the number of political parties. The

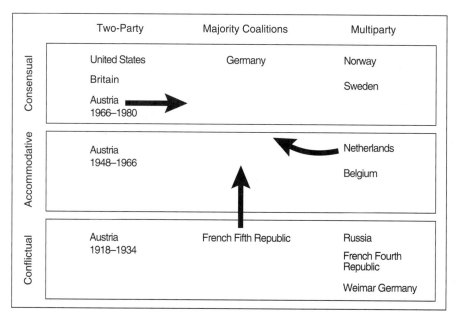

	Two-Party	Majority Coalitions	Multiparty
Consensual	United States Britain Austria 1966–1980	Germany	Norway Sweden
Accommodative	Austria 1948–1966		Netherlands Belgium
Conflictual	Austria 1918–1934	French Fifth Republic	Russia French Fourth Republic Weimar Germany

F I G U R E   5 . 3   Classifying Party Systems by Number of Parties and Antagonism Between Parties

majoritarian two-party systems are either dominated by just two parties, as in the United States, or they have two substantial parties and election laws that usually create legislative majorities for one of them, as in Britain. **Majority-coalition systems** are those where parties establish open pre-electoral coalitions so voters know which parties will attempt to work together to form a government. The purely **multiparty systems** have combinations of parties, voter support, and election laws that virtually ensure that no single party wins a legislative majority. Interest aggregation by party bargaining after the election is critical for shaping policy directions. Germany and France, as we have already mentioned, are among the multiparty systems in which voter support of party coalitions at the electoral level has often had a major impact on forming governments and policies.

The degree of antagonism or polarization among the parties is another important characteristic of party systems. In a **consensual party system** the parties commanding most of the legislative seats are not too far apart on policies and have a reasonable amount of trust in each other and in the political system.[16] These are typically party systems like those shown toward the top of Figure 5.2 Bargaining may be intense and politics exciting in these systems, but it seldom threatens the system itself.

In a **conflictual party system,** the legislature is dominated by parties that are far apart on issues or are highly antagonistic toward each other and the political system, such as the Russian party system. If a party system has mixed characteristics of a certain kind—that is, both consensual and conflictual—we classify it as **accommodative.** Arend Lijphart has used those terms to describe party systems in which political leaders are able to bridge the intense differences between antagonistic voters.[17]

The United States and Britain are contemporary examples of relatively consensual majoritarian party systems. They are not perfect two-party systems because minor parties exist in both nations. However, in Britain a single party usually wins a legislative majority and controls the legislature and the executive with disciplined party voting. In the Unites States, the shifting programs of presidential party candidates alter the degree of consensus from election to election. Moreover, the looser cohesion of American parties and the frequently divided control of legislature and executive lead to post-election bargaining that is similar to consensual multiparty systems.

Good examples of consensual multiparty systems are found in Norway and Sweden. In these countries there are four or five parties—socialists, agrarian/center, liberals, conservatives, and small communist movements. A subset of these parties has usually been able to construct long-lived governments, singly or in coalition.

Austria between 1918 and 1934 is the best example of a majoritarian conflictual party system. Antagonism between the Socialist Party and the other parties was so intense that in the mid-1930s it produced a brief civil war. The Austrian experience also illustrates how party systems can change over time. After World War II, the leaders of the two major parties negotiated an elaborate coalition agreement of mutual power sharing—checks and balances—to control its conflicts. After some 20 years of the consociational "Grand Coalition," party antagonism had declined to the point that more normal majority politics could be tolerated, although some consociational elements remained. Later the Austrian party system moved toward a consensual system, with some single-party majorities and some coalitions. Most recently, the Freedom Party, a controversial populist party of the far right, won substantial support by attacking the consensual style of the party system. The party's entry into a coalition government after the 1999 election damaged Austria's relations with other members of the European Union, because of the party's extreme political views.

France, Italy, and Weimar Germany are good historical examples of conflictual multiparty systems, with powerful Communist parties on the left and conservative or Fascist movements on the right. Cabinets had to form out of centrist movements, which were themselves divided on many issues, thus making for instability, poor government performance, and loss of citizen confidence in democracy. These factors contributed to the overthrow of democracy in Weimar Germany, the collapse of the French Fourth Republic, and government instability and citizen alienation from politics in Italy.

More recently, some of the emerging party systems in Central and Eastern Europe have tended to follow this pattern of conflictual, multiparty competition. For instance, in the 1995 parliamentary elections in Russia, 43 parties appeared on the ballot—ranging from unreformed communists on the left to nationalist parties on the right—and seven parties won representation in Parliament. The hope is that this is a transitional period as a new party system is established, not a precursor to the instability that has haunted other polarized party systems.[18]

The mixed consociational system can enable a deeply divided nation to find a way to peaceful democratic development. In the Netherlands, for example, the leaderships of competing movements found bases of accommodation that provide mutual guarantees to the various groups. In Austria and Lebanon after World War II, suspicious and hostile groups—the socialists and Catholics in Austria, and the Christians and Muslims in Lebanon—worked out a set of consociational understandings making it possible for stable governments to be formed. Austria's accommodation was based on a two-party system and Lebanon's on many small, personalistic religious parties. After 1975, however, Lebanon was penetrated and fragmented by the Middle Eastern conflict and fell victim to civil war.

South Africa adopted consociational practices in its transition to democracy. Leaders of the major political parties of the white minority and two major segments of the black majority negotiated (with great difficulty) arrangements for a democratic election and a multiparty coalition government to follow it. A typically consociational feature of the "Interim Constitution" of the transition guaranteed a share in power and government—cabinet posts—to all parties winning over 5 percent of the vote in the election. Later, this feature was abandoned. As the contrasting examples of Austria and Lebanon suggest, such practices (and the ability even to agree to attempt them) offer hope but no guarantees of long-term success to deeply divided democracies.

All this suggests that, although the number of parties affects the degree of political stability, the degree of antagonism among parties is more important. Where multiparty systems consist of relatively moderate antagonists, stability and effective performance seem possible. Where systems consist of highly antagonistic elements, collapse and civil war are ever-present possibilities, regardless of the number of parties. When crises develop, the commitment of party leaders to work together to defend democracy can be critical for its survival. It may be easier, however, to arrange such commitments in a multiparty, representational setting.[19] Some of the new democracies of Eastern Europe and Latin America and Asia, especially those divided by language or ethnicity, face similar challenges.

AUTHORITARIAN PARTY SYSTEMS

Authoritarian party systems are also specialized interest aggregation structures. They deliberately attempt to develop policy proposals and to mobilize support for them, but they do so in a completely different way from competitive party systems. With authoritarian party systems, aggregation takes place within the ranks of the party or in interactions with business groups, landowners, and institutional groups in the bureaucracy or military. The citizens have no real opportunity to shape aggregation by choosing between party alternatives, although controlled elections are often organized.

Authoritarian party systems can be distinguished among themselves according to the degree of top-down control within the party and the degree of the party's control over other groups in society. At one extreme is the **exclusive governing party,** which insists on control over political resources by the party leadership. It recognizes no legitimate interest aggregation by groups within the party nor does it permit any free activity by social groups, citizens, or other government agencies. In its most intensive form, sometimes called totalitarianism, it penetrates the entire society and mobilizes support for policies developed at the top. Its policies are legitimated by an encompassing political ideology that claims to know the true interests of the citizens, whatever their immediate preferences.[20] At the other extreme is the **inclusive governing party** that recognizes and attempts to coordinate various social groups in the society. It accepts and aggregates certain autonomous interests, while repressing others and forbidding any serious challenges to its own control.

Exclusive Governing Parties

Few parties have long maintained the absolute central control, penetration, and ideological mobilization of the most intensive (totalitarian) form of the exclusive government party. However, the ruling Communist parties of the USSR before 1985, of Eastern Europe before 1989, of China before 1980, of North Korea, Vietnam, and Cuba today fall toward the controlling end of the authoritarian party scale. Today, while withdrawing from direct administration of much of the economy, the Chinese regime, for example, still does not recognize the legitimacy of any other large political groups within Chinese society. Interest articulation by individuals, within bounds, may be permitted; the mobilization of wide support before the top elite has decided on policy is not permitted.[21]

The penetrating and controlling single-party systems can play important roles in mobilizing support for policies. An unchallenged ideological focus provides legitimacy and coherence; the party penetrates and organizes most social structures in the name of that ideology and in accordance with centralized policies. As a tool designed for unified mobilization, the exclusive governing party has been used by many leaders who were committed to massive social change. A party that successfully mobilized a colonial people behind independence, for example, might be used to change an underdeveloped society.

Even at the stage of ideological mobilization, the exclusive governing party may experience more internal aggregation than is commonly recognized or legitimately permitted. Internally, various groups may unite around such interests as region or industry, or behind leaders of policy factions. Either openly or covertly, beneath the supposedly united front, power struggles may erupt in times of crisis, with different leaders mobilizing backing for themselves and their positions. Succession crises are particularly likely to generate such power struggles, as demonstrated at the death of Stalin in the Soviet Union and Mao Zedong in China. In addition, the Chinese Communist Party several times has had to rely on the army, even on coalitions of regional army commanders, to sustain its control.

As the experiences of many new nations show, moreover, the creation of an exclusive governing party as an agent for social transformation is extremely difficult. The seduction of power regularly leads to political excesses that are not checked by competitive democratic politics and may distort ideological objectives. The exclusive governing parties in some African states also had limited capacity to control society. Furthermore, the loss of confidence in Marxist-Leninist ideology and in the Soviet model of authoritarian development led all eight of the African regimes that had once invoked it to abandon that approach by the early 1990s.[22]

As exclusive governing parties age, many enter a stage of more "mature" exclusive authoritarianism that maintains control but places less emphasis on mobilization. Some may degenerate into vehicles for personal rule and exploitation by the family and supporters of the ruler.[23] Finally, as shown by the collapse of communism in the former Soviet Union and Eastern Europe, if and when the party leaders lose faith in the unifying ideology, it may be difficult to maintain party coherence.

Inclusive Governing Parties

Among the preindustrial nations, especially in nations with notable ethnic and tribal divisions, the more successful authoritarian systems have seemed to have inclusive party systems. These systems recognize the autonomy of social, cultural, and economic groups and try to incorporate them or bargain with them, rather than control and remake them. In the more successful African one-party systems, such as Kenya and Tanzania, aggregation around personalistic, factional, and ethnic-based groups was permitted within decentralized organizations of the party.

Inclusive party systems have sometimes been labeled authoritarian corporatist systems. Like the democratic corporatist systems (see Chapter 4), some of these systems encourage the formation of large organized interest groups that can bargain with each other and the state. Unlike the democratic corporatist systems, however, these authoritarian systems provide no political resources directly to the populace. Independent protest and political activity outside of official channels are suppressed. The party leaders permit only limited autonomous demands within the ranks of the party and by groups associated with it.

The degree of legitimate aggregation permitted in the inclusive authoritarian systems may be substantial and take many forms. The party typically tries to gather various social groups under the general party umbrella and negotiate with social groups and institutions outside the party. Some of these inclusive parties have attempted aggressive programs of social change. Others have been primarily arenas for aggregating various social interests. Many inclusive party governments permit other parties to offer candidates in elections, as long as they have no real chance of winning. Indeed, one of the interesting features of politics in the last twenty-five years, along with the increasing number of liberal democracies, has been the growth of "electoral authoritarianism," in which a facade of democracy provides "some space for political opposition, independent media, and social organizations that do not seriously criticize or challenge the regime."[24] The PRI in Mexico was long a successful example of an inclusive governing party featuring electoral authoritarianism until its recent transition.

The relative stability of some inclusive authoritarian party systems should not obscure their frequent failures to build a stable governing structure. In many countries these parties coexist in uneasy and unstable coalitions with the armed forces and the civilian bureaucracy. In some countries the party has become relatively unimportant window dressing for a military regime or personal tyranny. Seldom have these parties been able to solve the economic or ethnic problems that face their nation.

These political systems were often created by unifying struggle against colonialism, and their viability has declined as colonialism has become more distant. As memories of the independence struggle have faded and the leaders of independence movements have departed, the ties of ideology and experience that held

B O X   5 . 3   Mexico's PRI

One of the oldest and the most elaborately inclusive authoritarian parties was the Partido Revolucionario Institucional (PRI) in Mexico. The PRI dominated the political process and gave other parties no realistic chances of winning elections for more than 50 years. The PRI maintained popular support after the creation of a broad coalition within the party by Lázaro Cárdenas in the 1930s; it was also careful to control the counting of the ballots. Its actions were not shaped by electoral competition, at least until the 1990s. However, the party incorporated many social groups within it, with separate sectors for labor, agrarian, and popular interests. While some discontent was suppressed, other dissatisfied individuals were deliberately enticed into the party. The party also gave informal recognition to rather distinct and well-organized political factions grouped behind such figures as former presidents. Various Mexican leaders mobilized their factions within the PRI and in other important groups not directly affiliated with it, such as big business interests. Bargaining was particularly important every six years when the party chose a new presidential nominee. The legal provision that the incumbent president could not succeed himself guaranteed some turnover of elites and may have facilitated more legitimate and open internal bargaining. In recent decades, however, rising discontent illustrated the difficulties in coordinating all interests through a single party. The urban and rural poor who had not shared in Mexico's general growth joined with others who want a more fully democratic system. An armed uprising of peasant guerrillas in early 1994 shocked the political establishment and led to more promises of genuine democratic competition. Legislative elections in 1997 were more open than earlier contests, and ended the 70-year rule of the PRI, which then lost the presidency in the 2000 election. The PRI seeks to play a new role as a competitive democratic party.

these parties together have weakened. These events, in conjunction with the world-wide expansion of democracy, have led to a general loss of legitimacy for the single-party model. In some cases the failure of authoritarian parties has permitted the emergence of some real party competition. More frequently, electoral authoritarianism with varying degrees of manipulation and control has been introduced to provide a veneer of legitimacy for internal and external consumption. In more than a few, the outcome has been a resort to naked coercion by government agencies or private forces, with the military serving as final arbiter.[25]

THE MILITARY AND INTEREST AGGREGATION

After World War II, parliamentary and democratic governments were instituted among most of the nations of the Third World. In many countries the lack of effectiveness and authority of these civil governments led to their breakdown and their replacement by **military governments.** With its control of instruments of force, and in the absence of a strong constitutional tradition, the military was an effective contender for power. Even in those regimes where civilian authority was

---

B O X   5 . 4   **Trying to Make Democracy Work**

The military government in Nigeria responded to the democratization wave of the 1990s by initiating state-level elections in 1991, and federal legislative elections in 1992. However, the military mandated a restricted process under which politicians from former civilian regimes were disqualified (as tainted by corruption). Voters were thus left with a choice of only two parties, both created by the government. Turnout was adversely affected by a spreading cynicism about the meaningfulness of the vote. Citizens' doubts were confirmed when the military annulled the presidential election of June 1993, even before the votes were announced, and appointed an Interim National Government to organize new elections. In November 1993 a military coup by Defense Minister General Sani Abacha overturned the Interim National Government, banned all political activity, dissolved the legislature, dismissed the 30 elected state governments, and thus ended even a limited role of elections in interest representation. In spring 1999 the military government allowed an election for president. The victor was a former army general, who is now trying to implement democratic reforms. But continuing ethnic violence and political murders threaten to destabilize democracy again.)

---

reestablished, the military generally constituted a significant power contender, and exercised influence in the political process. In Brazil, for example, the military played a crucial interest aggregation role in the democratic processes before 1964 and was the dominant aggregating and policymaking actor for the next 20 years. In many other nations, including Syria, Pakistan, Indonesia, Guinea, Zaire, Paraguay, and Haiti, the military has long been the dominant, or at least a major, interest aggregator. Nonetheless, a striking development in recent years has been the decline of military regimes as an official form of government, with Pakistan and Myanmar the outstanding exceptions.

The military's virtual monopoly of coercive resources gives it great potential power, even if it chooses to exercise it behind the scenes. Thus, when agreement fails on aggregation either through democratic or authoritarian party systems, the military may emerge by default as the only force able to maintain orderly government. The soldiers then remain the basic force underpinning the personal tyranny of a civilian president or a dominant party. Or the armed forces may use their power to further institutional or ideological objectives. Military rulers may try to create military and/or bureaucratic versions of authoritarian corporatism, linking organized groups and the state bureaucracy with the military as final arbiter of disagreement. They may undertake "defensive" modernization in alliance with business groups or even undertake more radical modernization. In Latin America almost all the corporatist versions of authoritarian aggregation have had a strong military component and only rarely a dominating role for the authoritarian party.

The major limitation of the military in interest aggregation is that their internal structures are not designed to mobilize support across a range of issues or outside their coercive control. The military is primarily organized for the downward processing of commands under threat of coercion. It is not set up to aggregate internal differences, to build a compromise, to mobilize wide support of government policy, or even to communicate with social groups outside the command hierarchy. Nor does the military regime have the surface claim of legitimacy that elections provide for the international community. Thus the military lacks many of the advantages in mobilizing voluntary support held by party systems. These internal limitations may be less serious when the military is dealing with common grievances and putting pressure on—or seizing power from—incumbent authorities. These limitations become a major problem, however, when a military government needs to mobilize backing for economic development or other broad government programs. For these reasons military governments frequently prove unstable, are forced to share power with other institutions, or encourage the formation of cooperating authoritarian parties.

TRENDS IN INTEREST AGGREGATION

As we have previously noted, the democratic trend in the world gained momentum with the collapse of authoritarian regimes in Eastern Europe at the end of the 1980s. Figure 5.4 classifies the world's regimes by the predominant interest aggre-

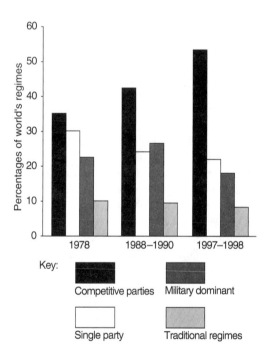

FIGURE   5 . 4   Change in Predominant Interest Aggregation Structure—Moving Toward Democracy in the World?

Source: Adapted from Raymond D. Gastil, *Freedom in the World 1979, 1988–1989, 1997–1998* (New York: Freedom House, 1979, 1989, 1998).

gation structure at three points: the end of the 1970s, the end of the 1980s, and the late 1990s. The percentages should be viewed as estimates, often based on limited information. But the figure provides a rough idea of the frequency of the three major forms: competitive parties, single-party, and military-dominated regimes. The "residual" category of traditional governments consists mostly of small kingdoms in the Middle East, South Asia, and the Pacific.

In 1978 about one-third of the world's 150-plus independent countries had competitive party and electoral systems as their predominant interest aggregation structures. These regimes were the main form in Western Europe and North America (including the Caribbean), not uncommon in Latin America and Asia, but rare in Africa and the Middle East. Nearly as many countries had some versions of a single-party regime. Single-party systems were the main form in Eastern Europe and relatively common in Africa and Asia. In slightly less than a quarter of the countries the military dominated interest aggregation, either formally (military governments) or in practice (military-dominated civilian governments). The military-dominated regimes accounted for about a third or more of the countries in Africa and Latin America.

A decade later, the trend is obviously away from single-party governments. Across the world they decline from 30 to 24 percent of the world's nations, although still accounting for nearly 40 percent of African nations. As we already know, the decline of exclusive governing party regimes is even more striking. The democratic trend toward competitive party and electoral systems is also notable, with an increase from 36 to 41 percent of the world's political systems (and more experimenting with some competition). The proportion of military governments actually increases slightly, from 23 to 26 percent of the world's countries.

The trend toward democracy took off beginning in 1989 with the dramatic changes occurring in Eastern Europe, and new pressures for democracy in the developing world. The proportion of competitive regimes is now well over 50 percent, with decline in the proportions of all other forms. The majority of the remaining single-party systems are loosely corporatist, with a few exceptions such as China and Cuba. The decline of ideological underpinnings for authoritarian governments, as well as the withdrawal of support from the Soviet Union, has contributed to this trend, especially in Africa.

Many African nations moved toward a more democratic and free system during the 1990s. This trend has continued, as has a notable decline in formally military regimes. Larry Diamond classified about a third of the African states as electoral democracies at the end of 2001.[26] However, the bulk of African nations fall into one of the varieties of "electoral authoritarianism" discussed above, with severe constraints on civil freedom and electoral opposition. A few remain unabashed authoritarian systems or mired in deadly civil war (as in Sudan and Zaire).

Perhaps in deference to the decline in the legitimacy of authoritarianism, the military throughout the world is now more likely to dominate from behind the scenes than through direct rule. Latin America also has experienced the genuine replacement of military regimes by competitive party regimes in such important countries as Argentina, Brazil, Chile, and Uruguay. Although the era of confidence in the military as a solution to development seems to have passed, military domination remains a likely outcome when other types of government are unable to solve internal conflicts.

Where there has been "backsliding" on the road to democracy, such as the assaults on democratic competition by Peru's President Fujimori in the 1990s, or the overthrow of Pakistan's elected president by the army in 1999, the military has usually been at least part of the antidemocratic movement. With such examples in mind, we cannot assume that the democratizing trend will continue relentlessly. Multiparty regimes that seem unable to cope with economic and social problems often lose their legitimacy. Such is now the challenge facing the new competitive regimes of Eastern Europe and the former Soviet Union, as well as the Third World.

SIGNIFICANCE OF INTEREST AGGREGATION

How interests are aggregated is an important determinant of what a country's government does for and to its citizens. The factors that most interest us about government and politics—stability, revolution, participation, welfare, equality, liberty, security—are very much consequences of the pattern of interest aggregation.

One importance outcome of the aggregation process is the narrowing of policy options. Through interest aggregation, the desires and demands of citizens are converted into a few policy alternatives. The consequence is that many possible policies have been eliminated and only a few remain. In addition, this means that political resources have been accumulated in the hands of the relatively few political actors who decide policy. The policy alternatives that reach this stage are serious matters for political consideration because they have the backing of significant sectors of society. For instance, a policy alternative such as the United States government taking over the steel production industry has never been "serious," because no group with major political resources has favored it, even though this policy has been implemented in other nations.

Narrowing and combining policy preferences are easily seen in the working of competitive party systems. Of the many possible policy preferences, only a few are promoted by parties after the parties choose leaders and establish election platforms. In the elections, voters support some of these parties and thus shape the strength of party representation in the legislature. Even at the legislative stage, some further consolidation and coalition building takes place between party factions or party groups. At some point, however, most policy options have been eliminated from consideration. Either they were never backed by parties or the parties supporting them did badly in the elections.

In noncompetitive party systems, military governments, and monarchies, aggregation works differently, but with the similar effect of narrowing policy options. It may be that on some issues, aggregation will virtually determine policy, as when a military government or a faction of an authoritarian party can decide the government's program. In other cases the legislative assembly, military council, or party politburo may contain several factions of similar strength that negotiate to determine policy outcomes. The narrowing of policy choices also implies that the influence and access of certain social interests are determined by the process of interest aggregation.

Another consequence of interest aggregation is that the pattern of polarization in the political culture often carries over to the policy making body. In a relatively consensual society like Germany, the parliament is made up of mainly moderate and tolerant parties. Thus the policy making style of the legislature tends to encourage cooperation and consensus building. In more conflictual Italy, the stalemated Parliament was long dominated by two parties very distant from each other—the Communists and the Christian Democrats. Thus, the workings of the government are often a reflection of the patterns of interests within the society.

But politics shapes its environment as well as reflecting it. Interest aggregation often alters the amount of polarization that the political culture projects into policy-making. That is one reason why politics is so fascinating. Well-organized and well-led political parties might, at least for a while, be able to dominate politics and limit the strength of extremist groups in the legislature, as in the accommodative model that we mentioned earlier. Conversely, well-organized extremists might be able to appeal to the fears and prejudices of some groups and get their support at the polls, thus gaining more legislative strength in an otherwise consensual country.

The ultimate implication of aggregation processes may be in the representativeness and adaptability of the government, and thus its stability. Authoritarian interest aggregation tends to create political power structures that do not reflect popular opinion. In a highly divided and conflict-ridden society, such unrepresentativeness may be proposed as a great virtue. Leaders of military coups often justify their overthrow of party governments by claiming to depolarize politics and rid the nation of conflict it cannot afford. Similarly, heads of authoritarian parties typically claim that their nation must concentrate all its energies and resources on common purposes and that party competition would be too polarizing.

In contrast, proponents of democratic interest aggregation argue that the best hope for mutual accommodation of conflicting social and political interests lies in free expression and participation in fair electoral competition, followed by negotiation using constitutional resources. Without such democratic aggregation, suppression of dissent leads to injustice and the frustration of the excluded, the corruption of the included, and eventually to violence and greater instability.

Democracy thus leads policy makers to act as the people wish. In a polarized political culture, the cost of interest aggregation that reflects division and uncertainty may be seen as a price to pay for citizen control. As the frequent instability in authoritarian and military governments indicates, however, it may be easier to do away with the appearance of polarization than the reality. Cultural divisions may end up being reflected through military factions or intraparty groups, instead of through party competition, and the citizens may end up without either freedom and participation or stability.

KEY TERMS

accommodative party
 systems
associational groups
authoritarian party
 systems
competitive party systems
conflictual party systems
consensual party systems

exclusive governing party
inclusive governing party
institutional groups
interest aggregation
majoritarian two-party
 systems
majority-coalition systems

military government
multiparty systems
patron-client network
plurality election rules
proportional
 representation
single-member districts

SUGGESTED READINGS

Converse, Philip E. and Roy Pierce. *Political Representation in France.* Cambridge, MA: Harvard University Press, 1986.

Cox, Gary. *Making Votes Count: Strategic Coordination in the World's Electoral Systems.* Cambridge: Cambridge University Press, 1997.

Dalton, Russell J. and Martin P. Wattenberg. *Parties Without Partisans: Political Change in Advanced Industrial Democracies.* New York: Oxford University Press, 2000.

Downs, Anthony. *An Economic Theory of Democracy.* New York: Harper and Row, 1957.

Farrell, David. *Electoral Systems: A Comparative Introduction.* New York: St. Martin's Press, 2001.

Farrell, David, Ian Holliday, and Paul Webb, eds. *Political Parties in Democratic States,* Oxford: Oxford University Press, 2002.

Gallagher, Michael, Michael Laver, and Peter Mair. *Representative Government in Modern Europe,* 3rd ed. New York: McGraw-Hill, 1995.

Jackson, Robert H. and Carl G. Rosberg. *Personal Rule in Black Africa.* Berkeley: University of California Press, 1982.

Kitschelt, Herbert. *The Transformation of European Social Democracy.* New York: Cambridge University Press, 1994.

Klingemann, Hans-Dieter, Richard Hofferbert, and Ian Budge. 1994. *Parties, Policy and Democracy.* Boulder, CO: Westview Press.

Laver, Michael and Norman Schofield. *Multiparty Government.* New York: Oxford University Press, 1990.

Lijphart, Arend. *Electoral Systems and Party Systems.* New York: Oxford University Press, 1994.

———. *Patterns of Democracy.* New Haven, CT: Yale University Press, 1999.

Linz, Juan J. *Totalitarian and Authoritarian Regimes.* Baltimore, MD: Johns Hopkins University Press, 2002.

——— and Alfred Stepan, eds. *The Breakdown of Democratic Regimes.* Baltimore, MD: Johns Hopkins University Press, 1978.

Nordlinger, Eric A. *Soldiers in Politics: Military Coups and Governments.* Englewood Cliffs, NJ: Prentice-Hall, 1976.

O'Donnell, Guillermo, Philippe C. Schmitter, and Laurence Whitehead. *Transitions from Authoritarian Rule: Prospects for Democracy.* Baltimore, MD: Johns Hopkins University Press, 1986.

Powell, G. Bingham, Jr. *Contemporary Democracies: Participation, Stability and Violence.* Cambridge, MA: Harvard University Press, 1982.

———. *Elections as Instruments of Democracy.* New Haven, CT: Yale University Press, 2000.

Riker, William H. *Liberalism Against Populism.* San Francisco, CA: W. H. Freeman, 1982.

Sartori, Giovanni. *Parties and Party Systems.* Cambridge, England: Cambridge University Press, 1976.

Ware, Alan. *Citizens, Parties, and the State.* Princeton, NJ: Princeton University Press, 1988.

ENDNOTES

1. Luis Roniger and Ayse Gunes-Ayata, eds., *Democracy, Clientelism, and Civil Society* (Boulder, CO: Lynne Rienner, 1994); S. Eisenstadt and L. Roniger, *Patrons, Clients and Friends* (Cambridge, England: Cambridge University Press, 1984); Lucian W. Pye, *Asian Power and Politics* (Cambridge, MA: Harvard University Press, 1985); Martin Shefter, "Patronage and Its Opponents," in *Political Parties and the State* (Princeton, NJ: Princeton University Press, 1994); see also the studies of the personal networks of leaders in the politics of the former Soviet Union, such as T. H. Rigby and Rokdan Harasimin, *Leadership Selection and Patron Client Relations in the USSR and Yugoslavia* (Beverly Hills, CA: Sage, 1981).

2. William Thompson, *The Grievances of Military Coup-Makers* (Beverly Hills, CA: Sage, 1973).

3. The extensive literature on party strategies owes its largest debt to Anthony Downs, *An Economic Theory of Democracy* (New York: Harper and Row, 1957). More generally, see Dennis C. Mueller, *Public Choice II* (Cambridge, England: Cambridge University Press, 1989) and Gary Cox, *Making Votes Count* (New York: Cambridge University Press, 1997.)

4. Russell J. Dalton, Scott C. Flanagan, and Paul Allen Beck, eds., *Electoral Change in Advanced Industrial Societies* (Princeton, NJ: Princeton University Press, 1984); Mark Franklin et al., *Electoral Change* (Cambridge, England: Cambridge University Press, 1992); Herbert Kitschelt, *The Transformation of European Social Democracy* (New York: Cambridge University Press, 1994); Wolfgang C. Mueller and Kaare Strom, *Policy, Office or Votes? How Political Parties in Western Europe Make Hard Decisions* (New York: Cambridge University Press, 1999).

5. Maurice Duverger, *Political Parties: Their Organization and Activity in the Modern State,* [1954] trans. Barbara and Robert North (New York: Wiley, 1963). For more recent discussions of electoral systems and consequences, see Rein Taagepera and Matthew Shugart, *Seats and Votes* (New Haven, CT: Yale University Press, 1989); Cox, *Making Votes Count;* and the references in Note 11 below.

6. Ian Budge, David Robertson, and Derek Hearl, *Ideology, Strategy and Party Change: Spatial Analyses of Post-War Election Programmes in 19 Democracies* (New York: Cambridge University Press, 1987); Richard Katz and Peter Mair, eds., *How Parties Organize: Change and Adaptation in Party Organizations in Western Democracies* (Thousand Oaks: Sage Publications, 1994).

7. Despite their virtues, elections cannot solve perfectly all the complex problems in fairly aggregating interests. For example, giving each citizen one vote does not take account of the varying intensities with which different people may hold their opinions. Moreover, a very large literature in economics and political science has demonstrated various problems, notably that for some distributions of preferences about three or more alternatives, there is no fair rule for aggregating the votes to select a single, unequivocally best, outcome ("Arrow's Paradox"). Important original works in this literature were Duncan Black, "On the Rationale of Group Decision Making," *Journal of Political Economy* 56 (1948) 23–34; and Kenneth Arrow, *Social Choice and Individual Values* (New Haven, CT: Yale University Press, 1951). For an accessible, although controversial, discussion of some implications for political science, see William H. Riker, *Liberalism Against Populism* (San Francisco: W. H. Freeman, 1982). More recently, see Kenneth A. Shepsle and Mark S. Bonchek, *Analyzing Politics: Rationality, Behavior and Institutions* (New York: W. W. Norton, 1997), Part II.

8. Richard Topf, "Electoral Participation," in H. Klingemann and D. Fuchs, eds., *Citizens and the State* (Oxford, England: Oxford University Press, 1995); Mark Franklin, "Electoral Participation," in Lawrence LeDuc, Richard Niemi, and Pippa Norris, eds, *Comparing Democracies 2: Elections and Voting in Global Perspective* (Beverly Hills: Sage Publications, 2002), pp. 216–35.

9. However, the initiation of semi-competitive elections for Chinese village leadership positions since 1987 has in some areas had significant impact on the correspondence of opinions between citizens and local leaders. See Melanie Manion, "The Electoral Connection in the Chinese Countryside," *American Political Science Review* 90 (1996): 736–48.

10. Russell J. Dalton, *Citizen Politics: Public Opinion and Political Parties in Advanced Industrial Democracies*, 3rd ed. (Chatham, NJ: Chatham House, 2002; Philip E. Converse and Roy Pierce, *Representation in France* (Cambridge, MA: Harvard University Press, 1986); Michael Lewis-Beck, *Economics and Elections: The Major Western Democracies* (Ann Arbor: University of Michigan Press, 1988).

11. For analyses of the implications of election laws for party representation and government majorities, see Douglas Rae, *The Political Consequences of Election Laws* (New Haven, CT: Yale University Press, 1967); Taagepera and Shugart, *Seats and Votes*, 1989; Arend Lijphart, *Electoral Systems and Party Systems: A Study of Twenty-seven Democracies, 1945–1990* (Oxford, England: Oxford University Press, 1994).

12. Hans-Dieter Klingemann, Richard Hofferbert, and Ian Budge, *Parties, Policy and Democracy* (Boulder, CO: Westview, 1995); Gallagher, Michael, Michael Laver, and Peter Mair. *Representative Government in Western Europe*, 2nd ed. New York: McGraw-Hill, 1995, Ch. 13. See also Richard Rose, *Do Parties Make a Difference?*(Chatham, NJ: Chatham House, 1984), ch. 5.

13. The literature on coalitions, their formation and durability, has now become very large. See especially Michael Laver and Norman Schofield, *Multiparty Government: The Politics of Coalition in Europe* (New York: Oxford University Press 1990); and Wolfgang C. Mueller and Kaare Strom, *Coalition Governments in Western Europe* (New York: Oxford University Press, 2000).

14. Generally, see G. Bingham Powell, Jr., *Elections as Instruments of Democracy* (New Haven, CT: Yale University Press, 2000), Chs. 3, 4.

15. On elections and the representation of votes and preferences, as well as the trade-off with accountability, see Powell, *Elections as Instruments of Democracy*, Chs. 5–10.

16. This classification is adapted from Arend Lijphart, *Democracy in Plural Societies* (New Haven, CT: Yale University Press, 1977); and Arend Lijphart, *Patterns of Democracy* (New Haven, CT: Yale University Press, 1999).

17. Lijphart, *Democracy in Plural Societies.*

18. There is a burgeoning literature on the new party systems of Eastern and Central Europe; see especially Herbert Kitschelt, Zdenka Mansfeldova, and Radoslaw Markowski, *Post-Communist Party Systems: Competition, Representation and Inter-party Cooperation* (Cambridge, England: Cambridge University Press, 1999).

19. See Lijphart, *Patterns of Democracy*, 1999; G. Bingham Powell, Jr., *Contemporary Democracies* (Cambridge, MA: Harvard University Press, 1982), chs. 8 and 10; and Juan J. Linz and Alfred Stepan, eds., *The Breakdown of Democratic Regimes* (Baltimore, MD: Johns Hopkins University Press, 1978).

20. Juan Linz, *Totalitarian and Authoritarian Regimes* (Boulder, CO: Lynne Rienner, 2000; Amos Perlmutter, *Modern Authoritarianism: A Comparative Institutional Analysis* (New Haven, CT: Yale University Press, 1981), especially pp. 62–114.

21. See Melanie Manion, "Politics in China", Chapter 13 below; for the earlier period, see, for example, Franz Schurman, *Ideology and Organization in Communist China* (Berkeley: University of California Press, 1966).

22. On the efforts in Africa, see Crawford Young, *Ideology and Development in Africa* (New Haven, CT: Yale University Press, 1982), ch. 2.

23. Juan Linz calls these "sultanistic" regimes, see *Authoritarian and Totalitarian Regimes* 2000, 151–157; Houchang Chehabi and Juan Linz, eds, *Sultanistic Regimes* (Baltimore: Johns Hopkins, 1998; and Robert H. Jackson and Carl G. Rosberg, *Personal Rule in Black Africa* (Berkeley: University of California Press, 1982).

24. Larry Diamond, "Thinking About Hybrid Regimes," *Journal of Democracy* 13 (2002): 26. In general see the articles by Diamond; Andreas Schedler; Steven Levitsky and Lucian Way; and Nicolas van der Valle in a section of this issue of *Journal of Democracy* devoted to "Elections without Democracy," pp. 21–80.

25. See the references in notes 22–24

26. Diamond, "Thinking About Hybrid Regimes," 30–31.

Government
and Policymaking

Policymaking is the pivotal stage in the political process, the point at which bills become law, or edicts are issued by the rulers. Later, policies are implemented and enforced. To understand public policy, we must know how decisions are made. Where is power effectively located in different political systems? What does it take to change public policy: a simple majority vote in the legislature or approval also by an independently elected executive? Or is it a decree issued by the monarch, a signed agreement by military commanders, or a decision by the party central committee? Or is it merely the whim of the personal dictator?

This chapter focuses on decision rules and on the policymaking role of government agencies such as legislatures, chief executives, bureaucracies, and courts. Government agencies are at the core of policymaking. While parties, interest groups, and other actors may be very active in articulating and aggregating interests, government officials, legislators, and their staffs do most of the actual initiation and formulation of policy proposals. Interest group demands for tax relief or for the protection of endangered species cannot succeed unless they are transformed into law or policy by government officials according to some accepted decision rules. They cannot be effective until these policies are appropriately implemented by other officials. Yet, government action does not flow in one direction only. The interaction between government and citizens is a two-way process, including an upward flow of influence and demands from the society, as well as a downward flow of decisions from the government.

CONSTITUTIONS AND DECISION RULES

A constitution is the basic rules concerning decision making, rights, and the distribution of authority in a political system. We sometimes use this word to refer to a specific document laying out such principles—for example, the one adopted by the founding fathers of the United States in 1787. But a constitution need not be embodied in a single document and in fact rarely is. We should therefore think of a constitution as a set of rules and principles, whether it is a specific written document, a set of customs or practices, or, as is usually the case, both. Even a military

127

or other dictatorship typically attempts to have set procedures for having decrees proposed, considered, and adopted. Written, or codified, constitutions are particularly important in political systems based on the *rule of law*. This means that government can take no action that has not been authorized by law and that citizens can be punished only for actions that violate an existing law. Under a codified constitution, the constitution is the supreme body of laws.

A constitution contains a set of **decision rules**—the basic rules governing how decisions are made, setting up agencies and offices with specific powers, assigning them territorial and functional jurisdiction, and the like. All governments have decision rules. Decision rules may be simple or complex, and any given political system may have many such rules, or a smaller repertoire of rules that they use in many different circumstances. For example, the U.S. Congress has many different decision rules that apply under different circumstances, such as a simple majority in each house to pass a bill initially, but a two-thirds majority to override a presidential veto. The British House of Commons uses a much smaller set of rules (mainly simple majority rule). Decision rules may be more or less formal and precise. Most legislatures have formal and precise decision rules, whereas cabinets at the head of the executive branch often have informal and flexible rules.

Perhaps the most important rules that constitutions establish are those that govern the policymaking process. Policymaking is the conversion of social interests and demands into authoritative public decisions. Constitutions establish the rules by which this happens. They confer the power to propose policies on specific groups or institutions, and they give others the right to amend, reject, or approve such proposals, or to implement, police, or adjudicate them. The branches of government in modern democracies are largely known by the formal functions they play in this policy process. The legislative branch makes public policies; the executive branch implements and executes them; and the judicial branch adjudicates disputes that arise from them. In reality, however, the functions that different branches of government play are not so easily identified and distinguished from one another. For example, the executive branch is often accountable for most of the policy formulation and initiation (especially in parliamentary democracies), even though officially this function belongs to the legislature.

Knowing what policymaking function a political institution (such as a legislature) plays, however, may still leave us with a very rudimentary understanding of how policies get made. We also need to know how decisions are made within that institution. Within any given branch of government or other political institution, there are numerous rules that affect the policymaking process. The most important of these may be voting rules. In most modern legislative chambers, and in many courts, voting rules are *egalitarian*, which is to say that each member has the same voting power (though presiding officers, such as the Speaker of the British House of Commons, may have the power to break a tie vote). Simply speaking: one person, one vote. That is hardly ever true in government departments (ministries), however. There, decision making is *hierarchical*, and everybody is supposed to defer to his or her superior. In a pure hierarchy, only the vote of a person at the very top (for example, the minister) counts.

When decisions are made through voting, rules are still needed to determine the outcome. Many institutions operate through simple majority voting, which means that in a choice between two options, whichever option gets the larger number of votes wins. An absolute majority means that a winning proposal (for example, a legislative bill) must have the support of a majority of those eligible to vote, including those that might choose to abstain. Qualified majorities of three-fifths, two-thirds, or even three-fourths, are sometimes required for particularly consequential decisions. For example, the U.S. Constitution requires two-thirds majorities in both houses of Congress in order to amend the constitution or override a presidential veto. The most extreme voting rule is unanimity, which means that any one member can block any decision. Different voting rules have different attractions. Qualified majority rules, requiring over 50 percent, can protect against hasty decisions, or against decisions that disadvantage large proportions (perhaps close to half) of the voters. On the other hand, qualified majority rules can give a small minority the power to block proposals favored by a large majority, and the more restrictive voting rules are (as the percentage to approve approaches unanimity,) the less likely it is that any decision can be made at all.

Decision rules affect political activity because they determine what political resources to seek and how to acquire and use them. Individuals and groups seeking to influence policy have to operate within the framework of these rules. In a federal and decentralized system such as the United States, a pressure group may have to approach both the legislative and the executive branch, and it may have to be active both at the state and the federal level. If instead decisions are made by decree from the commander of the armed forces or the central committee of a single party state, groups will need to influence these crucial policymakers.

It is important that decision rules be transparent and stable. If they are not, citizens will not know what to expect from government. That may in turn cause them to be less trusting and less willing to invest or make other commitments. It may also lead to serious conflicts, and ultimately government may break down and issues be decided by force. The importance of having predictable decision rules was suggested by Thomas Jefferson in his introduction to the first Manual of the House of Representatives: "A bad set of rules is better than no rules at all."

Making Constitutions

Constitution making is a fundamental political act: It creates or transforms decision rules. Most of the constitutions that are in force today were formed as the result of some break, often violent, with the past—war, revolution, or rebellion against colonial rule. New decision rules have to accommodate new internal or external powers. Thus, the defeated powers and the successor states of World Wars I and II all adopted new constitutions or had new constitutions imposed on them. Britain is unusual in having not a formal written constitution but only a long-accepted and highly developed set of customs and conventions, buttressed by important ordinary statutes. This reflects the British record of gradual, incremental, and, on the whole, peaceful political change. Nevertheless, the major changes in British decision rules, such as the shift of power from the Crown to Parliament in the seventeenth century, and the Reform Acts of 1832 and 1867, which established party and cabinet government and vastly extended the right to vote, followed on periods of civil war or unrest.

Perhaps the greatest exception to the association between disruptive upheavals and constitution creation is the peaceful development over the last 40 years of the constitution of the European Union, whose growing powers are altering the decision rules affecting almost 400 million Europeans in 15 countries. But while there has been no violence associated with the formation and growth of the European Union, its origins lie in the bitter lessons of World Wars I and II.

The decades since World War II have seen much constitutional experimentation. Not only the defeated powers, but many new states, such as India and Nigeria, that achieved independence with the break up of colonial empires of Britain, France, and Portugal, introduced new political arrangements. Some of the new states in the developing areas, such as Nigeria, have subsequently changed their form of government several times. France has had two constitutions in this period, the second of which—the Fifth Republic of 1958—appears more stable than previous French constitutions. In the last two decades the worldwide trend toward democracy, the end of the Cold War, and the dissolution of the Soviet Union have precipitated a new round of constitutional design. The recent constitutional crafting in Eastern Europe, Russia, and the other Soviet successor states as well as in South Africa and elsewhere, have reignited old polemics about the virtues and faults of different constitutional arrangements, or about the very wisdom of constitutional engineering.[1]

Democracy and Authoritarianism

The most important distinction in policymaking functions is between democratic and authoritarian systems. Democracy means "government by the people." In small political systems, such as local communities, "the people" may be able to share directly in debating, deciding, and implementing public policy. In large political systems, such as contemporary states, democracy must be achieved largely through indirect participation in policymaking. Policymaking power is delegated to officials chosen by the people. Elections, competitive political parties, free mass media, and representative assemblies are political structures that make some degree of democracy, some "government by the people," possible in large political systems. Such indirect democracy is not complete or ideal. Moreover, the democratic opportunities in less economically developed societies are often meaningful to educated elites or to those living near the centers of government, but less relevant to the average citizen in the countryside. But the more citizens are involved and the more influential their choices, the more democratic the system.

In democratic systems, competitive elections give citizens the chance to shape policy through their selection and rejection of key policymakers. In large societies, competitive elections with full adult suffrage are a necessary condition for meaningful "government by the people." In **authoritarian regimes,** on the other hand, the policymakers are chosen by military councils, hereditary families, dominant political parties, and the like. Citizens are either ignored or pressed into symbolic assent to the government's choices.

Transitions toward democracy have been a major feature of world politics in the last 25 years, beginning in Southern Europe, extending to Latin America and Asia, and more recently to Eastern Europe and the former Soviet Union. This movement toward democracy is a "Third Wave" of worldwide democratization.[2] Both of the previous waves have been followed by reversals, though the overall number of democracies has grown over time. The first wave began in the nineteenth century and culminated with the establishment of many new democracies after the Allied victory in World War I. After World War II, a second democratic wave included many newly independent ex-colonial states, as well as the defeated authoritarian powers. Since about 1975, a third wave has undermined the legitimacy of authoritarian regimes everywhere, especially since the collapse of the Soviet Union in 1991. But note the case of Nigeria, where attempts to establish civilian and democratic regimes have fallen twice to military coups (1966 and 1983), and where a transition toward democracy was again aborted by the military in 1993. Nigeria is not unique. It can be difficult to consolidate stable democratic regimes, especially in poor societies.[3] Today's Third Wave of democratization may well experience many reversals of the sort Nigeria has experienced. In such systems as China and Egypt democracy has not yet taken hold.

Separation of Government Powers

The basic decision rules of democratic political systems differ along three important dimensions: (1) the separation of powers between different branches of government; (2) the geographic distribution of authority between the central (national) government and lower levels, such as states, provinces, or municipalities; and (3) limitations on government authority. We shall discuss these dimensions in order, beginning with the separation of authority between executive and legislative institutions.

The theory of **separation of powers** has a long and venerable history going back at least to the work of Locke and Montesquieu.[4] Separation of power, they argued, has the virtue of preventing the injustices that might result from an unchecked executive or legislature. Madison and Hamilton elaborated this theory in *The Federalist*,[5] which described and defended the institutional arrangements proposed by the U.S. Constitutional Convention of 1787. Political theorists in the course of the nineteenth and first part of the twentieth centuries reflecting on the two successful historical cases of representative democracy—Britain and the United States—gradually codified what we may call the "classic" separation of powers theory that dominated the political science of the pre–World War II period. This theory argued that there are essentially two forms of representative democratic government—the presidential and the parliamentary.

The **democratic presidential regime** provides two separate agencies of government—the executive and the legislative—separately elected and authorized by the people. Each branch is elected for a fixed term; no one branch can by ordinary means unseat the other; and each has specific powers under the constitution. Ultimate power to authorize legislation and approve budgets in modern democracies resides with the legislature, whose relationships with the executive are then critical for concentration or dispersal of power. Different presidential regimes provide their presidents with a variety of different powers over government appointments and policymaking, such as the authority to veto legislation or to make policy by executive decree under some conditions.[6] In a country such as the United States, both legislature and executive (Congress and the Presidency) have large and significant roles in policymaking. In some other democratic presidential systems, such as Brazil, the president may have such a variety of constitutional powers, including the power to make laws through "emergency" decrees, that he or she can reduce the role of the legislature. But coordination between the separate institutions of executive and legislature must somehow be achieved to make policy.

The **parliamentary regimes,** on the other hand, make the executive and legislative branches interdependent. First of all, only the legislative branch is directly elected, whereas the prime minister and his or her cabinet (the collective leadership of the executive branch) emerge from the legislature. The cabinet is chaired by the prime minister who is the head of government and selects the other cabinet members.[7] Typically, neither branch has a fixed term of office. The cabinet can be voted out of office at any time, and most often this is true of the legislature (the parliament) as well.

The critical feature that makes this possible is the **confidence relationship** between the prime minister and the parliamentary majority. (See Box 6.1.) In a parliamentary system, the prime minister and his or her cabinet must at all times enjoy the confidence of the parliamentary majority. Whenever the parliamentary majority for whatever reason expresses its lack of confidence (through a no-confidence vote), the prime minister and all the other cabinet members have to resign. On the other hand, the prime minister typically has the power to dissolve parliament and call new elections at any time. These two powers, the parliamentary majority's dismissal power and the prime minister's dissolution power, make the two branches mutually dependent. It induces agreement between them by forcing the executive branch to be acceptable to the parliamentary majority. Thus parliamentary democracies do not experience the form of divided government that is common under presidentialism, when the party that controls the presidency does not control the legislature, or vice versa. Instead, the chief executive (prime minister and cabinet) becomes the agent of the parliamentary majority, and in most parliamentary systems consists largely of members of parliament. Conflicts between parliament and the executive are less likely to occur, and decision making tends to be more efficient than under presidentialism. Since the same party (or parties) controls both branches of government, the cabinet tends to dominate policymaking, and the legislature may be less influential than under a presidential constitution.

Not all democracies fit neatly into the presidential or parliamentary category. Some, such as France, are often characterized as mixed or **"semi-presidential."** In some of these mixed types, the president and the legislature are separately elected (as in presidential systems), but the president then has the power to dissolve the legislature (as in parliamentary systems). In such systems, the cabinet may be appointed by the president (as under presidentialism), but subject to dismissal by the legislature (as under parliamentarism). Shugart and Carey identify several kinds of mixed systems with independently elected presidents who have substantial policymaking power but must share control over the executive branch with the legisla-

BOX 6.1 The Confidence Vote in Parliamentary Democracies

Prime ministers in parliamentary democracies lead precarious political lives. Unlike presidents in presidential systems, prime ministers can be voted out of office at any time, and for any reason, by a parliamentary majority. There are two ways in which this can happen. One is when parliament passes a motion expressing a lack of confidence in the prime minister—a no-confidence motion. The other possibility is when parliament defeats a motion expressing confidence in the prime minister—a confidence motion. No-confidence motions are typically introduced by the parliamentary opposition in the hope of bringing down the prime minister. Confidence motions, on the other hand, are normally introduced by prime ministers themselves, and it is not at all self-evident why they would do so. Since one possible result of a confidence motion is being kicked out of office, it may seem like a form of Russian roulette.

In reality, however, the confidence vote can be a powerful weapon in the hands of the prime minister. It is typically attached to a bill (a policy proposal) that is favored by the prime minister but not by the parliamentary majority. By attaching a confidence motion to the bill, the prime minister forces the members of parliament to choose between the bill and the fall of the cabinet. This can be a particularly painful choice for dissident members of the prime minister's own party. If they vote for the bill, they may bring down their own government, and perhaps immediately have to face the voters to boot. British prime ministers have often resorted to the confidence motion in order to bring rebellious party members into line. In 1993, Conservative Prime Minister John Major faced a parliamentary crisis over the ratification of the Maastricht Treaty, which expanded the powers of the European Union. Major had only a slim majority in the House of Commons, and many "Euroskeptics" in his own party were opposed to the Maastricht Treaty. About 20 of these Conservative dissidents voted with the opposition and helped defeat the Maastricht Treaty in the House of Commons. Immediately after this embarrassing defeat, however, Major introduced a confidence motion on his Maastricht policy and announced that if he lost this vote, he would dissolve the House of Commons and hold new elections. Many of the Conservative dissidents feared that their party would do poorly in such an election and that they might personally lose their seats. Major's confidence motion passed by a vote of 339 to 299, and the House of Commons approved the Maastricht Treaty. Thus, the confidence vote actually helps explain why party discipline tends to be stronger in parliamentary than in presidential systems.

---

ture. A variety of arrangements exist for such shared control; their consequences are often sharply affected by which party or coalition controls the presidency and legislature. Many of the new constitutions of the emergent democracies of Eastern Europe and Asia are of this mixed type.

Reading across Figure 6.1, we see political systems classified by the separation of policymaking powers between executive and legislative institutions, from concentrated to dispersed. The vertical dimension of the table shows geographic division of power, which is discussed in the next section. In authoritarian governments

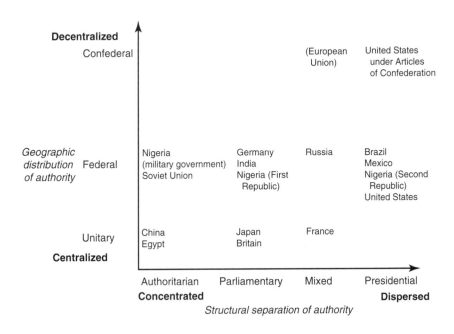

FIGURE 6.1   Division of Governmental Authority

on the left, executive, legislative, and judicial power are typically concentrated. Two of the twelve countries discussed in this book—China and Egypt—have authoritarian governments not chosen in competitive elections. Britain, Germany, Japan, and India are parliamentary systems in which executive and legislative powers are concentrated in cabinets responsible to the popularly elected lower houses of parliament. At the extreme right of Figure 6.1 are pure presidential systems such as Brazil, Mexico, and the United States. Nigeria seems to be in transition to a presidential democracy. In between, we find mixed systems such as France and Russia.

In the debate over the best system of representative democracy, many political theorists traditionally favored the British-style parliamentary system. This version of parliamentarism, coupling plurality voting rules that usually create clear single party majorities in Parliament with a Cabinet and prime minister responsible to Parliament, can result in fairly stable governments responsible to the public will. Parliamentarism coupled with proportional representation—as in Germany and France between the two world wars—seemed more crisis prone. Such crises occurred because of the emergence of large extremist political parties, which resulted in cabinet instability and even breakdown. On the other hand, the Scandinavian countries demonstrated that parliamentary systems with proportional representation can be quite stable when ideological conflict between the political parties remains moderate, whereas dominating parliamentary majorities, as in Northern Ireland, can sometimes threaten minority groups and intensify conflict.[8] In comparison to both versions of parliamentary government, the U.S. presidential system has often been criticized for periodically producing divided government, which could result in stalemate or "gridlock."

The Third Wave of democratization has reopened these parliamentary-presidential debates. Advocates of parliamentarism, particularly of the proportional variety, argue that it provides a consensual framework in which different economic, ethnic and religious groups can find representation and negotiate their differences. Parliamentary systems also have the flexibility to change governments between elections if the people disapprove of actions of the executive. Since many of the current transitional democracies are deeply divided, a parliamentary, proportional representation system may be particularly suitable. Presidentialism, they argue, is more susceptible to social conflict and democratic breakdown.[9] Under conditions of divided government, a confrontation between the two legitimately elected institutions representing the people can tear a political system apart. Or, a strong president can use executive powers to repress competition. Other scholars point out that while many scholars prefer the parliamentary solution, practical politics is coming out on the side of elected presidents with some political power.[10] Even in the domain of the former British empire (such as in Nigeria) and in most of Eastern Europe and the Soviet successor states, the constitutions provide for powerful presidents. Latin America has been dominated by presidential regimes for more than a century, and a 1993 referendum in Brazil reaffirmed its commitment to presidentialism. Presidentialism also offers the citizens a more direct choice of chief executive, and it puts more effective checks on the power of the majority in the legislature.

The relationships between executives and legislatures are not the only important non-geographic choices about dividing or sharing policymaking powers. In some smaller European democracies—such as Austria or Sweden—we find a form of "corporatist" democracy.[11] These are arrangements where the "class struggle" between workers and management, so threatening to democratic stability, could be abated by a social partnership. Through deliberation and bargaining over wages, benefits, prices, and social policy, top leaders from labor, management, and government would attempt to set economic policy (see Chapter 4). Thus often severe and disruptive conflicts could become technical rather than ideological questions, resolvable by deliberation and compromise.

A major trend in the division of policymaking powers in recent years has been the growth of **independent central banks.** Central banks, such as the Federal Reserve in the United States, have the critical task of regulating the supply of money and the interest rates, as well as many financial transactions for government and society. In most countries such bank policy was long controlled by the chief executive as part of the government bureaucracy. But in the last twenty years, and especially since the early 1990s, many countries have given their central banks substantial independence and set for them the primary task of using monetary policy to maintain price stability and limit inflation. Their independence from the executive is encouraged by giving bank governors long terms of office free from the possibility of dismissal, as well as stipulated policy objectives and responsibilities.[12] Such independence reassures investors, domestic and foreign, and seems to constrain inflation, but it limits the economic policy alternatives of the chief executive and cabinet.

Geographic Distribution of Government Power

According to the geographic division of power, we have confederal systems at one extreme, unitary systems at the other extreme, and **federal systems** in the middle. (See the vertical dimension of Figure 6.1.) The United States under the Articles of Confederation was confederal. Ultimate power rested with the states. The central government had authority over foreign affairs and defense but depended on financial and other support from the states. Under the Constitution of 1787, the American government changed from confederal to federal, which is to say that both central and state governments had separate spheres of authority and the means to implement their power. Today, the United States, Germany, Russia, India, Nigeria, Mexico, and Brazil are federal systems in which central and local units each have autonomy in particular spheres of public policy. These policy areas and powers are, however, divided among central and local units in varying ways. Britain, France, China, Japan, and Egypt are unitary systems with power and authority concentrated in the central government. Regional and local units have only those powers specifically delegated to them by the central government, which may change or withdraw these powers at will.

Most of the world's states are unitary. In fact, only 18 states are federal, or fewer than one in ten. But whereas the federal states are relatively few in number, they tend to be large and politically important. Thus, federal states account for more than one-third of the world's population and 41 percent of its land area. Generally speaking, the larger and the more diverse a state is, the more likely it is to be federal. Federalism is commonly thought to have a number of advantages. In multinational or otherwise divided societies, it may help protect ethnic, linguistic, or religious minorities, particularly if they are geographically concentrated. It may generally serve as a check on overly ambitious rulers and thus protect markets and citizen freedoms. Moreover, federalism may allow subunits (such as states) to experiment with different policy programs. Governments may thus learn from the experiences of others. In addition, citizens may be free to "vote with their feet" and choose the policy environment that best fits their preferences. However, while federalism promotes choice and diversity, it does so at the expense of equality. Since federalism allows local governments to pursue different policies, the implication is that citizens may get systematically different treatments and benefits from different local governments. Unitary governments may also be in a better position to redistribute resources from richer regions to poorer regions, if that is desirable.

In comparing confederal, federal, and unitary systems, however, we must keep in mind the distinction between formal and actual distribution of power. In unitary systems, in spite of the formal concentration of authority at the center, regional and local units may acquire power that the central government rarely challenges. In the American federal system over the last century, power has steadily moved from the states toward the center. In recent years there has been an effort, under the slogan of a new federalism, to move power from the federal government back to the states. Even in unitary systems there have been efforts to shift some power to provincial and local governments. This has been a response to democratic pressures, demands for greater grassroots influence. Thus, the real differences between federal and unitary systems may be considerably less significant than their formal arrangements suggest. Mexico is an example of the discrepancy between formal and actual federalism. Until recently the Partido Revolucionario Institucional (PRI) had centralized control in this formally federal system. Recent developments in Mexico, with oppositional parties winning ground in some states and the PRI power monopoly under challenge, have produced some "real" federalism to go along with the formalities.

Limitations on Government Power

Unlike authoritarian regimes, democracies are characterized by some legal or customary limitation on the exercise of power. Systems in which the powers of various government units are defined and limited by a written constitution, statutes, and custom are called **constitutional regimes.** Civil rights—such as the right to a fair trial and freedom to speak, petition, publish, and assemble—are protected against government interference except under specified circumstances.

The courts are crucial to the limitations on governmental power. As illustrated in Table 6.1, governments may be divided into those, at one extreme, in which the power to coerce citizens is relatively unlimited by the courts, and those, at the other extreme, in which the courts not only protect the rights of citizens but also police other parts of the government to see that their powers are properly exercised. The United States and India are examples of systems in which high courts rule effectively on challenges that other parts of the government have exceeded the powers allocated by the constitution. This practice of **judicial review** is authorized to various degrees in about half of the world's democracies and seems to be growing in popularity. But judicial review is often weakened by lack of independence of the appointment or tenure of judges, as in Japan, or by their ineffectiveness in overcoming executive power. Some other constitutional regimes have independent courts that protect persons against the improper implementation of laws and regulations, but cannot legally overrule the assembly or the political executive, as in Britain. The substantive rights of persons in these systems are protected by statute, custom, self-restraint, and political pressure—which are also essential to the effectiveness of courts even where judicial review is authorized. In authoritarian systems policymakers do not usually allow courts to constrain their use and abuse of power, even where brave judges attempt to rule against them.

T A B L E   6 . 1   Judicial Limitation of Governmental Authority

Unlimited		*Limited*
Nonindependent Courts	**Independent Courts**	**Judicial Review**
China	Britain	United States
Egypt	Finland	India
Nigeria		Germany
		France
		Japan
		Russia

Arend Lijphart characterizes only four of the 36 democratic systems he examines as having "strong" judicial review: Germany, India, the United States, and Canada after 1982.[13] The Supreme Court of India has been singled out as most similar to the United States Supreme Court, having successfully overruled the Prime Minister and assembly by declaring over 100 national laws and ordinances unconstitutional.[14] The German Constitutional Court has also had a substantial impact on national and state policymaking, both through its rulings and through government's anticipation of those rulings. About a quarter of Lijphart's democracies had either strong or medium strength judicial review. In both France and Germany new legislation may be challenged in court by opposition members of parliament even before it takes effect, a process called "abstract" judicial review. Lijphart classified a little over half of his democracies as having "weak judicial review," with the powers of courts constrained by very limited constitutional authority, as in Sweden, or limited independence of government-appointed judges, as in Japan. In the remaining democracies, including Britain, courts enjoyed no power of judicial review of legislation, although, as suggested in Table 6.1, they may still protect individuals from government abuse not specifically authorized by law.

In many of the new democracies of Eastern Europe judicial review was proclaimed in the constitution, but proved harder to implement in practice. There have been striking successes in constraining governments in some countries, as in Bulgaria, but failures in others, such as Albania and Belarus. In Nigeria the courts long retained a striking degree of judicial independence under a succession of otherwise undemocratic military regimes, but were shown little respect under the Abacha regime of the mid-1990s, which established special military tribunals to prosecute its perceived enemies. Similarly, the president has used military and security courts, as well as executive decrees and a long-standing State of Emergency to limit efforts by courts to exert judicial independence in Egypt. China, on the other hand, after explicit rejection of any limits on "mass justice" from the late-1950s to 1970s, has gradually attempted to introduce a very limited "rule by law," as a way of encouraging stability and economic growth and controlling corruption. But the practice falls far short of the promise of even partial limitation on governmental authority.

All written constitutions provide for amending procedures. Most framers of constitutions have recognized that basic decision rules must be adaptable, because of potential ambiguities, inefficiencies, changes in citizen values, or unforeseen circumstances. On the other hand, if amendments are too easy to make, then important constitutional protections may be jeopardized. Therefore, many constitutions provide that certain arrangements may not be amended—for example, the provision in the U.S. Constitution granting each state equal representation in the Senate. Amending procedures vary widely, ranging from the complex to the simple. Perhaps the simplest case is that of the United Kingdom, where an ordinary parliamentary statute may alter the constitution. Thus the Parliament Act of 1911 reduced the power of the House of Lords to that of proposing amendments and delaying legislation for one parliamentary session. The current effort to eliminate the power of the hereditary peers is similarly taking place through ordinary legislation. Due to the

Lords' power to delay legislation, the new reforms may require enactment in two successive parliamentary sessions.

Some constitutions prescribe qualified majorities, such as a two-thirds majority, for constitutional amendments. Others require that an amendment be approved twice with an interval of time between passages. Brazil requires its legislature to vote an amendment in two separate occasions with a three-fourths vote each time. In some cases, constitutional amendments must be approved by a popular vote. The U.S. Constitution has the most difficult formal procedure, requiring initiation by two-thirds of both houses of the Congress (or by the never-employed procedure of a national convention called by two-thirds of the states), and approval by three-fourths of the state legislatures, or three-fourths of specially elected states' conventions. Constitutions that have complicated amending procedures, such as the American one, are called "rigid." On average, they tend to be amended less frequently than their "flexible" counterparts.[15]

One of the main points of Figure 6.1 and Table 6.1 is that constitutions may concentrate or disperse government power along several dimensions. There are necessary trade-offs involved in making such constitutional choices. Probably no one who favors democracy and individual liberties would argue for extreme centralization of power in an omnipotent dictator, as in Thomas Hobbes's *Leviathan* (Chapter 1). However, constitutional democracies that concentrate power to a somewhat lesser degree, such as the British system, have some important advantages. Their governments tend to be effective and efficient, and by relying on majority rule, they tend to treat all citizens equally. No small group can hold up a decision favored by a solid majority. On the other hand, constitutions that disperse power have their own advantages. They are more likely to check potential abuses of power, such as the tyranny of a majority, and policies will tend to be more stable over time.

Checking the Top Policymakers

In many authoritarian systems, there is no legal and institutionalized way to remove the top political leaders if they become unpopular or overstep whatever bounds they may face. Moreover, authoritarian leaders can usually change or simply ignore the constitution itself, when it restricts their desires. Democracies have various procedures for keeping the leaders in check, but the procedures vary between types of systems. In parliamentary systems, chief executives can be removed virtually at any time through a vote of no confidence if they lose the support of a parliamentary majority. In Germany, Social Democratic Chancellor Helmut Schmidt was ousted by Helmut Kohl of the Christian Democratic Party in October 1982. In Britain Prime Minister Margaret Thatcher's own Conservative Party replaced her with John Major in 1990.

Democratic presidential systems fall somewhere in between. Unlike prime ministers under parliamentary constitutions, presidents have fixed terms of office. Most presidential systems do allow presidents to be removed before their term is up, but typically only if they are guilty of serious criminal or other wrongdoing. The procedure through which this is done is called **impeachment.** Impeachment typically involves three components: (1) impeachable offenses are usually identified as presenting unusual danger to the public good or safety; (2) the penalty is removal from office (sometimes with separate criminal penalties;) (3) impeachment cases are decided by the legislature, but require more than ordinary majorities and may also involve the judiciary in some way. In the American system, impeachment procedures can be used against the incumbents in top offices, even the president (as in the cases of Presidents Nixon and Clinton) or a Supreme Court justice, if their activities stray too far beyond legal bounds.

The establishment of the impeachment power has been associated with the rise of presidential separation-of-powers systems, and with the need in such systems for an extraordinary check against abuse of power on the part of high executive officers. (However, its modern origin was in eighteenth century Britain; see Box 6.2.) The framers of the American constitution viewed the normal checks and balances as insufficient protection against serious corruptions of power. Impeachment typically combines legislative and judicial powers against an executive out of control. The positive value of impeachment is that it provides a way of legally mobilizing political power against a threat to the constitutional or legal order. On the other hand, the danger is that it can be used for less pressing purposes. It can be tempting under a separation-of-powers system, when the executive and legislative are controlled by different political parties, and particularly when these parties are hostile to one another, to employ the institution out of primarily partisan motives. To prevent abuse of the impeachment procedure, the odds are typically stacked in

---

BOX 6.2   Impeachment

Impeachment is often thought of as a procedure that is typical of presidential rather than parliamentary systems. Nevertheless, its modern origins lie in Britain. The framers of the American constitution adopted impeachment from their British institutional heritage. In English constitutional tradition, impeachment was a process affecting top executive and civil officers accused of "high crimes and misdemeanors," for which the penalty was removal from office. Impeachment was quite separate from judicial control over criminal behavior.

An illustrative impeachment case was in process in the British Parliament at the very time that the U.S. Federal Constitution was being drafted, while the *Federalist Papers* were written, and while the states were engaged in ratification. Warren Hastings, Governor General of India (1774–1784), was accused and impeached for "high crimes and misdemeanors" by the Whig Party, which then controlled the House of Commons. The House of Lords tried the case over a seven-year period (1787–1795) but failed to convict Hastings. The institution then fell into disuse in Britain as her system of parliamentary government evolved. In a parliamentary system, cabinet members and ministers hold office only when they have the confidence of a parliamentary majority. A no-confidence vote can bring them down at any time and for any reason. Parliament can therefore much more easily hold the top political elite accountable through the threat of a no-confidence vote rather than impeachment.

favor of the defendant. Impeachment is often a cumbersome procedure, and it typically takes a large majority to convict—in the United States, a two-thirds majority in the Senate. No U.S. president has yet been convicted by the Senate and removed from office, although that fate has befallen other federal officials, such as judges.

Brazil, Mexico, and many other Latin American nations with strong presidents have impeachment traditions imbibed from the United States. In Mexico, the president, the state governors, and federal judges are subject to impeachment. Brazil also has an impeachment process similar to that of the United States, except that it takes a two-thirds vote to charge the president and other high civil officers with impeachable offenses. A two-thirds vote is also required in the Senate to convict. The clause was invoked in 1992 when President Collor was impeached on charges of large-scale corruption. He resigned before trial in the Senate. While impeachment is associated with constitutions having powerful presidencies with fixed terms of office, it has also been adopted in semi-presidential regimes, and even in purely parliamentary regimes.

In the long run the ultimate control of democratic order is periodic and competitive elections. This need to achieve and regularly renew their mandates is the fundamental device that leads politicians to respond to the needs and demands of citizens. It is deeply imperfect. It may be difficult to tell when elected officials are incompetent, deceitful, or just unlucky. The complexities of policymaking may baffle the attempt of even trained observers to assign responsibility for successes or failures. The multiplicity of political issues may leave citizens torn between their candidate choices. Or, none of the choices may seem very palatable. Yet, deeply imperfect as it is, this remarkable recruitment structure, through its effects on information, group activity, and party competition, gives every citizen some influence on the policymaking process. For this reason we consider it the most significant democratic structure.

ASSEMBLIES

Three important types of government institutions are frequently involved in policymaking: (1) the legislative assembly; (2) the chief executive; and (3) the higher levels of bureaucracy. The distribution of policymaking predominance among these three institutions varies from country to country and from issue area to issue area. Legislative **assemblies** have existed for thousands of years. Ancient Greece and Rome had them, as did many other ancient societies, and indeed the Roman Senate has given its name to modern assemblies in the United States and many other countries. The Icelandic Althingi, first assembled in A.D. 930, is the oldest existing assembly. The British Parliament dates back to the Model Parliament of 1295 and beyond. Almost all contemporary political systems have assemblies, variously called senates, chambers, diets, houses, and the like. Assemblies may also be known as "legislatures" (regardless of what role they actually play in legislating) or as "parliaments" (mainly in parliamentary systems). Their formal approval is usually required for major public policies. They are generally elected by popular vote, and hence are at least formally accountable to the citizenry. Today more than 80 percent of the countries belonging to the United Nations have such governmental bodies. The almost universal adoption of legislative assemblies suggests that in the modern world a legitimate government must formally include a representative popular component.

Assembly Structure

Assemblies vary in their size—from less than 100 to more than 1000—and their organization. Legislatures may consist of one (in which case they are called unicameral) or two (bicameral) chambers. Most democracies, and some authoritarian systems, have bicameral (two-chamber) assemblies. Federal systems normally provide simultaneously for two forms of representation: often one chamber in which representation is based on population, and a second in which representation is based on geographic units. Even in unitary systems (such as France), **bicameralism** is common, but the purpose of the second chamber is to provide a check on policymaking rather than to represent subnational units. The bicameral U.S. Congress grew out of both federalism and the desire to separate the power of the federal government. The House of Representatives directly represents the citizens, with districts roughly equal in population size. In the Senate, on the other hand, the 50 U.S. states are equally represented. The U.S. congressional chambers check and balance one another as well as the other branches of government. Thus the Senate must approve treaties and executive appointments made by the president; both the Senate and the House must consent to a declaration of war; and the House must initiate all measures involving taxation and appropriations.

The American system, in which the two chambers have roughly equal powers, is unusual. In most bicameral systems one chamber is dominant, and the second (such as the Russian Council of the Federation or the French Senate) has more limited powers that are often designed to protect regional interests. While representatives in the dominant chamber are popularly elected, those in the second chamber are sometimes chosen by the regional governments (as in Germany) or in other indirect ways. The prime minister in most parliamentary systems is responsible only to the more popularly elected chamber, which therefore has a more important position in policymaking than the second chamber. (See the discussion of the vote of confidence procedure above and in Box 6.1.) In such systems members of the prime minister's cabinet are usually chosen from the majority party or parties' leadership in this chamber.

Assemblies also differ in their internal organization, in ways that have major consequences for policymaking. There are two kinds of internal legislative organization: party groups and formal assembly subunits (presiding officers, committees, and the like). There is often an inverse relationship between the strength of parties versus other subunits (such as committees). The stronger parties are, the weaker are committees, and vice versa. British members of Parliament vote strictly along party lines much more consistently than members of the U.S. Congress. As in most parliamentary systems, British members of Parliament rarely vote against the instructions of their party leaders. Because cabinets generally hold office as long as they can command a parliamentary majority, deviating from the party line means risking the fall of the government and new elections. (See

Box 6.1 on the Confidence Vote.) In presidential systems, the president and the legislators are independently elected for fixed terms of office. Thus the fate of the governing party is less directly tied up with voting on legislative measures. In American legislatures, party discipline operates principally on procedural questions, such as committee assignments or the selection of a presiding officer. On substantive policy issues, Democratic and Republican legislators are freer to decide whether or not to vote with their party leaders.

All assemblies have a committee structure, some organized arrangement that permits legislators to divide up their labor and to specialize in particular issue areas. Without such a sublegislative organization, it would be impossible to handle the large flow of legislative business. As we have seen, however, the importance of committees varies. In some legislatures, such as the United States, committees are very influential. This is at least in part because they are highly specialized, have jurisdictions that match those of the executive departments, and have large staff resources. Strong committees tend to have a clear legislative division of labor that matches the executive branch, and they are often arenas in which the opposition can be influential. British committees are much weaker than their opposite numbers in the United States, since they have small staffs, are dominated by the governing party, and get appointed for one bill at a time. Hence, they cannot accumulate expertise in a particular policy area. German and Japanese committees are stronger than those of Britain but weaker than their American counterparts.[16]

Assembly Functions

Assembly members deliberate, debate, and vote on policies that come before them. Most important policies and rules must be considered and at least formally approved by these bodies before they have the force of law. Assemblies typically also control public spending decisions, so that control of the purse strings (budgeting) is one of their major functions. In addition, some assemblies have important appointment powers, and some (like the British House of Lords in criminal cases) may serve as a court of appeals. Although laws typically need assembly approval, in most countries legislation is actually formulated elsewhere, usually by the political executive and the upper levels of the bureaucracy. When we compare the importance of assemblies as policymaking agencies, the U.S. Congress, which plays a very active role in the formulation and enactment of legislation, is at one extreme. The other extreme is represented by the National People's Congress of the People's Republic of China, which meets infrequently and does little more than listen to statements by party leaders and rubberstamp decisions made elsewhere. Roughly midway between the two is the House of Commons in Britain. There, legislative proposals are sometimes initiated or modified by ordinary members of Parliament, but public policy is usually initiated and proposed by members of the Cabinet (who are, to be sure, chosen from the members of the parliamentary body). The typical assembly provides a deliberating forum, formally enacts legislation, and sometimes amends it.

Assemblies should not be viewed only as legislative bodies. All assemblies in democratic systems have an important relationship to legislation, but not necessarily a dominant role. Their political importance is based not just on this function, but also on the great variety of other political functions they perform. Assemblies can play a major role in elite recruitment, especially in parliamentary systems where prime ministers and cabinet members typically serve their apprenticeships in parliament. Legislative committee hearings and floor debates may be important sites for interest articulation and interest aggregation, especially if there is no cohesive majority party. Debates in assemblies can be a source of public information about politics and thus contribute to the socialization of citizens generally and elites in particular. However, as in policymaking, the assemblies of different nations play very different roles in their respective political systems. The British House of Commons ordinarily does not make much of an independent impact on policymaking, because it is controlled by the ruling party's majority. The Commons and its debates are, however, central to public debate, and one of its chief functions is to prepare politicians for executive office. Through its committees, the U.S. Congress plays a major role in making laws and budgets, but must share other functions with many other institutions in the decentralized American system. The People's Congress in China plays only a limited socialization role.

Representation: Mirroring and Representational Biases

Contemporary legislative assemblies, especially in democratic systems, are valued particularly because they represent the citizens in the national policymaking process. It is not obvious, however, what the ideal linkage between citizens and government officials should be. One body of thought holds that government officials should mirror the characteristics of the citizens as far as possible. This principle, also known as *ascriptive representation*, is held to be particularly important with respect to potentially conflictual divisions such as race, class, ethnicity, gender, language, and perhaps age.

However, ascriptive representation is not the only concern in recruiting public officials. The limits of mirroring were inadvertently expressed by a U.S. senator. In defending a Supreme Court nominee that was accused of mediocrity, the senator lamely contended, "even if he were mediocre, there are a lot of mediocre judges and people and lawyers. They are entitled to a little representation, aren't they?" Most people would probably not go as far as to argue that government officials should mirror the general population in their abilities to do their jobs. Instead, we generally want political elites to be the best possible *agents* for their constituents. In this view, government officials should be selected for their ability to serve the interests of the citizens, whether or not they share the voters' background characteristics.

For politicians to be good agents, they need to have similar *preferences* to the citizens they represent and they need the appropriate *skills* to do their jobs. In democracies, political parties are the most important mechanism by which the preferences of citizens and leaders get aligned. As far as skills are concerned, education and experience are the most important factors. Political and governmental leadership, particularly in modern, technologically advanced societies, requires knowledge and skills that are hard to acquire except through education and training. Natural intelligence or experience may, to a limited degree, take the place of formal education.

Hence, it might be a good thing for government officials to be better informed, more intelligent, more experienced, and perhaps better educated than the people they serve. Just as medical patients tend to look for the most capable physician, rather than the one that is most like themselves, so, one could argue, citizens should look for the best qualified officeholder. In this view, selecting government officials, including representative policymakers, is like delegating to experts. It may be a hopeful sign that citizens in many modern democracies are increasingly willing to select leaders who do not share their background characteristics.

As in the case of so many other political choices, there is no obvious or perfect way to choose between mirroring and expert delegation. This is an old debate, and in many situations it is necessary to make a trade-off between the two. And different offices may require different considerations. Most people would, for example, probably put a higher emphasis on mirroring in their local assembly than in a regulatory agency overseeing nuclear technology.

The bad news is that political elites, even democratically elected members of legislative assemblies, hardly ever mirror the citizens they represent on any of the ascriptive characteristics. Even in democracies such as the United States, Britain, and France, political leaders tend to be of middle- or upper-class background or unusually well-educated and upwardly mobile individuals from the lower classes. There are exceptions. In some countries trade unions or leftist political parties may serve as channels of political advancement for people with modest economic or educational backgrounds. These representatives acquire political skills and experience by holding offices in working class organizations. Thus the Labour Party delegation in the British House of Commons and the Communist delegation in the French National Assembly have included substantial numbers of workers. And during the long domination of the executive by the Norwegian Labor Party, which held the prime ministership for all but seven years between 1935 and 1981, none of its prime ministers had even completed secondary school. But these are rare and vanishing examples. In most contemporary states, the number of working-class people in high office is small and declining.

Women have traditionally also been poorly represented in political leadership positions in most countries. History certainly offers examples of strong and influential female rulers, such as Queen Elizabeth I of England (who ruled from 1558 to 1603). Yet in most countries women did not have the right to vote until well into the twentieth century and have not held many political leadership positions. That has changed significantly in the last twenty-five years. In 1980, women on average held fewer than 10 percent of the parliamentary seats in the advanced industrial democracies. By 1990, that figure was up to about 15 percent, and by 1997 women had surpassed 20 percent. Women have also held the chief executive office in a growing number of countries, particularly in Europe and Asia. (See Box 6.3.) The most famous female chief executive is probably Margaret Thatcher, who was Britain's longest-serving prime minister (1979–1990) in modern times and a highly effective and influential political leader. But women's advancement has been uneven, and their representation remains low in the developing world. In many

Northern European countries, such as Sweden, women by the late 1990s accounted for 30 to 40 percent of the legislators and a similar proportion of cabinet members. In the United States, they had made similar gains in some states—most notably in Arizona, where women held five out of six statewide elective offices after the 1998 elections. But in Russia, Mexico, Brazil, and Japan, women still accounted for fewer than one legislator in ten in the 1990s.[17]

Political elites also tend to be unrepresentative with respect to age. In many countries, legislators (much less chief executives) under 40 are a rarity, whereas a large proportion of leading politicians are past normal retirement age. Japan is an extreme example. In 1990, there were about eight legislators over the age of 60 for every one member under 40. In many countries, university graduates—and often lawyers and civil servants in particular—are vastly overrepresented, whereas ethnic, linguistic, and religious minorities are often underrepresented. Representational biases are thus numerous and pervasive. And while women's representation is increasing, class biases are getting worse.

BOX 6.3   Women as Chief Executives

From about 1970 on, women have gained chief executive office in a growing number of countries. Interestingly, many of them have been from Asian and Middle Eastern countries, where women's roles in public life traditionally have been limited. Sinmavo Bandaranaike of Sri Lanka (1960–1965 and 1970–1977), Indira Gandhi of India (1966–1977 and 1980–1984), and Golda Meir of Israel (1969–1974) were among the pioneers. In the 1980s and 1990s, women also came to power in the Philippines, Pakistan, and Bangladesh, and again in Sri Lanka. In Burma, Nobel Peace Prize winner Aung San Suu Kyi won the elections of 1990 but the military prevented her from taking office.

Women have also made inroads in leadership positions in Europe and North America, though they are still few and far between in Africa and Latin America. The first female leader in a major European country was Prime Minister Margaret Thatcher of Britain (1979–1990). Her strong and decisive leadership made her one of Europe's most influential politicians in the 1980s. Thatcher, who now serves in Britain's House of Lords, was not a conventional feminist, however. She showed little interest in gender issues and appointed very few women to her cabinets. Women have come to power in other western countries as well. Both Ireland and Iceland have had female presidents. Canada, France, and Switzerland have had brief stints with female prime ministers. In Norway, Gro Harlem Brundtland held the prime ministership for a total of about ten years between 1981 and 1996. Brundtland, a physician and environmentalist, later headed the World Health Organization.

The career paths of Asian women leaders have tended to differ from those in Europe. Many of the former have come from prominent political families, such as the Gandhi family in India and the Bhuttos in Pakistan. In several cases, they have been the widows or daughters of important political leaders. In Europe, women leaders are more likely to have made independent political careers, and they can rely on stronger women's interest groups.

POLITICAL EXECUTIVES

In modern states, the executive branch is by far the largest, the most complex, and typically the most powerful branch of government. It is not easy to describe executives in simple ways, but it is sensible to start at the top. Governments typically have a small number of **chief executives,** officials who sit at the very top of the often-colossal executive branch. Such executives have various names, titles, duties, and powers. Some are called presidents, others prime ministers, chancellors, premiers, or secretaries general, and still others are chairmen or chairs. There are even a few kings who still have genuine power. Titles may mislead us as to what functions these officials perform, but they tend to be the main formulators and executors of public policy. We shall discuss the chief executives, including their cabinets, which are an important part of the policymaking process, especially in parliamentary systems, before turning to the subordinate parts of the executive, called the bureaucracy.

Structure of the Chief Executive

Democratic governments typically feature either a single chief executive (in presidential systems), or a split chief executive of two offices: a largely ceremonial head of state, who represents the nation on formal occasions, and a more powerful head of government, who determines public policies. Table 6.2 distinguishes among executives according to the bases of their power to affect policymaking. In the left column we see the chief executives in authoritarian systems, whose power ultimately rests on coercion. The middle and right columns show the chief executives

T A B L E   6 . 2   Bases of Legislative Power of Chief Executives

Authoritarian	Democratic: Partisan Influence	Democratic: Constitutional Powers
	Effective	
General Secretary, China	British Prime Minister	
	French Prime Minister	
	German Chancellor	
	Indian Prime Minister	
	Japanese Prime Minister	
	(Russian Prime Minister)	
	Ceremonial	
Chinese President		British Queen
		German President
		Indian President
		Japanese Emperor
	Ceremonial and Effective	
Egyptian President	French President	Brazilian President
		Mexican President
		Nigerian President
		Russian President
		U.S. President

in democratic countries. The middle column shows executives whose power rests primarily on their partisan influence in the legislature, which is the case of the prime ministers in most parliamentary systems. The right column includes chief executives whose ability to influence legislation resides in powers directly granted them by the constitution, rather than partisan connection alone. Strong presidents may have the ability to veto legislation, for example, or to issue decrees that have the force of law, or to introduce the budget. They usually have the power to appoint and dismiss members of the cabinet

Reading down the table, we see the distinction between executives with effective power over policy, purely ceremonial roles, or both effective and ceremonial power. Political executives are effective only if they have genuine discretion in the enactment and implementation of laws and regulations, in budgetary matters, or in important government appointments. Where they do not have these powers, they are symbolic or ceremonial. In presidential systems the ceremonial and effective roles are almost always held by the same person, the president, as we see in both authoritarian and democratic systems at the bottom of Table 6.2. In parliamentary democratic systems, and in some authoritarian systems, the two roles are separated between the "head of state," who is primarily a ceremonial official, and a "head of government," who makes and implements the decisions. The British, German, Indian and Japanese prime ministers appear in column two at the top right of the table, while their ceremonial counterparts appear at the center right. These distinctions are not absolute. Some constitutions, such as the German, give substantial formal powers to their prime ministers, while even largely ceremonial presidents can exert important influence if the parties are divided or by exercising special constitutional powers (or both, as has recently happened in India.) Moreover, partisan influence in the legislature is useful even to the strongest democratic presidents. Still, it is usually easy to determine the primary sources of legislative power, even where the formal names may be misleading.

As noted earlier, a few countries, such as France and Russia have both significant presidents and prime ministers. The balance of power between them depends on the constitutional powers of the president and on the partisan division in the legislature. In Russia the constitutional powers of veto and decree of the President are very great, and the legislature has seldom been unified against him; the Prime Minister has been mostly just another administrator, with little effective power. In France, however, the President's formal powers are much weaker; when the legislature has been unified under opposition parties it has elected a Prime Minister who has effectively dominated policymaking, reducing the President to a largely ceremonial role.

The Chairman of China's Communist Party is the most powerful political figure and the effective chief executive; the president is the head of state, which is a purely ceremonial role, without associated powers. However, in recent years the same individual (Jiang Zemin) held both offices, and also a key role as chairman of the Central Military Commission. A third role was the premier, or head of government, which was a largely administrative position.

Monarchies are much more rare at the end of the twentieth century than they were at its beginning. Some monarchs, such as the king of Saudi Arabia and some other Arab monarchs, still exercise real power. Most contemporary monarchs, however, have little or no actual political influence. Monarchs like the British queen or the Scandinavian kings are principally ceremonial and symbolic officers with very occasional political powers. They are living symbols of the state and nation and of their historical continuity. Britain's queen may bestow honors or peerages (appointments to the nobility) with a stroke of her wand, but these are recommended by the prime minister. When there is an election, or when a government falls, the queen formally appoints a new prime minister. Normally she has no discretion in selecting a prime minister, however, but is required by convention to pick the leader of the majority party in the House of Commons. The Japanese monarchy has also traditionally been dignified and exalted and played an important role as a national symbol. In contrast, the Scandinavian and Low Country monarchies are more humdrum. Because members of these royal families occasionally use more humble means of transportation, these dynasties are sometimes called "bicycle monarchies" (see Box 6.4).

In republican democracies with parliamentary systems, presidents perform the functions that fall to kings and queens in parliamentary monarchies. Thus German presidents give speeches on important anniversaries and designate prime ministers after elections or when a government has resigned. Like parliamentary systems,

---

BOX 6.4   Pomp and Circumstance Versus Bicycle Monarchies

Monarchies may be a dying breed, but Western Europe still has more of them than any other region of the world. Britain and Spain are monarchies, as are six of the smaller European democracies (the Netherlands, Belgium, Luxembourg, Denmark, Norway, and Sweden), plus a few microstates such as Monaco. Most of these monarchies have a long history, but two were created in the twentieth century: the Norwegian monarchy in 1905, and the Spanish one in 1975, as Spain transited from the Franco dictatorship to democracy. Monarchies are not all the same. The Spanish king may have more influence than any other European monarch, but few of them have any real power. The Swedish king was even stripped of all his remaining formal powers in a constitutional reform in the 1970s.

Monarchies vary more in style than in power. The British tend toward pomp and ceremony, with decorated horses carrying the Queen to Parliament in a gilded carriage. The Scandinavian and Low Country monarchies are often called "bicycle monarchies." The late King Olav V of Norway (who reigned 1957–1991) was a particularly folksy monarch. An Olympic ski jumper in his youth, he could even in later years often be seen cross-country skiing in the woods around Oslo (the capital of Norway), accompanied only by his dog. During the oil crisis of the 1970s, he insisted on taking public transportation from the royal palace to the ski trails (and on paying for his ticket). When he was still crown prince, he once gave an interview to an American journalist who showed up at the royal cottage without an appointment. While the journalist was interviewing him, the Crown Prince proceeded to do the family dishes.

communist countries have tended to separate the ceremonial and the effective executives. The president of the People's Republic of China, for example, has usually been a ceremonial officer. He greeted distinguished visitors and opens and presided over meetings of the People's Congress.

A system in which the ceremonial executive is separated from the effective executive has a number of advantages. The ceremonial executive symbolizes unity and continuity and can be above politics. The U.S. presidency, which combines both effective and ceremonial functions, runs the risk that the president will use his ceremonial and symbolic authority to enhance his political power or that his involvement in politics may make him a less effective symbolic or unifying figure.

Recruitment of Chief Executives

Historically, finding generally acceptable ways to select the individuals to fill the top policymaking roles has been critical to political order and stability. A major accomplishment of stable democracies has been to regulate the potential conflict involved in leadership succession and confine it to the mobilization of votes instead of weapons. When we refer generally to "recruitment structures," we are thinking of how nations choose their top policymakers and executives. Table 6.3 shows the recruitment structures in the countries selected for this book. The most familiar structures are the presidential and parliamentary forms of competitive party systems. In presidential systems, as in Brazil and the United States, parties select candidates for nomination, and the electorate chooses between these. Russia and France have directly elected presi-

T A B L E   6 . 3   Recruitment of Chief Executive

Country	Chief Executive Structure	Recruitment Structures	How Often Has This Type of Government Survived Succession?[b]
Brazil	President	Party and voters	Often
Britain	Prime minister	Party, House of Commons, voters	Very often
China	Party secretary[a]	Party and military	Often
Egypt	President	Party and military	Twice
France	President/Prime minister	Party, (Assembly,) voters	Often
Germany	Chancellor	Party, Bundestag, voters	Often
India	Prime minister	Party, Lok Sabha, voters	Often (one interruption)
Japan	Prime minister	Party, Diet, voters	Often
Mexico	President	Party and voters	Once
Nigeria	President	Military, party, voters	Never
Russia	President	Party and voters	Once
United States	President	Party and voters	Very often

[a]"Party secretary" refers to that position or a similar one as head of party in communist regime.

[b]"Often" means that at least three successions have taken place under that type of government.

dents but also give an important role to the prime minister, who is appointed by the president but can be removed by the legislature.

Mexico appears similar to other presidential systems, but the Partido Revolucionario Institucional (PRI) had such control over the electoral process that for half a century the voters merely ratified the party's presidential nominee. That nomination itself was announced by the outgoing president after complex bargaining between party factions and other powerful groups. Mexico seemed to be moving to give the voters an honest role in choosing between alternative candidates, but until the remarkable July 2000 election many voters remained skeptical that a non-PRI president could really come to power. As the table shows, Mexico now seems a newly democratic presidential system, with parties nominating candidates and voters genuinely choosing between them.

In both presidential and parliamentary democracies the tenure of the chief executive is limited, directly or indirectly. In the presidential system this happens directly, through fixed terms of office for the chief executive. In the parliamentary system there is a maximum term for the parliament, which then indirectly also limits the life of the cabinet, since the prime minister is accountable to the new parliamentary majority and can be removed by it.

Table 6.3 also illustrates the role of noncompetitive parties and military organizations in China and Egypt. The important role played by political parties illustrates the great need to mobilize broad political support behind the selection of chief executives. The frequent appearance of parties also reflects, no doubt, the modern legitimacy of popular sovereignty: the promise that the rulers' actions will be in the interest of the ruled.

Authoritarian systems rarely have effective procedures for leadership succession. The more power is concentrated at the top, the riskier it is to transfer it from one person to the next. Very often, authoritarian leaders do not dare to relinquish their power, and leadership succession occurs only when they die. In Communist regimes, the Communist Party selected the general secretary (or equivalent), who was the controlling executive force. Individual succession was not a simple matter. These systems did not limit the terms of incumbents, who were difficult to oust once they had consolidated their supporters into key party positions. Nonetheless, they always had to be aware of the possibility of a party coup of the type that ousted Nikita Khrushchev from the Soviet leadership in 1964. As a system, however, the Soviet leadership structure seemed quite stable until the dramatic 1991 coup attempt against Gorbachev. Although he was briefly restored to power, the events surrounding the coup stripped the Soviet presidency of power, and legitimacy passed to the presidencies and legislatures of the 15 constituent republics, most importantly to President Boris Yeltsin of Russia. Russia managed its first democratic transition surprisingly smoothly, from Yeltsin to his chosen successor Vladimar Putin, who was elected as the new president in April 2000.

The poorer nations show substantially less stability, and the regimes have usually had less experience at surviving succession crises. Nigeria is typical. It experienced a succession of military coups and governments from 1966 until 1979, then introduced a competitive presidential system, which was overthrown by a military coup shortly after its second election in 1983. The military government again moved toward civilian rule in the early 1990s but then annulled the 1993 presidential election before the results were announced. The military rulers finally allowed a return to civilian rule in 1999.

Many African nations are under military governments; some of them have experienced repeated coups. Military governments, stable or unstable, have also been common in Latin America and the Middle East. The Chinese Communist Party has remained in power for 50 years but has suffered several periods of internal strife, and the army has been involved in recruitment at all levels. India's democracy, having persisted through assassinations and other crises, has been an exception to the rule among poorer nations. It has provided a number of democratic successions with a single interruption (authoritarian emergency rule that postponed elections for several years) in the 1970s.

The Cabinet

In many political systems, the **Cabinet** is the most important collective decision-making body. Its power can be particularly great in parliamentary systems, where its formation is closely linked to selection of the prime minister. It typically contains the leaders (often called "ministers" or "secretaries of state") of all the major departments (sometimes called "ministries") into which the executive branch is divided. The Cabinet meets frequently—often several times per week—and it is typically selected and led by the head of government: the president in presidential systems and the prime minister in parliamentary ones. In some parliamentary systems the entire cabinet is collectively responsible to the legislature and the prime minister may be little more than "first among equals," especially under conditions of multi-party coalition governments. In other parliamentary systems, such as Germany, the constitution confers much more authority on the prime minister.[18] Confidence motions (Box 6.1) are usually introduced by the prime minister. In all cases the entire cabinet must resign when the government loses a vote of confidence or no-confidence.

How does the Cabinet get selected? In presidential systems, selecting Cabinet members is typically a presidential prerogative, though sometimes (as with the U.S. Senate), the legislature has to give its approval. The president can typically also dismiss Cabinet members at will, whereas the legislature's ability to do so is most often severely limited.

In parliamentary systems, on the other hand, the process is very different, since the prime minister and his or her cabinet need to maintain the confidence of the parliamentary majority. Therefore, Cabinet formation depends on the result of parliamentary elections and on the composition of Parliament. If a competitive party wins a parliamentary majority by itself, it will (if unified) be able to form a Cabinet of its own members and can then pass and implement its policies. Sometimes who controls the majority is determined directly by the elections. This will always be the case in pure two-party systems, where one party or the other will always have a parliamentary majority. It can also happen in multiparty systems, whenever one party gets more seats than all its competitors combined.

But the more parties there are, the less likely it is that one of them will have a majority on its own. We call the outcome in which one party controls a parliamentary majority by itself a majority situation. Whenever majority situations occur in parliamentary systems, the majority party almost always forms a *majority single-party cabinet* by itself.

Far more often, no party wins a majority of votes. In most multiparty countries, the typical election result is that no party has a parliamentary majority by itself—a minority situation. Most commonly under such circumstances, several parties (two, three, or as many as six or seven) join forces and form a *coalition cabinet* in which they are all represented. Sometimes, parties anticipate this need to form coalitions before the election. They may then make a formal agreement with one another and inform the voters that they intend to govern together if they collectively get enough votes. The allied parties may thus encourage their voters to support the coalition partners' candidates where their own party's candidates seem weak and often take advantage of special provisions of voting laws. Many German and French governments have come to power in this fashion. In such cases, the voters can have a direct voice in the choice of the future Cabinet, much as they do in two-party systems. Voters are thus given a major role in choosing the direction of government policy.

But parties often do not make such preelection commitments. Even when they do, they often fail to get the support they would need to control a parliamentary majority. If no party or preelection coalition wins control of the legislature through the election, then parties may bargain after the election, or between elections, to form a new Cabinet.

Whether bargaining takes place before or after the elections, the parties in parliamentary systems typically have a lot of options concerning the composition of the Cabinet. In minority situations, the result can be either a minority government or a majority coalition of several parties. In some cases, a single party decides that it can form a minority cabinet alone, often because the other parties disagree too much among themselves to offer any alternative. Figure 6.2 illustrates these various possibilities. In the minority case, the parties in the Cabinet must continually bargain with other parties to get policies adopted and even to remain in office. In majority coalitions, bargaining will take place primarily among coalition partners represented in the Cabinet. In both of these circumstances the power of the prime minister may depend on the bargains he can strike with leaders of other parties.

These complications illustrate two of the problems of combining parliamentary government with electoral systems of proportional representation. Such systems tend to produce minority situations. One problem with this is that the voters are often not given a very clear choice about who will control the executive branch. Instead, the parties may determine this behind closed doors after the election. Sometimes, the results are paradoxical, as when parties that have just lost votes in the elections are able to negotiate their way into a governing coalition. The second problem is that under minority situations, cabinets are sometimes unstable. Italy, for example, has on average had more than one change of government per year since World War II. Yet, such problems need not always emerge. In Germany, for example, cabinets have been quite stable and the voters have generally been given fairly clear options ahead of elections.

Party System	Election Result	Cabinet Type

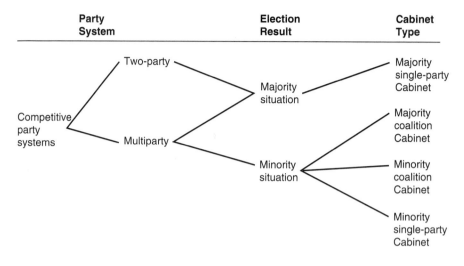

FIGURE 6.2   Cabinet Formation
in Parliamentary Democracies

Functions of the Chief Executive

Typically, the chief executive is the most important structure in policymaking. The executive normally initiates new policies and, depending on the division of powers between the executive and the legislature, has a substantial part in their adoption. In presidential systems, the president very often has veto powers. Thus the chief executive not only has the first word in policymaking, he or she also typically has the last word. In parliamentary systems, on the other hand, the executive is less likely to be able to exercise a veto. The political executive also oversees policy implementation and can hold subordinate officials accountable for their performance. The central decisions in a foreign policy crisis are generally made by the chief executive: the president (George W. Bush in the Iraq War) or the prime minister (Margaret Thatcher in the Falklands crisis). Political initiatives and new programs tend to originate in the executive. A bureaucracy without an effective executive tends to implement past policies, rather than to initiate new ones. Without politically motivated ministers, bureaucracies tend toward inertia.

The decision of a president, prime minister, cabinet, or central party committee to pursue a new foreign or domestic policy will usually be accompanied by structural adaptations—the appointment of a vigorous minister, an increase in staff, the establishment of a special cabinet committee, and the like. Where the political executive is weak and divided, as in Fourth Republic France or contemporary Italy, (at least until recently,) this dynamic force is missing. Initiative then passes to the bureaucracy, legislative committees, and powerful interest groups, and general needs, interests, and problems may be neglected. In a separation-of-powers system when the presidency and the congress are controlled by different parties, even a strong president may be hampered in carrying out an effective policy. And if the president is hamstrung, the assembly is rarely able to fill the gap.

Chief executives also perform important system functions. Studies of childhood socialization show that the first political role perceived by children tends to be the chief political executive—the president, prime minister, and king or queen. In early childhood the tendency is to identify the top political executive as a parent figure. As the child matures, he or she begins to differentiate political from other roles, as well as to differentiate among various political roles (see Chapter 3). The conduct of the chief executive affects the trust and confidence that young people feel in the whole political system and that they carry with them into adulthood. The role of the chief executive in recruitment is obviously important. Presidents, prime ministers, and first secretaries have large and important powers to appoint not only cabinet and politburo members and government ministers but often judges, senior civil servants, ambassadors, and military officers as well. Typically, political executives can bestow honors and distinctions on members of the government and private citizens. The political executive also plays a central role in communication, in explaining and building support for new policies, or in improving performance in various sectors of the society and economy.

THE BUREAUCRACY

Modern societies are dominated by large organizations, and the largest contemporary organizations are government **bureaucracies,** or their systems of public administration. These agencies, by which we mean all the members of the executive branch below the top executive (president/monarch, prime minister, and cabinet) are generally in charge of implementing government policy. The size of government bureaucracies has increased over the course of the twentieth century. This is partly due to government efforts to improve the health, productivity, welfare, and security of their populations. In part, it may also be part of the tendency for government agencies, once they have been established, to seek growth for its own sake. In reaction to this tendency, and as part of the concern about government inefficiencies, there has in recent decades been a movement to reduce government budgets and to downsize the bureaucracy.

Structure of the Bureaucracy

The most important officials in bureaucracies are the experienced and expert personnel of the top **civil service.** The British "government," which we can think of as its top executive positions, consists of approximately 100 "frontbench" members of Parliament, some 20 of whom serve in the Cabinet, with the remainder named as ministers, junior ministers, and parliamentary secretaries. This relatively small group of political policymakers oversees some 3,000 permanent members of the **higher civil service,** largely recruited directly from the universities. They spend their lives as an elite corps, moving about from ministry to ministry, watching governments come and go, and becoming increasingly important as policymakers as they rise in rank. Below the higher civil service are a huge body of more than half a million permanent public employees, ordinary civil servants, organized into about 20 government departments and a number of other agencies. The total number of British civil servants rose from 100,000 in 1900 to more than 700,000 in 1979, but it then declined by 1991 to about 550,000 under Conservative governments.

The importance of the permanent higher civil service is not unique to Britain, though perhaps it has been most fully institutionalized there. In France, too, the higher civil service is filled with powerful generalists who can bring long tenure, experience, and technical knowledge to their particular tasks. In the United States, many top positions go to presidential appointees rather than to permanent civil servants. Despite this difference and a greater emphasis on technical specialization, there are permanent civil servants in the key positions just below the top appointees in such agencies as the Internal Revenue Service, the Federal Bureau of Investigation, the Central Intelligence Agency, the National Institutes of Health, and all the cabinet departments. These people tend to be specialists, such as military officers, diplomats, doctors, scientists, economists, and engineers, who exert great influence on policy formulation and execution in their specialties. Below these specialists and administrators are the vast numbers of ordinary government employees, postal workers, teachers, welfare case agents, and so forth, who see that governmental policies are put into practice. In 1993, the United States had 18.8 million public employees of all kinds, federal, state and local, or about 15 percent of the total labor force. In many European countries, that proportion is even higher, approaching a third of the labor force in Norway, Denmark, and Sweden.

The Functions of the Bureaucracy

Bureaucracies have acquired great significance in most contemporary societies. One reason is that the bureaucracy is almost alone in implementing and enforcing laws and regulations. In so doing, they may have quite a bit of discretion. Most modern legislation is general and can be effectively enforced only if administrative officials work out its detail and implementation. Policy implementation and enforcement usually depend on bureaucrats' interpretations and on the spirit and effectiveness with which they put it into practice. But the power of bureaucracies is not restricted to their implementation and enforcement of rules made by others. In Chapters 4 and Chapter 5 we discussed how bureaucratic agencies may articulate and aggregate interests. Departments like those for agriculture, labor, defense, welfare, and education may be among the most important voices of interest groups. Moreover, administrative agencies in modern political systems do a lot of adjudication. Tax authorities, for example, routinely determine whether citizens have faithfully reported their income and paid their taxes, and these authorities assess penalties accordingly. While citizens may in principle be able to appeal such rulings to the courts, relatively few actually do.

Finally, bureaucracies are involved in communication. Political elites, whether executives or legislators, base many of their decisions on the information they obtain from the public administration. Similarly, interest groups, political parties, the business elites, and the public depend on such information. Most major agencies in modern governments have spokespersons whose job it is to inform and influence the media. With the increasing media power in modern societies, top government executives are eager to present their versions of events. Leaks of secret or confidential information and intelligence have become a veritable flood. Increasingly, however, large parts of the journalistic professions refuse to recognize any limits on the publication of private as well as political information. Thus political executives and bureaucracies can no longer control information in the ways that they formerly did. In dealing with the media, top administrators now must have more complex strategies and professional assistance. The art of "spin control" has replaced their reliance on classification and "executive privilege."

Bureaucracy and Performance

We commonly use the term "bureaucracy" to refer to all systems of public administration. Strictly speaking, however, bureaucracy refers to a particular way of organizing such agencies, a practice that gained favor in the latter part of the nineteenth century and the beginning of the twentieth century. According to the classical German sociologist Max Weber, bureaucracies have the following features: (1) decision making is based on fixed and official jurisdictions, rules, and regulations; (2) there are formal and specialized educational or training requirements for each position; (3) there is a hierarchical command structure: a firmly ordered system of super- and subordination, in which information flows upward and decisions downward; (4) decisions are made on the basis of standard operating procedures, which include extensive written records; and (5) officials hold career positions, are appointed and promoted on the basis of merit, and have protection against political interference, notably in the form of permanent job tenure. No organization is perfectly bureaucratic in this sense, but professional armies come reasonably close, as do tax revenue departments.

These features of bureaucracies have a number of salutary effects. They promote competence, consistency, fair treatment, and freedom from political manipulation. Keep in mind what life could be like without bureaucracies. Before the advent of modern bureaucracy, public officials were often a sorry lot. Some of them inherited their jobs; others got them through family or political connections. Yet others bought their posts and used them either to enrich themselves or gain social status (or both). Many saw them strictly as a sideline and devoted little time to their duties. No wonder, then, that public officials were often incompetent, uninterested in their jobs, corrupt, or all of the above. They often used their powers arbitrarily, to favor friends and neighbors, and to the disadvantage of others. Given the lack of rules and records, aggrieved citizens typically had few recourses.

But the negative connotations that the word "bureaucracy" has taken on suggest that such organizations have liabilities as well. Bureaucratic organizations have a tendency to become stodgy, rule-bound, inflexible, and insensitive to the needs of their clients. In many cases, bureaucrats also have few incentives to be innovative and efficient, or even to work very hard. Although bureaucracies are supposed to be politically and ideologically neutral, in fact they tend to be influenced by the dominant ideologies of the time, to have conservative propensities, and to pursue institutional interests of their own.[19] Bureaucracies may present special problems in periods of major social change. When the Bolsheviks (Communists) took power in Russia in 1917, they had to depend on military officers and officials of the Czarist regime until they could train their own. In post-Communist societies in the 1990s, the resistance and inertia of the old governmental and economic bureaucracies have hampered government reforms and transitions toward democracy and economic freedom. Many citizens are exasperated with bureaucracy and its propensities for inefficiency and lack of responsiveness. This frustration is reflected in popular cynicism as well as in periodic attempts to reform government.

Mark Nadel and Francis Rourke suggest a variety of ways that government and societal agencies may influence and control bureaucracies, externally or internally.[20] The major external government control is the political executive. Although presidents, prime ministers, and ministers formally command subordinate officials and may have the power to remove them for nonperformance of duty, executives and bureaucracies actually mutually depend on one another. Top executives typically try to persuade; rarely do they go to the extreme of dismissing or transferring civil servants. Centralized budgeting and administrative reorganization are other means of executive control. The threat to take away resources or authority may bring bureaucratic implementation into greater conformity with the aims of the political executive.

Modern authoritarian systems discovered that they could achieve more efficient and effective control by simultaneously manipulating political socialization, political recruitment, and political communication. Socialization efforts are made to instill loyalty and to limit and regulate information. But if recruitment is made a part of a larger pattern of control, it is hardly neglected. Leadership selection in the former Soviet Union was accomplished through a device called *nomenklatura*. Under this procedure important positions were kept under the direct supervision of a party agency whose officials had the final word on recruitment. Moreover, the party offered a complicated set of inducements to control the behavior of the chosen officials. These inducements made it difficult for any but the topmost officials to have much freedom of action. Soviet leaders used normative incentives, such as appeal to party, ideology, and national idealism; financial incentives, such as better salaries, access to finer food and clothing, better housing, and freedom to travel; and coercive control, such as reporting by police, party, and bureaucrats. They used demotion or imprisonment, even execution, as penalties. To avoid a coup by police or military forces, the varied layers of command and inducement structures were interwoven, so that no layer could act independently.

In democracies assemblies and courts also help control the bureaucracy. Legislative committee hearings or judicial investigations may bring bureaucratic performance into line with political desires. Sweden invented the institution of the **ombudsman** to prevent bureaucrats from doing injury or injustice to individuals.[21] This invention has been copied by a number of other states. In the Scandinavian countries, Britain, Germany, and elsewhere ombudsmen now investigate citizen claims that they have suffered injury or damage as a result of government action. Ombudsmen typically have no power of their own, but report to the legislature for remedial action. Their cases rarely lead to criminal conviction, but often government officials change their policies as a result of embarrassing publicity. Thus, ombudsmen offer a more expeditious and less costly procedure than court action. Among the extragovernmental forces that constrain bureaucracies are public opinion and the mass media, as well as interest groups of various kinds.

Not all controls on bureaucrats are external. Internal controls, such as advisory committees, are appointed to oversee the impartiality of their performance. Another way of controlling bureaucracy is to decentralize it, thereby bringing agencies closer to their clients. Finally, the attitudes of the bureaucrats themselves affect their responsiveness and responsibility. The norms and values that bureaucrats bring with them into public service, and the standards and obligations they are taught to respect, have an important bearing on bureaucratic performance.

All such controls on civil servants tend to be less effective outside the advanced industrial democracies. Authoritarian systems lack many of these controls, particularly external ones, such as elected political executives and legislators, independent courts, free mass media, and interest groups. Therefore, authoritarian regimes are particularly prone to bureaucratic inefficiency and inertia. Moreover, in many nonindustrial countries, mass media are neither independent nor influential, few citizens participate in politics, and lower-level government employees are poorly trained and paid—all conditions that encourage bribery, extortion, and bureaucratic mismanagement.[22]

Successful democracy requires that public policies made by national assemblies and chief executives be implemented fairly and effectively; democracy depends on the rule of law. When ruling parties demand kickbacks of public money from construction firms seeking public works contracts, the democratic process is subverted by rent-seeking politicians. (See Chapter 1 and Box 1.4.) Similarly, when tax officials and border authorities are open to cash payments to overlook tax deficiencies and customs violations, democratic law making is undermined. Citizens who must bribe teachers to get education for their children or health officials to get immunizations are deprived of benefits of democratic public policies. Such practices are all too common in the poorer nations of the world.

Failure of the rule of law is difficult to study systematically, but some comparative insight into corruption in public bureaucracies is provided by the surveys of perceptions of corruption on the part of business people, academics, and analysts in different countries. These have been combined into a Corruptions Perception Index, which rates about one hundred countries each year on a scale from 0 ("highly corrupt") to 10 ("highly clean"). Table 6.4 shows the ratings for 2002 (based on a three year moving average) of our usual twelve countries. As we see, all of our countries experience some levels of corruption, with even Britain's 8.7 less than ideal. (The top country rated in 2002 was Finland at 9.7.) But Britain, the United States, Germany and Japan (despite individually notorious cases in each), rate in the top half of the scale and countries. Brazil, Mexico, China and Egypt are far more corrupt, with scores in the range of 4.0 to 3.4, while Russia, plagued by many problems of its dual economic and political transitions, scores even worse, as does India. Nigeria, despite its recent efforts at democratic transition, is perceived as one of the world's most corrupt countries, with a score of 1.6. Comparisons of

T A B L E   6 . 4   Perceived Corruption
and Economic Development Level*

Country	Perceived Corruption Index (0 = Corrupt) (10 = Clean)	Economic Development Level (PPP)
Britain	8.7	24,468
United States	7.7	34,870
Germany	7.3	25,530
Japan	7.1	27,430
France	6.3	25,280
Brazil	4.0	7450
Mexico	3.6	8770
China	3.5	4260
Egypt	3.4	3790
India	2.7	2450
Russia	2.7	8660
Nigeria	1.6	830

*Economic development level from World Bank, downloaded from www.worldbank.org/data on Sept. 24, 2002;
Perceived Corruption Index from Transparency International, downloaded from www.transparency.org/cpi/index
on April 24, 2003.

the perceived corruption scores with the Purchasing Power Parity measure of economic wealth and productivity in column two show that corruption and the failure
of the rule of law are very strongly associated with poverty and underdevelopment,
as well as with direct indicators of popular misery (also see Table 7.3).[23]

The ills of bureaucracy, including inefficiency and inertia, are pandemic. This
is truly a dilemma because we are unlikely to invent any schemes for carrying out
large-scale social tasks without the organization, division of labor, and profession-
alism that bureaucracy provides. Its pathologies can only be mitigated. The art of
modern political leadership consists not only of defining and communicating appropriate goals and policies, but also of getting them implemented by a massive and
complex bureaucracy—how and when to press and coerce it, reorganize it, reward
it, teach it, or be taught by it.

KEY TERMS

assemblies

authoritarian regimes

bicameralism

bureaucracy

Cabinet

chief executives

civil service

confidence relationship

constitutional regimes

decision rules

democratic presidential
  regime

federal systems

higher civil service

impeachment

independent central banks

judicial review

ombudsman

parliamentary regimes

policymaking

semi-presidential regime

separation of powers

SUGGESTED READINGS

Aberbach, Joel, Robert D. Putnam, and Bert A. Rockman. *Bureaucrats and Politicians in Western Democracies*. Cambridge, MA: Harvard University Press, 1981.

Döring, Herbert, ed. *Parliaments and Majority Rule in Western Europe*. New York: St. Martin's Press, 1995.

Huber, John D. *Rationalizing Parliament*. Cambridge, England: Cambridge University Press, 1996.

Katzenstein, Peter. *Small States in World Markets*. Ithaca, NY: Cornell University Press, 1985.

Lijphart, Arend. *Democracy in Plural Societies*. New Haven, CT: Yale University Press, 1977.

————. *Patterns of Democracy: Government Forms and Performance in Thirty-Six Countries*. New Haven, CT: Yale University Press, 1999.

Linz, Juan and Arturo Valenzuela, eds. *The Failure of Presidential Democracy: Comparative Perspectives*. Baltimore, MD: Johns Hopkins University Press, 1994.

Mainwaring, Scott and Matthew Shugart, eds. *Presidentialism and Democracy in Latin America*. New York: Cambridge University Press, 1997.

March, James G. and Johan P. Olsen. *Rediscovering Institutions: The Organizational Basis of Politics*. New York: Free Press, 1989.

North, Douglass. *Institutions, Institutional Change, and Economic Performance*. Cambridge, England: Cambridge University Press, 1990.

O'Donnell, Guillermo and Philippe Schmitter. *Transitions from Authoritarian Rule*. Baltimore, MD: Johns Hopkins University Press, 1986.

Powell, G. Bingham. *Contemporary Democracies*. Cambridge, MA: Harvard University Press, 1982.

Riker, William H. *Federalism: Origin, Operation, and Significance*. Boston, MA: Little, Brown, 1964.

Sartori, Giovanni. *Comparative Constitutional Engineering*. New York: New York University Press, 1997.

Secondat, Charles de, Baron de Montesquieu. *The Spirit of the Laws*. London: Hafner, 1960.

Shugart, Matthew, and John Carey. *Presidents and Assemblies: Constitutional Design and Electoral Dynamics*. Cambridge, England: Cambridge University Press, 1992.

Strøm, Kaare. *Minority Government and Majority Rule*. Cambridge, England: Cambridge University Press, 1990.

Tsebelis, George and Jeannette Money. *Bicameralism*. Cambridge, England: Cambridge University Press, 1997.

Weaver, Kent and Bert Rockman, eds. *Do Institutions Matter? Government Capabilities in the United States and Abroad*. Washington: Brookings Institution, 1993.

Weber, Max. "Bureaucracy." In H. H. Gerth and C. Wright Mills, eds. *From Max Weber*. New York: Oxford University Press, 1976, pp. 196–244.

Weingast, Barry R. "Political Foundations of Democracy and the Rule of Law." *American Political Science Review* 91, no. 2 (June 1997): 245–63.

ENDNOTES

1. For a skeptical view of constitutional design, see James G. March and Johan P. Olsen, *Rediscovering Institutions: The Organizational Basis of Politics* (New York: Free Press, 1989), pp. 171–172. For a more sanguine argument, see Giovanni Sartori, *Comparative Constitutional Engineering* (New York: New York University Press, 1995).

2. Samuel Huntington, *The Third Wave: Democratization in the Late Twentieth Century* (Norman, OK: University of Oklahoma Press, 1991).

3. Adam Przeworski, Michael E. Alvarez, Jose Antonio Cheibub and Fernando Limongi, *Democracy and Development* (NY: Cambridge University Press, 2000).

4. John Locke, *Two Treatises of Government,* ed. Peter Laslett (Cambridge, England: Cambridge University Press, 1960); Charles de Secondat, Baron de Montesquieu, *The Spirit of the Laws* (London: Hafner, 1960).

5. *The Federalist: A Commentary on the Constitution of the United States* (Washington: National Home Library Foundation, 1937).

6. On presidential decree powers see John M. Carey and Matthew S. Shugart, *Executive Decree Authority* (New York: Cambridge University Press, 1998); for more general discussions of presidential powers see Matthew S. Shugart and John M. Carey, *Presidents and Assemblies: Constitutional Design and Electoral Dynamics* (Cambridge, England: Cambridge University Press, 1992); and Scott Mainwaring and Matthew S. Shugart, eds., *Presidentialism and Democracy in Latin America* (New York: Cambridge University Press, 1997.)

7. It is important to avoid confusion between the formal titles of government officials and the source of their selection and bases of their powers—which determine the type of political system. For example, Germany is a parliamentary system, whose executive is headed by a prime minister, although his official title is Chancellor; and as in many parliamentary systems the German head of state is a ceremonial president, chosen by the legislature, with little policymaking power. See also Table 6.2

8. Arend Lijphart, *Democracy in Plural Societies* (New Haven: Yale University Press, 1977); G. Bingham Powell, *Contemporary Demcracies* (Cambridge: Harvard University Press, 1982); Arend Lijphart, *Patterns of Democracy: Government Forms and Performance in Thirty-Six Countries* (New Haven: Yale University Press, 1999.)

9. Juan Linz and Arturo Valenzuela, eds., *The Failure of Presidential Democracy: Comparative Perspectives* (Baltimore, MD: Johns Hopkins University Press, 1994). Also see Przeworski, et. al., *Democracy and Development,* 2000, pp. 128–136.

10. Donald Horowitz, "Comparing Democratic Systems," in Larry Diamond and Mark F. Plattner, eds., *The Global Resurgence of Democracy* (Baltimore: Johns Hopkins University Press, 1993), pp. 127 ff.

11. Philippe Schmitter and Gerhard Lehmbruch, *Trends Toward Corporatist Intermediation* (Beverly Hills, CA: Sage, 1979).

12. See the discussion and references in Arend Lijphart, *Patterns of Democracy,* 1999, Ch. 13.

13. Arend Lijphart, *Patterns of Democracy,* 1999, p. 226.

14. George H. Gadbois, Jr., "The Institutionalization of the Supreme Court of India," in John R. Schmidhauser, ed., *Comparative Judicial Systems* (London: Butterworth Enterprises, 1987), pp. 111–142.

15. Donald S. Lutz reports that the U.S. Constitution, amended 26 times in 202 years (at the time of his writing in 1991) had been formally changed far less often than the cross-country average of about 2.5 amendments per year. "Toward a Theory of Constitutional Amendment," *American Political Science Review* 88 (1994), pp. 355–370. However, the Japanese constitution, of about average rigidity, had never been amended. Also see Ivo Duchachek, *Power Maps: Comparative Politics of Constitutions* (Santa Barbara, CA: ABC Clio Press, 1973), pp. 210 ff.

16. For a survey of parliamentary committees in Europe, see Ingvar Mattson and Kaare Strøm, "Parliamentary Committees," in Herbert Doring, ed., *Parliaments and Majority Rule in Western Europe* (New York: St. Martin's, 1995), pp. 249–307.

17. See Pippa Norris, "Legislative Recruitment," in Lawrence LeDuc, Richard G. Niemi, and Pippa Norris, eds., *Comparing Democracies* (London: Sage, 1996), pp. 184–215; and Richard E. Matland, "Women's Representation in National Legislatures: Developed and Developing Countries," *Legislative Studies Quarterly* 23, No. 1 (February 1998): 109–125.

18. See the different chapters in Michael Laver and Kenneth A. Shepsle, *Cabinet Ministers and Parliamentary Government* (New York: Cambridge University Press, 1994.)

19. See Joel Aberbach, Robert D. Putnam, and Bert A. Rockman, *Bureaucrats and Politicians in Western Democracies* (Cambridge, MA: Harvard University Press, 1981).

20. Mark V. Nadel and Francis E. Rourke, "Bureaucracies," in Fred Greenstein and Nelson Polsby, eds., *Handbook of Political Science,* vol. 5 (Reading, MA: Addison-Wesley, 1975), pp. 373–440.

21. See Frank Stacey, *The British Ombudsman* (Oxford, England: Clarendon Press, 1971); Roy Gregory and Peter Hutchesson, *The Parliamentary Ombudsman: A Study in the Control of Administrative Action* (London: Allen and Unwin, 1975).

22. On the difficulties involved in reducing administrative corruption in developing countries, see Robert Klitgard, *Controlling Corruption* (Berkeley, CA: University of California Press, 1989).

23. For statistical analysis explaining scores on the Corruption Perception Index, see Daniel Triesman, "The Causes of Corruption: A Cross-National Study," *Journal of Public Economics* 76 (June 2000): 399–457, who suggests lower levels of economic development, shorter exposure to democracy, and federalism among factors encouraging more perceived corruption.

Public Policy

In this chapter, we shift our focus to **public policies,** to all those authoritative public decisions that governments make. We shall refer to them as the **outputs** of the political system. Policies or outputs are normally chosen for a purpose; they are meant to promote end results that we shall refer to as political **outcomes.** Different policy instruments may be more or less efficient ways to reach the outcomes that policymakers ultimately want. We therefore want to know the relationships between political outputs and outcomes. Yet, the policies that a particular society adopts may not be what its citizens asked for or would have wanted. Whether a certain outcome is good or bad ultimately depends on normative criteria that we call **political goods and values.** And whatever values and goals policymakers and citizens have will surely affect their evaluation of the political outcomes they actually reach. Since politicians and citizens often disagree over political goods and values, it is important to keep these goals in mind when we study public policy. In this chapter, we shall discuss these aspects of public policy in order, but we begin by considering what governments do.

GOVERNMENT AND WHAT IT DOES

Governments do many things. Some of them are timeless, similar in kind to what happened in the ancient world. In the days of the Roman Empire, for example, defense against external and internal enemies was a major government responsibility. It continues to be so in most societies today. In other ways, governments today do things that were unthinkable in the past. For example, contemporary governments regulate telecommunications and air traffic, policy areas that were unknown until the twentieth century.

Governments as Producers

What governments do can be summarized under several labels. First, governments produce many goods and services, though exactly which varies a great deal. While in most societies, governments provide law enforcement and postal services, in many countries they go far beyond such service provision. In the former Soviet Union and other communist states, governments owned and operated most major industries and produced everything from military equipment to consumer goods such as clothing and shoes. In a capitalist society such as the United States, the government produces far fewer goods, particularly consumer products. In other advanced industrial societies, such as much of Western Europe, the government is a larger producer than in the United States, but a far smaller one than in the former Soviet Union. Governments control a number of industries in many states, but the range is very different. In recent decades, one study shows, governments in the United States employed only 1 percent of the persons engaged in mining and manufacturing and 28 percent of those working for public utilities supplying gas, water, and electrical power; whereas in France, the corresponding figures were 8 percent and 71 percent. Capitalist, free-market societies tend to have governments that are less active as producers than have socialist societies. Yet, there is no society in which the government produces no goods and services, and similarly no state in which all industries are run by the government. Even in the former Soviet Union, part of the agricultural sector was private, as were many simple consumer services such as babysitting. Other ostensibly communist societies, such as Poland in the 1980s or China today, feature a lot of private enterprise, particularly in the consumer goods sector.

Public Policies

The importance of governments goes far beyond their role as producers of goods and services. Indeed, this may not even be their most important role in most contemporary states. Governments also engage in various forms of public policy, which is the focus of this chapter. Public policies may be summarized and compared according to outputs—that is, according to the actions governments take to accomplish their purposes. We classify these actions or outputs under four headings:

1. the **extraction** of resources—money, goods, persons, and services—from the domestic and international environments;
2. the **distribution**—of money, goods, and services;
3. the **regulation** of human behavior—the use of compulsion and inducement to enforce extractive and distributive compliance or otherwise bring about desired behavior; and
4. the **symbolic** policies—political speeches, holidays, rites, public monuments and statues, and the like—used by governments to exhort citizens to desired forms of behavior, often to build a sense of community or to celebrate exemplary conduct (see Chapter 1).

Night Watchman State, Police State, Welfare State, Regulatory State

Political systems have different policy profiles. Some governments produce a lot of goods and services but regulate little. Elsewhere, the government may be heavily engaged in extraction and distribution, but relies on the private sector to produce most goods and services. We can classify states broadly according to their mix of policies and activities. For example, it is customary to contrast the **night watch-man state** of the nineteenth century with the more expansive forms of government that have emerged in the twentieth century. The night watchman state is a Lock-ean state (see Chapter 1), primarily concerned with regulation aimed at preserving law, order, and commerce, and the protection of its citizens.

The twentieth century saw the creation of the **police state,** the **welfare state,** and the **regulatory state.** The police state regulates much more intrusively and ex-tracts resources more severely. The most oppressive forms of the police state have been associated with the totalitarian ideologies (Nazism, fascism, and commu-nism) that have also left their mark on the past century. Fascist and communist governments typically call on their citizens to devote a lot of time to military or other community service.

The welfare state, which is found particularly in more prosperous and demo-cratic societies, engages itself extensively in distributive activities to provide for the health, education, employment, housing, and income support of its citizens. For this purpose, it also has to extract (tax its citizens) more extensively. The wel-fare state originated in Germany in the late nineteenth century but has spread to most developed societies. Finally, the regulatory state has evolved in all advanced modern societies in response to the growing complexity of modern life.

In the first chapter of this book, we discussed three important challenges fac-ing many contemporary states: building community, fostering development, and securing democracy and human rights. Many public policies are wholly or in part directed at these challenges. Public policies are designed to strengthen national identity and community by reinforcing the status of a common language or cul-ture, or by promoting allegiance to a shared political heritage. A host of economic policies aims to promote economic and social development and to distribute its benefits more or less broadly. Finally, other policies seek to establish or enhance mechanisms (democratic institutions) that enable citizens to control political deci-sions. In the past century most Western nations have been transformed from au-thoritarian, or oligarchic, regimes to democracies. Government policy has increas-ingly been used to meet popular needs and demands. Yet we cannot infer that everything democratic governments do is in the best interest of their citizens.

EXTRACTION

Let us now turn to the four types of public policy we have identified above, begin-ning with extraction. All political systems extract resources from their environ-ments and specifically from their members. When simple societies go to war, for ex-ample, individuals of specific age groups (most commonly young men) may be called on to fight. Anthropologists have estimated that in some hunter-gatherer so-cieties, such obligations have been so onerous that about half of all males have died in warfare (Thomas Hobbes would not have been surprised). Such direct extrac-tion of services is still found in modern states, in the form of compulsory military service, jury duty, or compulsory labor imposed on those convicted of crime.

The most common contemporary forms of resource extraction, however, are taxation and borrowing. **Taxation** is the extraction for governmental purposes of money or goods from members of a political system, for which they receive no immediate or direct benefit. Tax policies are designed to meet a lot of different objectives, which sometimes conflict. On the one hand, governments often want to collect as much tax revenue as possible from their citizens in order to finance various services. On the other hand, they do not want to kill the goose that lays the golden egg. The more governments tax their citizens, the less these people are inclined to work, and if the tax burden becomes too onerous, they may leave the country altogether. Another common trade-off in tax policies is between efficiency and equity. *Efficiency* means extracting the most tax revenue possible at the lowest cost to economic production. *Equity* means taxing in such a way that, as much as possible, no one is unfairly burdened, and particularly so that those who have the least are spared. In most societies, the tax system is designed to redistribute wealth in favor of the less well-off. Therefore, income taxes are generally progressive, which means that citizens with greater incomes are taxed at higher rates than those who earn less. Yet, there is a limit to how progressive income taxes can be. Highly progressive income taxes can reduce people's incentive to work and hurt capital formation. Therefore, they are often inefficient.

Personal and corporate income taxes and taxes on capital gains and wealth are called **direct taxes,** since they are directly levied on persons and corporations. Such taxes, as well as property taxes, tend to be progressive. But although corporate income taxes are meant to be progressive, corporations often avoid them through creative accounting or by moving their operations to countries where taxes are lower. If personal income taxes become too high, similar things can happen. **Indirect taxes** include sales and value-added taxes, excise taxes, and customs duties. Their distributive effects depend on who purchases the relevant commodities and services. Since the poor spend more of their income on food and clothing than do those who are better off, sales (or value-added) taxes on such necessities are regressive (which means that the poor pay relatively more than the rich). But indirect taxes on luxury goods may be progressive, since the poor rarely purchase yachts, fine jewelry, or private planes. Payroll taxes, which are often used to finance pensions (e.g., social security in the United States), tend to hit the middle class, since the wealthy often receive a larger share of their income in the form of interest or capital gains. Such taxes on wages also penalize people in the labor force relative to retirees and homemakers and can therefore hurt employment or drive businesses into the "underground economy" in which they do not report their incomes.

Political systems that rely heavily on sales and payroll taxes are less likely to attain a progressive tax structure overall. On the other hand, such taxes are less "visible" than income taxes and seem to generate less resentment and tax avoidance. In many countries, particularly where the government does not have good financial records, indirect taxes are easier to collect. Finally, the more mobile a tax object is, the more difficult it is to tax. Financial investments tend to be highly mobile, which makes them difficult to tax. Land and buildings, on the other hand, are not very mobile at all, and many states tax them substantially.

Besides redistribution and efficiency, tax policies are often designed to promote certain social values, such as charity, energy conservation, or home ownership.

For example, many countries stimulate home ownership by making mortgage interest payments tax deductible. The rationale is that home ownership promotes stable families who take an active interest in their neighborhoods. On the other hand, if such tax incentives are too generous, they can cause economic distortions and reduce output. Families may overinvest in housing, so that businesses are starved of capital. Moreover, mortgage deductions are primarily a middle-class benefit of little use to the truly poor, since they rarely own their own homes.

Figure 7.1 shows the central government revenues as a percentage of **gross domestic product (GDP),** the total value of goods and services produced by a country's residents in a year. For the average country in Figure 7.1, about a fifth of the GDP is extracted by the central government's taxes, but in some countries the proportion is much higher. Regional and local taxes add to the tax burden. In federal systems, such as Brazil, Germany, India, Russia, and the United States, these can increase the total tax burden by a third or more.[1]

Governments also derive revenues from non-tax sources (the lighter columns in Figure 7.1), such as administrative fees and income from business enterprises that they run. The total size of government revenue from all these sources in some advanced capitalist countries is not radically smaller than that of Eastern European countries when they were under Communist control.

Growing tax burdens have led to taxpayer revolts and some scaling back of government extraction. But Sweden still extracts more than 50 percent of its GNP

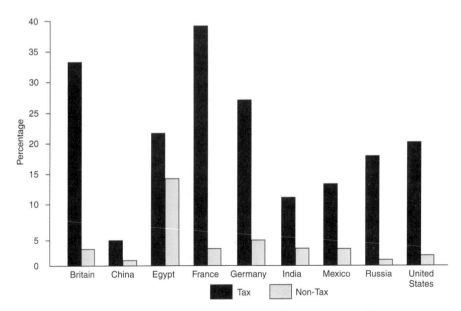

F I G U R E   7 . 1   Central Government Revenue as a Percentage of GDP and by Source of Revenue for Selected Countries, 1997

Source: World Bank, *World Development Report, 1999–2000* (New York: Oxford University Press, 2000), table 14, pp. 256–57.

in taxes and France comes close to the 50-percent mark. Britain and Germany (after taking account of their subnational governments) are among a number of advanced industrial societies that collect revenue at around the 40-percent level of GDP, while the United States and Russia extract about a third. Outside the European–North American area, central government revenue rarely exceeds 20 percent of GDP. Egypt, with its substantial public sector, is an exception. Much of its revenue comes from public enterprises and foreign aid. The central government revenue of India is under 15 percent, or about a third more if we add state and local governments.

The tax profiles of different states depend on the kinds of taxes imposed, the distribution of income and wealth, the consumption patterns of different population groups, and the mobility of capital and labor. In Germany and Britain most of the revenue comes from social security and income taxes, but Germany relies far more heavily on social security payments and Britain more on income taxes. India and Mexico receive most of their revenue from indirect taxes. Heidenheimer, Heclo, and Adams classify the tax systems of the advanced free-market economies of the **Organization for Economic Cooperation and Development (OECD)** countries into three categories: (1) heavy social security tax systems (including Germany, Austria, the Netherlands, France, and Italy), which receive one-third to one-half of their revenue from social security, which is imposed more or less equally on both employers and employees; (2) the United States and Japan, which fall the farthest below average in total tax burden and rely heavily on direct taxes rather than on sales and consumption taxes; and finally (3) countries such as Sweden and Norway, which impose the highest tax burdens of all the OECD countries and rely on all three types of taxation—direct, indirect, and social security payments but impose particularly burdensome social security payments on employers.[2]

Although overall tax burdens continue to grow, income tax rates have decreased in Western countries since the early 1980s, as there has been a shift from direct income taxes to less visible indirect consumption taxes. From 1975 to 1990 British top marginal income tax rates declined by 43 percentage points, U.S. federal rates by 42 points (though they then rose by about 13 points by the end of the Clinton administration, but are scheduled to come down by about 4.5 points under President George W. Bush), Swedish rates by 35 points, and Japanese rates by 25 points. The average decline in top tax rates for all OECD countries was 18 percent.[3] Tax rates have come down because of the spread of economic views that stress the importance of entrepreneurial incentives for productivity. Lower marginal income tax rates stimulate economic activity and lessen incentives for tax evasion, but they may cause growing income inequalities.

DISTRIBUTION

Government not only takes—it also gives away, and that is what we call distribution. Distributive policies include the allocation by governmental agencies of various kinds of money, goods, services, honors, and opportunities to individuals and groups in the society. They can be measured and compared according to the quantity of whatever is distributed, the areas of human life touched by these benefits,

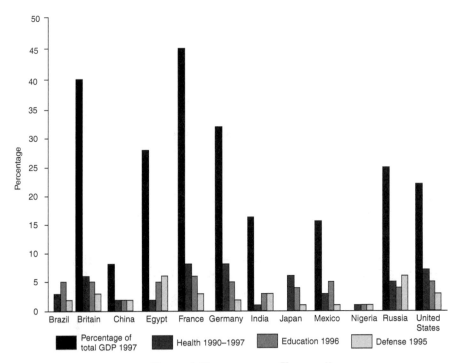

F I G U R E   7 . 2   Central Government Expenditures
as a Percentage of GDP and by Object of Expenditure, 1990–1997

Source: World Bank, *World Development Report: 1999–2000* (New York: Oxford University Press, 2000), Table 14, pp. 256–257; Table 7, pp. 242–243; Table 6, pp. 240–241; Table 17, pp. 262–263.

the sections of the population receiving these benefits, and the effectiveness of the distributive program.

Figure 7.2 reports central governmental expenditures on health, education, and defense as a percentage of GDP. Clearly, central government expenditures depend a great deal on economic development. Developed countries generally allocate from one-half to two-thirds of their central government expenditures to education, health, and welfare. France, Germany, and Britain spend more than two-thirds of their budgets here, as compared with just under one-half in the United States, where a larger share of health care is in the private sector. Developing countries such as India and Nigeria spend very little on health, but typically a little more on education. Low-income countries face a tragic quandary: While they urgently need to upgrade the skills of their workforces, their commitments in education and health are insufficient to make rapid headway. The government in a country such as Nigeria seems hardly to touch its people. India's efforts are only slightly greater. Sadly, the countries that "need" it the most have the least to spend on education and health.

National security spending shows a different pattern. Particularly among less-developed countries, spending varies as much with the international environment as with overall economic means. Some states that are locked in tense international confrontations, such as in the Middle East, or that are trying to exert international influence, make extraordinary defense efforts. Because of its worldwide security commitments, the United States is by far the heaviest military spender, though since the end of the Cold War, U.S. defense spending has decreased. Relative to the size of the national economy, however, Egypt spent more on defense in 1995 than did the United States. Japan, which spends as much as most Western countries on health and education, was very low in defense efforts. Prior to the watershed year of 1989, the Soviet Union and the Communist countries of Eastern Europe spent less on education, health, and welfare than the democracies of Western Europe. As the emerging democracies of the former Communist bloc have introduced market economies, their government revenue and expenditure patterns have become more similar to the West.

Poor nations, with limited budgets and many pressing demands, cannot easily spare the resources for health and education. Also, in both absolute and relative terms, social security expenditure in poor nations tends to be limited. But in these societies the aged and the infirm typically receive some care through the extended family. Just as our GNP measures fail to include the subsistence economy and therefore underreport the wealth of the poorest countries (see Chapter 1), our measures of educational and health expenditures may similarly underreport the efforts of the poorest states. Many developing societies still have a preindustrial welfare safety net for many citizens.

The Welfare State

The twentieth century has witnessed a vast increase in the scope of distributive policies in industrial societies. This has largely been associated with the growth of the welfare state. The welfare state generally refers to a set of government, and sometimes private, policies in the areas of old age pensions (known in the United States as social security), health, sickness, and accident insurance, unemployment benefits, and the like. Over time, welfare state policies have come to include such benefits as housing subsidies, child and childcare benefits, and other distributive policies. The first modern welfare state programs were introduced in Germany in the 1880s. In response to Germany's rapid industrialization and urbanization, the government began offering social insurance programs that protected workers against unemployment, accidents, sickness, and old age poverty. During the twentieth century, most industrialized states have adopted and greatly expanded welfare state policies, particularly in the period from the Great Depression of the 1930s until the 1970s.

Figure 7.3 shows that the welfare state in advanced capitalist (OECD) countries has continued to grow during the 1980s and 1990s, albeit at a somewhat slower rate. As the figure shows, welfare state spending consists of two major categories: cash transfers to individuals and families, and direct government spending on services. Though both categories have grown, the transfer programs remain the largest. Among the individual programs that make up the welfare state, old-age

F I G U R E   7 . 3   The Welfare State in OECD Countries
(OECD Average Transfers and Spending as Percent of GDP)

Source: "Privatising Peace of Mind," *The Economist* (October 24, 1998): 4.

pensions (social security) and health care loom particularly large. In many European countries with jobless rates of up to 10 or 15 percent, unemployment benefits are another major government outlay.

Not all welfare states are alike. Even among the advanced industrial countries, some welfare states are more extensive than others, and different political systems emphasize different programs and benefits. All the wealthier nations make efforts to assist the aged, the disabled, and the unemployed; however, differences in expenditures reflect policy and historical experience. The U.S. model stresses equality of opportunity through public education. In contrast, on the European continent, social security and health programs have traditionally taken precedence over education. The United States made a much greater effort, and much earlier, in mass education than did most European nations. On the other hand, Americans began spending on social insurance and public services much later, and still do less in this area. Americans have historically put much more emphasis on equality of opportunity and less on welfare obligations than Europeans. This may reflect the U.S. heritage as a nation of immigrants, many of whom have arrived poor and been expected to prosper by their own efforts.

Also, it is important to keep in mind that many welfare services in the United States are provided by private foundations, churches and other religious organizations, and individuals. In 1997 Americans made private donations of $143 billion to nonprofit organizations. More than three-fourths of these gifts came from living individuals, many of them persons of very limited means. The nonprofit sector of the

U.S. economy accounts for 8 percent of the gross domestic product, more than twice as much as in 1960. It employs close to 10 percent of the American workforce, more than the federal and state governments combined.[4] The nonprofit sector exists in other developed states as well, but generally on a much smaller scale.

Since World War II especially, governments have greatly expanded their spending on a wide range of benefits. Education is one of the most important of these. Developing societies have made large efforts to provide at least primary education for all their citizens, while most of the more developed societies have also experienced a huge increase in secondary and university enrollments. A few decades ago, fewer than 5 percent of young adults in most European countries were able to pursue a university or college education. Today, those numbers have risen to 40 percent or more (see Table 7.5). In most of these countries, the majority of colleges and universities are public. Consequently, government spending on secondary and higher education has risen very substantially.

As government expenditures have grown to between one-third and one-half of the national product in most industrial democracies, they have caused serious concern about the costs of welfare state programs and the ability of future generations to pay for them. One of the most serious problems is that at the same time that senior citizens are qualifying for greater pension benefits and health care costs are rising rapidly, the ranks of the elderly are swelling relative to those in the workforce. This is reflected in the dependency ratio, which is the proportion of those outside the workforce (because they are too young or too old) to those in the working-age population. Figure 7.4 shows that over the next decades, dependency ratios will increase in all advanced industrial societies, and particularly in such countries as Japan. That means that fewer and fewer working people will have to pay higher and higher taxes just to support existing health and welfare programs. In the United States, Medicare and Social Security may incur large deficits in the future. In other countries, social welfare programs are already costing more than their designated taxes are bringing in.

Another problem with some welfare state policies is that they give citizens few incentives to behave responsibly. For example, generous unemployment or sick leave policies may give people little incentive to work. Norway and Sweden are among the leading countries in the world in life expectancy and public health statistics. Yet, workers in these countries are on sick leave about twice as often as those elsewhere in Europe, as the average Swedish worker misses about five or six weeks of work per year. And in Norway, more than 10 percent of the working-age population is on disability pensions. The reason, at least in part, is that unusually generous sick leave benefits let workers keep virtually their entire pay from the first day that they miss work, and that it is relatively easy to qualify for disability benefits. But these policies are costly. In Sweden, sick pay and disability benefits account for more than 10 percent of the government's total spending.

These widely perceived problems with the welfare state have stirred efforts to prevent further increases in spending obligations (entitlements) and to contain the costs of those already in effect. Conservative parties in particular have stressed setting limits on public expenditures and labor costs.[5] Thus the gradual expansion of welfare benefits that characterized most of the twentieth century can no longer be taken for granted.

*Typical OECD country
†Population aged 0–14 and 65 and over as percentage of working-age population

FIGURE 7.4   The Shrinking Working Population

Source: "Privatising Peace of Mind," *The Economist* (October 24, 1998): 9.

REGULATION

Regulation is the exercise of political control over the behavior of individuals and groups in the society. Governments regulate the lives of their citizens in many ways. Although we usually associate regulation with legal coercion or its threat, there are other ways to regulate as well. Governments may control behavior by offering material or financial inducements or by persuasion or moral exhortation. For example, many governments try to reduce tobacco use by a combination of methods: (1) bans on smoking, sales, or advertising, (2) sales ("sin") taxes, and (3) information campaigns to convince citizens of the hazards of tobacco use.

Regulation occurs for a number of reasons, as we have discussed in Chapter 1. As social contract theorists such as Hobbes and Locke realized, government regulation can facilitate many beneficial activities. Economic production and commerce, for example, rely on government regulation to establish and protect property rights and to enforce contractual obligations. At the same time, citizens and consumers often demand regulations that protect them against fraud, manipulation, and obnoxious externalities such as toxic waste and environmental degradation. Increasingly, governments and international organizations, such as the European Union, have been involved in setting product standards, particularly for such products as pharmaceuticals and food. Governments also regulate to protect their citizens, and often particularly children and women, against physical and other abuse, and some protections are extended to animals and the natural environment as well.

Government regulation has proliferated enormously over the last century or so, due to new objective needs as well as citizen demands. Industrialization and urban concentration have caused problems in traffic, health, and public order. Industrial growth has created problems of industrial safety, labor exploitation, and pollution. Moreover, the growth of science and the belief that humanity can harness and control nature have led to increased demands for governmental action. Finally, changes in citizen values can lead to demands for new kinds of regulation. Thus, in recent decades regulation in the United States has extended to include gun control, protection of voting rights, prohibition of discrimination in employment, pollution, and the like. At the same time, however, in most modern nations regulation of birth control, abortion, divorce, blasphemy, obscenity, and sexual conduct has lessened.

But even though there are many similarities in regulative policies across the world, states often differ substantially in their policy profiles. Patterns of regulation vary not only with industrialization and urbanization, for example, but also with cultural values. In the study of public policy, we describe and explain such differences between political systems by asking the following questions:

1. What aspects of human behavior and interaction are regulated and to what degree? Does the government regulate such domains as family relations, economic activity, religious activity, political activity, geographic mobility, professional and occupational qualifications, and protection of person and property? These questions have to do with the *domain* of government regulation.

2. What social groups are regulated, with what procedural limitations on enforcement and what rights? Are these sanctions applied uniformly, or do they affect different individuals or groups differently? Are there rights of appeal? Such questions help us identify the *subjects* of regulation.

3. What sanctions are used to compel or induce citizens to comply? Does the government use exhortation and moral persuasion, financial rewards and penalties, licensing of some types of action, physical confinement or punishment, or other forms of coercion? These questions help us map the *instruments* or *mechanisms*, of regulation.

Although all modern states use sanctions, they vary in their goals and strategies. Yet, one aspect of regulation is particularly important politically: government control over political participation and communication. Recall from earlier chapters that democracy requires political competition. Governments in authoritarian systems often suppress political competition by prohibiting party organization, voluntary associations, and political communication. Government regulation in this area therefore has a crucial effect on democracy. Yet, focusing on the suppression of rights should not give us the idea that governmental regulation is always negative. Our civilization and amenities depend on regulation. Government regulation commonly promotes such values as the safety of persons and property, sanitation, prevention of environmental pollution, safe disposal of toxic wastes, maintenance of occupational safety, and equal access to housing and education.

Table 7.1 shows the political rights and civil liberties ratings for the countries included in this book, based on expert judgments. Political rights refer to citizen opportunities to participate in the choice of political leaders—voting rights, the right to run for office, and the like. Civil liberties refer to protec-

T A B L E 7 . 1 Political Rights and Liberties Ratings for Selected Countries 2001–2002

Country	Political Rights	Civil Liberties
Brazil	3	3
Britain*	1	2
China	7	6
Egypt	6	6
France	1	2
Germany	1	2
India	2	3
Japan	1	2
Mexico	2	3
Nigeria	4	5
Russia	5	5
United States	1	1

*Rating for Britain explicitly excludes Northern Ireland, which was rated 3, 3.

Source: Expert ratings of political rights and civil liberties for each country on 1 (highest) to 7 (lowest) scale, provided by Freedom House from their website, www.freedomhouse.org. Ratings are as of November 14, 2002.

tions in such areas as freedom of speech, press, assembly, and religion, as well as to procedural rights, such as trial by a jury of peers and bans on arbitrary or cruel treatment. The rich democratic countries all have ratings of 1 or 2 for both political and civil rights. India and Mexico, which has improved significantly in recent years, follow next. At the other extreme, China and Egypt strongly suppress both political rights and civil liberties. China in particular has tried to control the media comprehensively and sets few limits on government regulation vis-à-vis the individual. Brazil, Nigeria, and Russia are rated in the middle. These rankings, of course, vary over time. Nigeria's military governments of the 1990s were repressive and frequently brutal, earning scores of 7 and 6 before power was turned over to an elected civilian president in 1999. Rights and liberties in the United States have improved since the civil rights movement of the 1960s.

There is a strong correlation between political and civil rights. No country that scores high on participatory rights is very low on civil liberties, and no country low on participatory rights is high on civil liberties. This suggests a strong relationship between popular participation and the rule of law and equitable procedure. In a cross-national study of governmental repression in 153 countries during the 1980s, Steven C. Poe and C. Neal Tate concluded that democratic political institutions and conditions of peace and social order best explained positive civil and political rights records. Authoritarian states and those involved in internal or international war were the most frequent civil rights violators. A high level of economic development also helped explain a strong rights record.[6]

COMMUNITY-BUILDING AND SYMBOLIC POLICIES

A fourth type of output is symbolic policies. Much communication by political leaders takes the form of appeals to the courage, wisdom, and magnanimity embodied in the nation's past; or appeals to values and ideologies, such as equality, liberty, community, democracy, communism, liberalism, or religious tradition; or promises of future accomplishment and rewards. Political leaders appeal to such values for different reasons—for example, to win elections or get their own pet projects enacted. But at the same time many symbolic appeals and policies have the purpose of building community—for example, by boosting people's national identity, civic pride, or trust in government.

Symbolic outputs are also intended to enhance other aspects of performance: to make people pay their taxes more readily and honestly, comply with the law more faithfully, or accept sacrifice, danger, and hardship. Such appeals may be especially important in times of crisis. Some of the most magnificent examples are the speeches of Pericles in the Athenian Assembly during the Peloponnesian War, or those of Franklin D. Roosevelt in the depths of the Great Depression, or of Winston Churchill in World War II, when Britain stood alone after the fall of France. But symbolic policies are important even in less extreme circumstances. Public buildings, plazas, monuments, holiday parades, and civic and patriotic indoctrination in schools all attempt to contribute to the population's sense of governmental legitimacy and its willingness to comply with public policy.

OUTCOMES: DOMESTIC WELFARE

While we can describe different government policies, it is not always clear what their consequences will be. How do extractive, distributive, regulative, and symbolic policies affect the lives of citizens? Unexpected economic, international, or social events may frustrate the purpose of political leaders. Thus a tax rebate to increase consumption and stimulate the economy may be nullified by a rise in the price of oil. Increases in health expenditures may have no effect because of unexpected epidemics or rising health costs, or health services may not reach those most in need. Sometimes policies have unintended consequences that may be undesirable, as when the introduction of benefits for troubled social groups lead others to simulate the same troubles. Consequently, to estimate the effectiveness of public policy, we have to examine actual welfare outcomes as well as governmental policies and their implementation.

Table 7.2 compares a number of welfare indicators. The first two columns report measures of economic well-being or its lack: growth in private consumption and the share of the population living on less than $2 per day. The severe problems of Nigeria are particularly notable: not only does the vast majority of the population live on less than $2 a day, which is also true in India, but private consumption spending actually declined in the 1990s. The latter columns report the availability of critical public facilities: safe water and sanitation. Table 7.3 reports

T A B L E   7 . 2   Welfare Outcomes for Selected States, 1990–1998

Country	Growth in Private Consumption per Capita % Annual 1980–1997[*]	Population Below $2 per Day %, ca. 2000	Access to Safe Water (%) Mid–1990s	Access to Sanitation (%), Mid–1990s
Brazil	0.2	25.4	72	67
Britain	1.8	ND	100	100
China	4.5	53.7	90	21
Egypt	1.3	52.7	64	11
France	1.1	ND	100	96
Germany	ND	ND	ND	ND
India	1.9	86.2	81	16
Japan	ND	ND	96	100
Mexico	0.0	34.8	83	66
Nigeria	−2.6	90.8	39	36
Russia	ND	25.1	ND	ND
United States	1.1	ND	ND	ND

[*]Corrected for distribution.

Source: World Bank, *Entering the 21st Century: World Development Report 1999–2000* (New York, Oxford University Press, 2000), pp. 232–233; *World Development Indicators 2000*, Tables 2.4, 2.15. Retrieved May 12, 2000 from http://www.worldbank.org/data/wdi2000/pdfs/tab2_4.pdf,2_15.pdf; World Bank, *Building Institutions for Markets: World Development Report 2002* (New York, Oxford University Press, 2002), pp. 234–235; Table 2.

T A B L E 7 . 3   Health Outcomes for Selected Countries, 1990–1998

Country	Public Health Expenditure as % of GDP	Physicians per 1000 Citizens	Life Expectancy at Birth, 1999	Infant Mortality per 1,000 Live Births	Infant Health: % Malnutrition Under Age 5	Fertility Rate
Brazil	3.4	1.3	67	33	6	2.3
Britain	5.9	1.6	77	6	ND	1.7
China	2.0	2.0	70	31	16	1.9
Egypt	1.8	2.1	67	49	15	3.2
France	7.1	2.9	79	5	ND	1.8
Germany	8.3	3.4	77	5	ND	1.4
India	0.6	.4	63	70	53	3.2
Japan	5.9	1.8	81	4	ND	1.4
Mexico	2.8	1.2	72	30	14	2.8
Nigeria	0.2	.2	47	76	39	5.3
Russia	4.5	4.6	66	17	3	1.2
United States	6.5	2.6	77	7	ND	2.0

Source: World Bank, *Entering the 21st Century: World Development Report 1999–2000* (New York, Oxford University Press, 2000), pp. 232–33; World Bank, *World Development Indicators 2000*, Tables 2.14, 2.16, 2.18. Retrieved May 12, 2000 from http://www.worldbank.org/data/wdi2000/pdfs/tab2_14.pdf;2_16.pdf;2_18.pdf; World Bank, *Building Institutions for Markets:World Development Report 2002* (New York, Oxford University Press, 2002), pp. 232–33; Table 1.

T A B L E   7 . 4   Communication and Information, 1995–1998

Country	Newspapers	Televisions	Telephones, Main Lines	Personal Computers
Brazil	40	316	121	30.0
Britain	329	645	557	263.0
China	ND	272	70	8.9
Egypt	40	122	60	9.1
France	218	601	570	207.8
Germany	311	580	567	304.7
India	ND	69	22	2.7
Japan	518	707	503	237.2
Mexico	97	261	104	47.0
Nigeria	24	66	4	5.7
Russia	105	420	197	40.6
United States	215	847	661	458.6

Note: Per 1,000 people unless otherwise indicated.

Source: World Bank, *World Development Indicators 2000*, Tables 5.10, 5.11, 5.12. Retrieved May 12, 2000 from http://www.worldbank.org/data/wdi2000/pdfs/tab5_10.pdf,5_10.pdf,5_12.pdf.

on health outcomes, including life expectancy, infant mortality, the health of children, and fertility. Table 7.4 tells us about access to communication and information, such as telephones, newspapers, television, and personal computers. Table 7.5 compares educational efforts and the extent to which countries at various levels of economic development succeed in increasing literacy. All of these data show how governmental and private efforts, in societies at different levels of economic development and of differing social structures and cultures, affect human life chances. Although natural resources and socioeconomic structure constrain these outcomes, government and private efforts can make a big difference.

In Chapter 1, we saw how income distribution tends to be most unequal in medium-income developing societies, such as Brazil, and more equal in advanced market societies as well as in low-income developing societies, such as India (Table 1.4). In his studies of European economic history, Simon Kuznets showed that in the early stages of industrialization income distribution became more unequal, whereas in later stages of industrialization income distribution again came closer to equality.[7] This "Kuznets curve" is explained by the fact that in the early stages of modernization, the large sector of traditional farmers tends to be left behind as industry and commercial agriculture begin to grow. At higher levels of economic attainment, however, the number of poor farmers is reduced compared with the industrial and service sectors. In addition, when trade unions and political parties develop in democratic countries, they tend to bring about public policies that make income distribution more equal through taxation, wage policy, and welfare state policies.

Economic development affects economic prosperity, public health provisions such as sanitation and availability of potable water, and access to the outside world

T A B L E 7 . 5   Education and Literacy, 1997–1998

Country	Public Education Expenditure As Percent of GDP, 1997	Percentage of Relevant Age Group Enrolled, Secondary, 1997	Percentage of Relevant Age Group Enrolled, Tertiary, 1997	Percentage 15 Years and Above Illiterate, All, 1998	Percentage 15 Years and Above Illiterate Female, 1998	Female Share of Labor Force, 1998
Brazil	5.1	66	15	16	16	35
Britain	5.3	92	52	ND	ND	44
China	2.3	70	6	17	25	45
Egypt	4.8	75	23	46	58	30
France	6.0	99	51	ND	ND	45
Germany	4.8	95	47	ND	ND	42
India	3.2	60	7	44	57	32
Japan	3.6	100	43	ND	ND	41
Mexico	4.9	66	16	9	11	33
Nigeria	0.7	33*	4	39	48	36
Russia	3.5	88	41	1	1	49
United States	5.4	96	81	ND	ND	46

*"Gross," rather than "net," enrollment.

Source: World Bank, *World Development Indicators 2000,* Tables 2.9, 2.10, 2.12, 2.13. Retrieved May 12, 2000 from http://www.worldbank.org/data/wdi2000/pdfs/tab2_9.pdf,2_10.pdf, 2_12.pdf,2_3.pdf; total literacy from http://www.worldbank.org/data/databytopic/ILIT.pdf.

through telephone and television, roads, and other infrastructure. During the 1990s, the average public health expenditure per capita for the economically developed countries was $2505, compared with $182 for the developing countries. The average number of physicians per 1000 persons in the developed world was 2.8, as compared with 1.3 in the developing world. While most of the people of the developed world had access to safe water, this was true for only about half of the population of the less-advantaged areas. In Nigeria, for example, only 39 percent of the population has access to safe water. The country has a high birth rate, but almost one out of ten infants fails to survive the first year of life; and more than one-third of Nigerian children under the age of five suffer from malnutrition. On the average, Nigeria has only a single physician per 20,000 inhabitants, and its citizens have a life expectancy at birth of just 47 years (compared with 75-80 years in advanced industrial countries).

Nigeria demonstrates the ills of poverty, but some poor countries cope more successfully with their challenges than others. The importance of culture for public policy is suggested by the comparison between China and India. With a similarly low GNP per capita, Chinese average life expectancy is 70 years and infant mortality is 31 per 1,000 live births, while those of India are 63 years and 70 per 1,000, respectively. China has five times as many physicians as India relative to its population. Half of India's children under five are undernourished, as compared to a fifth of those in China.

While the incidence of infant mortality and malnutrition is much lower in advanced economies, these problems are still serious among the poor in advanced industrial countries such as the United States. Although Table 7.3 does not show this (because it shows only government, not private, health spending), the United States spends the largest proportion of its GNP on health care of any state (approximately 15 percent). At the same time, however, the United States has a somewhat higher infant death rate than Japan and Western Europe, due to more widespread poverty, drug abuse, and unequal access to health care. As Table 7.3 shows, Japan has an exceptional record in health outcomes. It has the longest life expectancy and the lowest infant mortality rate among all our countries. But its fertility rate of 1.4 means a declining population. (With no net migration, a fertility rate of approximately 2.1 results in a steady-state population.)

Table 7.4 provides a brief picture of the communications infrastructure. In the developed countries on the average there is a telephone for every two persons; in Nigeria there are as few as four to a thousand. Television has become widely available even in countries at middling development levels (e.g., Brazil and Mexico). Personal computers, however, are much more rare outside the advanced industrial economies. Whereas the relative incidence of television sets is less than three times higher in the United States than it is in Brazil, the relative frequency of personal computers is 15 times higher.

Table 7.5 provides us with a picture of educational attainment. The first column, showing public education expenditure as a percentage of GDP, gives a rough measure of the "priority" given to education. Remember, however, that private schools, which in some countries are very common, are not counted here. Countries such as Egypt devote similar percentages of their GNP to education as do the advanced industrial societies. Hence we may say that they are making proportionally similar efforts to educate their populations. But the differences in dollar expenditures per student are very large. China and India spend less generously on education, even relative to the size of their economies. Nigeria spends the least of all and requires only children from ages 6 to 12 to attend school. The outcomes are largely what we might predict from these differences in output. Nigeria has only a third of the appropriate age cohort in secondary education, by far the poorest record of these countries. India's figures are double that. The figures for Egypt are even better—75 percent in secondary schools, and 23 percent in colleges, universities, and other postsecondary educational and training institutions. At the high end in educational outcomes, France, Germany, Japan, and Britain have virtually all of their primary and secondary school-age children in schools, and about half of the college-age population is in some form of advanced education. In the United States, college education is even more common.

The payoffs of development and investment in education are clearly reflected in literacy rates. Nearly half of all Egyptians, Indians, and Nigerians are unable to read or write. Yet China, with a similarly low GNP and small investment in education, has only 17 percent illiteracy. But because they are often based on the number of school years completed, not on actual reading ability, literacy figures are a crude measure of skill and competence and must be treated with caution. The high official literacy figures in the United States, for example, conflict with studies showing substantial functional illiteracy among American adults.

Women in developing countries are especially likely to lag behind in literacy. For example, fewer than half of all adult females in Egypt and India are reported to be literate. The discrepancy between male and female literacy rates tells us something of the status of women. Where women make up a smaller proportion of the labor force (as shown in the last column in Table 7.5), female illiteracy also tends to be most common. Faced with poverty, disease, and the absence of a social safety net, parents in poor countries traditionally want to have many children, to ensure that some survive and can support them in old age. But large families tend to mean that women have few opportunities to educate themselves or hold jobs outside the home. The self-interest of parents in having large families often also conflicts with population control and economic development. Modernizing the status of women generally makes them better informed and more capable of making choices that lead to a more stable and healthy population. As women are educated and/or enter the labor force, they recognize the advantages of smaller families and become more aware of the importance of education and adequate health care.

Table 7.5 also reveals the sobering difficulties of trying to change societies, even in an area such as literacy, where modern methods and technology are available. It is hard for a poor country to spend a high percentage of its GNP on education, because it must then make sacrifices elsewhere. And the effects are limited if much of the country's productive effort has to go into feeding a rapidly growing population. No matter how large the educational effort may be, it does not translate into much per child, because the resource base is small and the population is growing rapidly. Moreover, since most older people are illiterate, the net effect on literacy is slow.

DOMESTIC SECURITY OUTCOMES

As Thomas Hobbes would have reminded us, maintaining domestic law and order and protecting persons and property are among the most basic government responsibilities. Without them the conduct of personal, economic, and civic life are impossible. It is therefore worrisome that until recently crime rates have been on the increase in many advanced industrial countries, as well as in the developing world. Thus in the United States the crime rate increased by almost 15 percent between 1982 and 1991. In France the 1990 incidence of crimes against persons and property was almost twice that of 1975. In Russia the crime rate doubled between 1985 and 1993, as that country experienced the collapse and remaking of a moral and legal order. The country now has a murder rate three to four times as high as the United States. Brazil and Mexico also have considerably higher murder rates than the United States, while those of such European countries as England, France, and Germany are a small fraction of the American numbers. China has similarly low murder rates, whereas Japan and Egypt are even lower.

High crime rates are primarily a problem of the larger urban areas where much of the population of modern countries resides. In modern and modernizing societies, despite increasing expenditures on law enforcement, the physical safety of our persons and possessions has over the past several decades been declining. Wealth and income may increase rapidly, but the liabilities of modernization include the anxiety over personal safety that is so common in urban life. The causes of this development are complex. Rapidly increasing migration into the major cities, either from the domestic countryside, or from poorer foreign countries, has increased diversity and conflict. Such urbanization is found in virtually all advanced industrial countries, but its pace is even more explosive in many developing countries such as Brazil and Nigeria, and the problems of poverty and infrastructure are far more severe. The newly arrived city-dwellers often find themselves uprooted from their cultures, unwelcome, without a job, and living in squalor. The weakening and even the breakdown of the nuclear family have impaired the capacity of modern cultures to transmit effective standards of conduct to the young. Also, inequality of income and wealth, unemployment, and the hopelessness of life prospects in the big city lie behind this general decline in public order and safety. In the former Communist countries the situation is compounded by the fact that traditional standards of law and morality have collapsed.

Yet, crime rates have recently come down significantly in the United States and some other countries. The number of murders per 100,000 inhabitants in the United States peaked at 9.4 in 1994, and declined to 6.8 in 1997 (see Figure 7.5). There are several reasons that crime rates have recently come down in the United States and elsewhere. One is a strong economy, in which more young people have been able to find jobs. A second reason is stricter law enforcement. This is reflected in part in the number of police officers relative to total population, which ranges from one police officer for every 350 persons in the United States, to 820 in India, and 1,140 in Nigeria. In the United States, both federal and state governments have also sought to reduce crime by increasing the length of imprisonment. By removing the criminally prone from the streets, these authorities have succeeded in cutting the crime rate, but at the cost of an exploding prison population. According to a recent study, the United States now imprisons more people than any other country—perhaps half a million more than communist China. The total prison population in the United States is around 1.8 million, including more than 1 million in custody primarily in state prisons, and 600,000 in local jails, awaiting sentencing or serving short sentences. This population has been increasing at a rate of more than 50,000 per year. Similarly, the French prison population almost doubled between 1983 and 1990.[8] A third cause of lower crime rates has been a decrease in the number of youth at the age at which most crimes are committed. Yet, as the 15–25-year-old

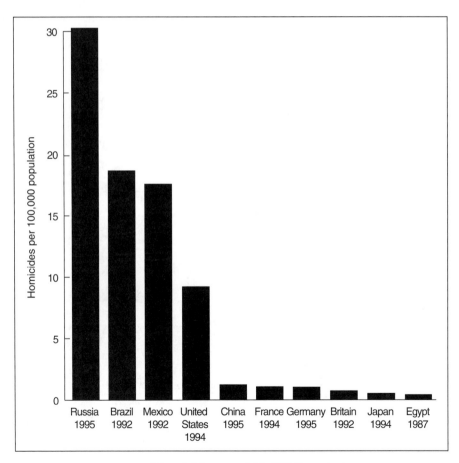

F I G U R E   7 . 5   Homicides per 100,000 Population
in Selected Countries, 1987–1995

Source: United Nations Demographic Yearbook, 1996 (New York: United Nations, 1996).

male population in the United States is now on the rise, we can expect violent crime to increase once again.

INTERNATIONAL OUTPUTS AND OUTCOMES

Most states engage in a great variety of international activities. Such economic, diplomatic, military, and informational activities may result in prosperity or depression, war or peace, secularization or the spread of particular beliefs.[9] The most costly outcome of the interaction among nations is warfare. Table 7.6 reports the numbers of deaths from international and internal collective violence for our twelve selected countries for almost the entire twentieth century (1900–1995). The figures are mostly civilian and military deaths from interstate warfare but also include the slaughter of civilians in the efforts to implement communism in the Soviet Union, the holocaust of European Jews under the German Nazis (the National Socialist Party) during World War II, many "ethnic cleansing" episodes in Europe and Africa, and civil wars in all parts of the world.

Table 7.6 shows the people of USSR-Russia, by a margin of more than two-to-one, to be the greatest victims of the tormented history of the twentieth century. The enormous Russian casualties during World War I destroyed the legitimacy of the Czarist regime. Its collapse was followed by the 1917 Bolshevik Revolution, the Civil War (1918–1921), and Stalin's Great Terror (particularly in the 1930s), each of which cost the lives of millions. Soviet suffering climaxed in World War II with a total of seventeen million civilian and military dead. All told, the Soviet Union/Russia suf-

T A B L E 7 . 6   Deaths from Collective Civilian-Military Violence for Selected Countries, 1900–1995

Country	Civilian Deaths	Military Deaths	Unspecified Deaths	Total Deaths
Brazil	—	1,000	2,000	3,000
Britain	131,000	1,350,000	—	1,481,000
China	4,047,000	2,671,000	818,000	7,536,000
Egypt	51,000	28,000	—	79,000
France	490,000	1,830,000	—	2,320,000
Germany	2,232,000	7,150,000	—	9,382,000
India	889,000	71,000	37,000	997,000
Japan	510,000	1,502,000	—	2,012,000
Mexico	125,000	125,000	10,000	260,000
Nigeria	1,005,000	1,000,000	6,000	2,011,000
Russia/USSR	12,028,000	11,901,000	96,000	24,025,000
United States	—	524,000	—	524,000
TOTALS	21,508,000	28,153,000	969,000	50,630,000

Source: Adapted from Ruth Leger Sivard, "Wars and War Related Deaths, 1900–1995," *World Military and Social Expenditures 1996* (Washington: World Priorities, 1996), pp. 18–19. U.S. deaths add Korean and Vietnam war totals, from U.S. Department of State figures, to Sivard report of World War I and II deaths.

fered more than 24 million civilian and military deaths in the wars and political horrors of the twentieth century.

Germany suffered the second-largest number of deaths from twentieth-century collective violence. More than three million, mostly military, occurred in the First World War. In World War II Germany suffered almost five million military deaths and another one and three-quarter million violent civilian deaths for a total of almost nine and one-half million. Other countries with huge losses include China, with a vast number of civilian casualties, and Japan, whose more than two million deaths occurred mainly among military personnel during World War II but include half a million civilians, notably many residents of Hiroshima and Nagasaki. French and British sufferings were of roughly similar magnitude, with the French losses somewhat higher than those of Britain. Both countries took horrendous military casualties in the trench warfare of World War I. Since the Civil War the United States has largely avoided the horrors of large-scale fighting on its own soil but still suffered over 120,000 deaths in World War I and close to half a million in World War II. While in the Korean and Vietnam wars, America suffered only moderate losses by these terrible standards, Korean and Vietnamese military and civilian dead were in the millions.

After World War II, the most devastating conflicts have occurred in the Third World. Many African countries, newly independent from about 1960, but with borders arbitrarily drawn by colonial powers, have serious problems of national cohesion and have suffered from chronic civil war. Large-scale civil war in Nigeria 1967–1970 cost perhaps more than a million lives, and more sporadic conflict has continued to the present time. In 2002, for example, when the country hosted an international beauty contest, it led to violent clashes between Muslims and Christians and hundreds of deaths. The partition of formerly British India into India, Pakistan, and Bangladesh has been associated with numerous deadly conflicts within and between the three countries. Some two million lives, mostly civilian, have been lost, half of them in India. The aftermath of the Cold War has witnessed a wave of instability and conflict in Eastern Europe and Central Asia. The breakup of the Soviet Union and Yugoslavia has resulted in bloody border wars and secessional conflicts (e.g., in Croatia, Bosnia, and Kosovo in the former Yugoslavia, and Chechnya in Russia). These conflicts have brought another wave of ethnic slaughter, religious clashes, and struggles for power between different warlords.

The Uppsala Conflict Data Project reports 103 armed conflicts (defined as involving at least 25 deaths) in the world from 1988 through 1997. Only six of these, including the continuing clashes between India and Pakistan, were interstate conflicts; most were civil wars occurring within current state boundaries. In 1997, a fairly typical year, there were 33 conflicts in progress, of which seven involved more than 1000 deaths.[10] The deadly costs of international warfare have gradually escalated. One authority estimates that more than 90 percent of the war deaths since 1700 have occurred in the twentieth century. Civilian deaths caused by war have increased even more rapidly than military ones. In the last decades of the century, more than three-quarters of the war deaths have been civilian.[11]

The United Nations in the post–Cold War world has intervened in some of these conflicts by providing peace-keeping missions when the parties to conflicts are ready to accept these mediations; more rarely as peace-makers when the conscience of the world cannot blink at cruel televised events. A case in point was the UN intervention in Bosnia and later in neighboring Kosovo; or in the transformation of the peace-keeping mission in the civil war in the West African state of Sierra Leone into a peacemaking effort. The UN's effectiveness in controlling both domestic and international collective violence depends on the maintenance of consensus among the great powers. How tenuous this consensus can become is illustrated in the troubled efforts of the UN to disarm Iraq after the Gulf War of 1990–1991 and later to prevent Saddam Hussein's government there from producing weapons of mass destruction.

The economic costs of national security are also high. Most major countries face a massive national debt that often includes large deferred costs of borrowing for earlier wars and the maintenance of national defense. Current defense expenditures, plus the interest costs of past conflicts, might have been spent on more constructive public objects or left for private consumption or investment. Yet, states feel that they need to spend significantly on national defense because they are still governed by the "security dilemma"—they have to "take out insurance" against the possibility that their neighbors might be aggressive. While military expenditures in the world have declined since the collapse of the Soviet Union, the horrors of September 11, 2001, have led to a new costly mobilization of resources against international terrorism.

POLITICAL GOODS AND VALUES

If we are to compare and evaluate public policy in different political systems, we need to consider the political goods that motivate different policies. That leads us back to the issues we discussed in Chapters 1 and 2, to the functions and purposes that governments serve. This book is organized around the concepts of system, process, and policy. We can think about values as "political goods" related to each of those levels of analysis.

At the system level, there is a long tradition in political analysis that emphasizes order, predictability, and stability. Citizens are most free and most able to act purposefully when their environment is stable, transparent, and predictable. We call these conditions **system goods** since they reflect the functioning and effectiveness of the whole political system. While people generally want some measure of change and new opportunities, most prefer stability to abrupt and unforeseeable change. Political instability—constitutional breakdowns, frequent leadership changes, riots, demonstrations, and the like—upsets most people's plans and can cost lives and material destruction. System goods have to do with the regularity and predictability with which political systems work, but also with their ability to adapt to environmental challenges.

Regularity and adaptability are typically somewhat in conflict. There are times when order and stability are at the top of the agenda. In the United States, the administration of Warren Harding after World War I was such a period, called "a return to normalcy." There was a similar withdrawal from mobilization after World

War II and the Korean War. On the other hand, the 1930s and the 1960s were periods of change and adaptation, in which the reach of governmental powers was extended. But the stress on change and adaptation can also be a call for reductions in the scope in government, as in the Thatcher administration in Britain or the Republican "Contract with America" of 1994–1995.

Another school of thought emphasizes goods associated with the political process—citizen participation and free political competition. Democracy is good and authoritarianism bad, according to this school of thought, because of the way citizens are treated in the process, and not because democracy, for example, produces better economic results. Democratic procedures and various rights of due process, then, are **process goods.** Process goods include participation, compliance, and procedural justice. We value participation not merely as a means to responsive government, but for its own sake, as it enhances citizen competence and dignity. Compliance with authority can also be a good, as individuals respond to the impulse to serve others, which can be one of humanity's most gratifying experiences. President John F. Kennedy in his inaugural address called on such impulses to serve and sacrifice when he said, "Ask not what your country can do for you; ask what you can do for your country." Procedural justice (trial by jury, habeas corpus, no cruel and unusual punishment) is another crucial process value, without which citizens would have much greater reasons to fear their governments.

Procedural goods also include *effectiveness* and *efficiency.* A preference for effectiveness means that we prefer policies that actually lead to their desired purpose to those that do not. Efficiency means that government policies should attain their objectives at the lowest possible cost. If two alternative policies would lead to the same result but at very different costs, we would prefer the policy with the lower cost. In designing government agencies, most of us would prefer institutions that are lean and inexpensive to bloated agencies that produce no better results.

A third and final focus is on **policy goods,** such as economic welfare, quality of life, freedom, and personal security. We value a political system that improves welfare, decreases inequalities, enhances public safety, enables people to live lives they want for themselves, and cleans up its environment, whatever the political process that produces these results. Well-meaning people do not always agree which of these policy goods are most important. Yet, there are at least two important criteria that most of us would agree that government policy should meet. The first is *fairness.* If government undertakes some public policy, we would like that policy to be fair. The problem is that people often disagree over what is fair. In some situations, and according to some people, fairness requires that all people are treated equally (as when family members attempt to divide a tempting pie). In other situations, fairness demands that individuals be treated according to their dessert or performance (as when grades are given in a college course). And in yet other situations, fairness means that people are treated according to their needs (for example, in cases of medical treatment). Thus fairness can imply *equal treatment* in some cases, *just desserts* (reward in proportion to merit or contribution) in others, and *treatment according to need* in yet others. Many distributive policies—for example, pension systems such as social security in the United States—rely on some combination of these criteria.

The debate over these various conceptions of fairness is never settled. In most cases, however, fairness would rule out practices that are *arbitrary* or *partial*. Few of us would find it fair if government officials threw dice to determine who would be imprisoned or given pensions, or if they made such decisions solely on the basis of their personal prejudices or connections. We can think of fairness in this sense as reflected in the process good of *procedural justice*.

The second consideration is the promotion and preservation of *freedom*. As anarchists, libertarians, and other government skeptics would remind us, public policies should promote and protect freedom and basic human and political rights. If two policies are equally efficient and fair, then we would prefer the one that respects the rights and liberties of the citizens to the greater extent. But even in a demo-cratic society, freedom is not always chosen over other political goods. The right to bear arms, protected in the Second Amendment to the U.S. Constitution, has recently become a hotly contested issue, as many Americans would like to prevent those most likely to cause harm from carrying lethal weapons. Similarly, freedom of speech is a Constitutional guarantee, but many citizens favor restrictions on speech that is insulting or offensive.

Liberty is sometimes viewed only as freedom from governmental regulation and harassment. Freedom is more than inhibition of government action, however, because private individuals and organizations may also commit infractions of liberty and privacy. In such cases, liberty may be fostered by government intervention. Much legislation against racial segregation and discrimination generally has been impelled by this purpose. Liberty to act, organize, obtain information, and protest is an indispensable part of effective political participation. Nor is it irrelevant to social, political, and economic equality. Prior to the breakdown of communism in Eastern Europe and the Soviet Union, it was a common view that the communist countries were trading liberty for equality, by contrast with capitalism, which was said to trade off equality for liberty. One important thing that has come to light after the collapse of communism is the extent of corruption and privilege, as well as economic stagnation, in communist societies. While they had surely traded off liberty for a basic security of employment, it was not clear that the communist bloc had otherwise gained much in the way of equality.

Table 7.7 draws on our three-level analysis of political systems to present a checklist of political goods or values. There is no simple way to say which value should prevail when they conflict. But it is different preferences between such values as freedom, fairness, and efficiency that set different cultures, parties, and political philosophies apart. One society or group of citizens may value fairness over liberty; another may make the opposite choice, as in Patrick Henry's famous exclamation, "Give me liberty or give me death!"

STRATEGIES FOR PRODUCING POLITICAL GOODS

All political systems embody strategies for producing political goods, but different political regimes are designed to produce different combinations of political goods. The framers of the U.S. Constitution believed that separation of powers

TABLE 7.7   Political Goods

Levels of Political Goods	Classes of Goods	Content and Examples
System level	System maintenance	The political system is characterized by regular, stable, and predictable processes domestically and internationally.
	System adaptation	The political system adapts to environmental change and challenges.
Process level	Participation in political inputs	The political system is open to and responds to a variety of forms of political action and speech, which may directly produce a sense of citizen dignity and efficacy.
	Compliance and support	Citizens fulfill their obligations (e.g., patriotic service) to the system and comply with public law and policy.
	Procedural justice	Equitable procedure (due process) and equality before the law.
	Effectiveness and efficiency	Processes have intended effects and are no more cumbersome, expensive, or intrusive than necessary.
Policy level	Welfare	Growth per capita; quantity and quality of health and material goods; distributive equity.
	Security	Safety of person and property; public order and national security.
	Fairness	Non-discrimination in government policy; mutual recognition of individuals from different ethnic, linguistic, or other groups; protection of vulnerable or disadvantaged citizens.
	Liberty	Freedom from regulation, protection of privacy, and respect for autonomy of other individuals, groups, and nations.

would protect liberty; Karl Marx believed that the "dictatorship of the proletariat" would lead to a just and harmonious society; Mussolini believed that a strong leader would increase national power and glory; and the Ayatollah Khomeini believed that a society modeled after the Koran, and administered by the clergy, would promote justice on earth and eternal salvation.

Since the collapse of the Soviet Union in 1991, democracy has seemed to be "the only game in town." Earlier in the twentieth century there have been several political ideologies in competition with political democracy—communism, fascism, corporatist authoritarianism, and the like. Fascism went down in flames in World War II. Communism all but collapsed in the late 1980s, drained of credibility by its policy failure and its corruption. Most of its successor regimes have democratized and established market economies. The dictatorships of Latin America, discredited by their cruelties and economic failures, have turned to the market and democracy. The postcolonial regimes of Sub-Saharan Africa, after a brief interlude of populist democracy in the 1960s, turned to authoritarian regimes of one kind or another. Then in recent years some of them have begun to experiment once again with democracy. But although democracy and the market economy have been the wave of the immediate past, other strategies may very well become credible once again. Below we spell out the major political-economic alternatives in the world today, beginning with the industrialized countries and moving on to the developing, or industrializing, ones.

Industrialized Nations

The industrialized democratic nations must reconcile pressures to maintain or increase government services with the need to accumulate resources for investment in economic growth. Many contemporary democratic industrial nations have relatively high unemployment and/or relatively slow rates of growth. The rise of the service economy and the emergence of environmental challenges have complicated the class structure and reduced the power of trade unions. Industrial pollution of land, air, and water divides nations differently, with a substantial part of the middle classes opposing growth that implies environmental degradation, and a substantial part of the working classes making the opposite choice. These dilemmas—both the old capital versus labor issues, and the newer service economy and environmental issues facing all advanced democracies—may be dealt with in a market-oriented fashion as in the Britain of Margaret Thatcher, and the United States of the Reagan era, or in a social democratic fashion as in Norway and Sweden.

But though there are policy differences between the market-oriented and social democracies, both types of democratic regimes have in the last decades reconsidered taxes, welfare, and regulation. The size, cost, and inefficiencies of government have become major political issues. In the United States both major political parties have embarked on efforts to limit and restructure government—the Republicans leading a campaign to contain spending and return powers to the state governments; and the Democrats with their efficiency program of "reinventing government." The environmental issue divides both right and left. In some European countries "Green," ecologically oriented, parties have emerged. In 1998, the German Greens became the first such party to win control of the executive branch of a major country, albeit as a junior partner, in a coalition government with the Social Democrats.

Industrial authoritarian nations come in leftist and rightist varieties. Franco Spain (1938–1975), Greece under the military dictatorship (1967–1974), the Chile of Pinochet (1973–1988), and the Brazil of "the generals" (1964–1985) are examples of right-wing authoritarianism. The military authoritarian regimes of Southern Europe and Latin America of the 1960s and 1970s suppressed popular political organization but granted considerable freedom to private enterprise. They sought to foster economic growth, though at the expense of increasing inequality of wealth and income. But their repressive policies eventually became unpopular. Where authoritarian right-wing regimes had produced good economic results, as in Spain and Chile, they were able to negotiate a peaceful transition to democracy. Elsewhere, as in Portugal and Argentina, they were toppled through popular unrest and revolutions.

Prior to the collapse of communism in Eastern Europe, the Soviet Union, Poland, and Hungary were industrialized authoritarian regimes of the left. Though many of these countries have now moved toward market economies and democracy, anti-Western groups in Russia and in states such as Belarus and Ukraine have seriously resisted such moves. In general, and across different regime types, the credibility of socialism and of high welfare expenditures has declined in the last decades, while that of the market economy has risen. It is still to be seen whether this is a pendular move, or whether the power of the state reached a historic high point in the 1980s. In most former communist states, the governments have now moved away somewhat from the market enthusiasm of the early days of reform. Democratic stability in Latin America and Eastern Europe may still hinge on their economic success. Thus, while there are currently few industrialized authoritarian regimes (whether radical or conservative), it would be a mistake to think that the category is no longer relevant.

Preindustrial Nations

The preindustrial nations face common challenges of modernization. There are some seven strategies of political development followed by preindustrial countries—one democratic and the six authoritarian regimes that follow.

Neotraditional Political Systems. Neotraditional political systems, the best exemplars of which are Saudi Arabia and the sheikdoms of the Persian Gulf, emphasize stability, the maintenance of an established order. Since these regimes are oil rich, they have so far been able to modernize selectively (for example, the military) and buy off opposition and discontent. But as they develop economically through their oil royalties, and as they provide health, educational, and other amenities to a substantial part of their populations, some political modernization may follow. This may in turn fuel the development of a political opposition and demands for reform.

Personal Rule. Most Sub-Saharan African states are not neotraditional, though they may contain traditional structures such as kingdoms or chiefdoms. The colonial boundaries inherited by most Sub-Saharan countries were artificial constructs that often included many different languages, ethnicities, and religions. The formally democratic regimes that were established after independence soon gave way to various versions of "personal rule."[12] The "personal ruler" is not simply a chief executive in the limited political sense; he has a "proprietary" relation to the regime, its institutions and agencies, and often exploits it for his personal purposes. Rent seeking is thus a serious problem in such countries, as in the case of President Mobutu of Zaire (see Chapter 1). Where these systems stabilize, the rulers maintain control through police suppression, patronage, spoils, and privileges distributed through clientelistic networks. Many of the personal rule regimes in Sub-Saharan Africa are characterized by low (or even negative) growth, low life expectancy, low literacy, and low health standards. Since these regimes are economically unproductive, they have little legitimacy and are susceptible to military coups.

Clerico-Mobilizational Regimes.   In the last decades, and principally in Islamic countries, a clerico-authoritarian mobilizational ideology has emerged. Clerico-mobilizational regimes are built on a religious authority for which they try to mobilize active support. They are antisecular in social matters (for example, regarding the status of women and family policies) and they restrict civil society through media censorship and suppression. They are authoritarian, but neither traditional nor technocratic. They want to control the modern media, use it for their own purposes, and clean up moral corruption. They are ambivalent in economic policy, urging market intervention from Koranic precepts, but in practice do not seriously interfere with banks and other economic institutions. They are nationalist and anti-Western.

This "fundamentalist" religious movement is represented in both branches of Islam—Shia and Sunni. The Shia version is exemplified in Iran, which is dominated by clerics and Islamic legislators and judges. Sunni Islam has similar radical theocratic movements, not only in the Middle East but in Afghanistan, Pakistan, and in the Islamic areas of Central Asia. Movements of this kind are also strong in the more secular states of Algeria, Egypt, and even Turkey. The fate of these new movements is still unclear. They may not be very effective in mounting an international coalition, and nationalism and the split between Shia and Sunni Muslims may impede collaboration.

Technocratic-Repressive.   Governments adopting this approach promoted economic growth previously in Indonesia and in parts of South America, where a coalition of military and civilian technocrats and business interests suppressed participation and pursued a growth-oriented investment policy at the cost of growing economic inequality. Such Middle Eastern countries as Syria and Egypt still pursue this strategy. In other countries that have gone democratic, economic or democratic failures may lead to reversions to technocratic-repressive strategies.

Technocratic-Distributive.   There also is a distributive, and more egalitarian, version of the modernizing authoritarian regime. One example is South Korea prior to its democratization. South Korea suppressed participation but encouraged some income redistribution along with growth. Early land reforms, rapid development of education, labor-intensive, export-oriented industrialization, and substantial American advice, support, and pressure marked the Korean experiment. Its economic success seems to have led to effective democratization.

Technocratic-Mobilizational.   The last category, the authoritarian technocratic-mobilizational strategy, has been exemplified primarily by preindustrial Communist countries, and in a milder form by Taiwan. In these states, there is a single political party mobilizing and involving citizens in the political process. Thus, Mexico was dominated by the Partido Revolucionario Institucional (PRI), which incorporates the major interest groups of labor, business, and agriculture into its party organization, for more than a half-century. Competitive participation is suppressed or limited. Though there are few such states today, we cannot rule out the possibility that they may return. China, Vietnam, North Korea, and Cuba are the last remaining Communist societies, dominated by single mobilizing political parties. China, Vietnam, and even Cuba have opened their socialist economies to market forces. China has seen enormous growth (see Chapter 13), but the question is how long it can avoid some political pluralism. The non-Communist mobilizational systems vary substantially in success and in their policy emphases. Taiwan has combined growth and distributive equity, and in recent years politics has become increasingly competitive.

Democratization in Developing Countries

Just as democracy has become the "only political game in town," democratization and its consolidation have become the main preoccupations of many contemporary political scientists. Current understandings of transitions to democracy emphasize the importance of leadership, choice, and bargaining, whereas they tend to play down the importance of economic and social factors. Many scholars argue that democratization can occur wherever the leaders, pressured or influenced by democratization elsewhere, begin moving in the democratic direction. The recent literature very persuasively emphasizes the uncertainty and unpredictability of democratic transitions.[13] While democratization is therefore uncertain, tentative, and reversible, "democratic consolidation" is a condition in which the main elites have accepted democracy and in which participatory behavior has been widely adopted among the general population.

Stable democracy seems to depend on the presence of a "civil society" based on free media and a lively associational life. These conditions in turn are associated with widespread literacy and rising economic standards. From this perspective a great many contemporary Third World democracies are not consolidated institutionally or culturally.[14] Yet, the democratization of Taiwan and South Korea suggests that industrialization, urbanization, education, and communication can indeed foster consolidation.[15] On the other hand, India, a democracy almost continuously since independence in 1947, demonstrates that even a relatively underdeveloped country can sustain democracy.

TRADE-OFFS AND OPPORTUNITY COSTS

One of the hard facts about political goods is that though each may be desirable, they cannot all be had simultaneously. A political system often has to trade off one value to obtain another. Spending funds on education is giving up the opportunity to spend them on welfare, or to leave them in the hands of consumers for their own use. These **trade-offs** and **opportunity costs** are also found in complicated decisions about investment for the future as opposed to present consumption, as when politicians have to decide how to fund future retirement benefits. Even more difficult are the trade-offs between security and liberty, or stability and adaptation, where the very concepts imply giving up some of the one for some of the other. Extreme liberty, as Hobbes would tell us, would make a highly insecure world where the strong might bully the weak and where collective action would be difficult. Yet, without liberty, security is of little value, as the prisoner is too well aware. Moreover, the trade-offs are not the same under all circumstances. Under some conditions increasing liberty somewhat will also increase security—for example, because riots against censorship will end. Under some conditions investment in education will be paid back many times in health and welfare, because trained citizens can better care for themselves and work more productively. Although in politics you cannot always "have your cake and eat it, too," one of the important tasks of social science is to discover the conditions under which positive and negative trade-offs occur.

Regrettably, political science has no way of converting units of liberty into units of safety or welfare. And because politics may involve violence on a large scale, we must acknowledge that we can never calculate the value of a political outcome gained at the cost of human life. People act as though they know how to make such conversions, but as political scientists we can only point to value judgments that people have been willing to make. The weight given to various goods differs across cultures and contexts. The advantage of a clear-cut ideology is that it provides a logical scheme that tells us how much one value should be traded against another, and thus offers orderly bases for choice. Such schemes may be invaluable for those pressed into action in the terrible circumstances of war, revolution, and famine. However, there is no ideology, just as there is no political science, that can solve all these problems objectively.

KEY TERMS

direct taxes

distribution

extraction

gross domestic product (GDP)

indirect taxes

neotraditional political system

night watchman state

opportunity cost

Organization for Economic Cooperation and Development (OECD)

outcomes

outputs

police state

policy goods

political goods and values

process goods

public policies

regulation

regulatory state

symbolic policies

system goods

taxation

technocratic

trade-off's

welfare state

SUGGESTED READINGS

Bratton, Michael and Nicholas Vandewall. *Democratic Experiments in Africa: Regime Transitions in Comparative Perspective.* New York: Cambridge University Press, 1997.

Castles, Francis G., ed. *The Comparative History of Public Policy.* Cambridge, England: Polity Press, 1989.

Dahl, Robert. *Democracy and Its Critics*. New Haven, CT: Yale University Press, 1989.

Diamond, Larry, ed. *Democracy in Developing Countries*. Boulder, CO: Lynne Rienner, 1992.

Flora, Peter and Arnold Heidenheimer. *The Development of Welfare States in Europe and America*. New Brunswick, NJ: Transaction Books, 1981.

Gourevitch, Peter. *Politics in Hard Times*. Ithaca, NY: Cornell University Press, 1986.

Heidenheimer, Arnold, Hugh Heclo, and Carolyn Teich Adams. *Comparative Public Policy*, 3rd ed. New York: St. Martin's Press, 1990.

Huntington, Samuel. *The Third Wave: Democratization in the Late Twentieth Century*. Norman, OK: Oklahoma University Press, 1991.

Jackson, Robert, and Carl Rosberg. *Personal Rule in Black Africa*. Berkeley, CA: University of California Press, 1982.

Katzenstein, Peter. *Small States in World Markets*. Ithaca, NY: Cornell University Press, 1985.

Lijphart, Arend. *Patterns of Democracy*. New Haven, CT: Yale University Press, 1999.

Lindblom, Charles E. *Politics and Markets*. New Haven, CT: Yale University Press, 1978.

Mainwaring, Scott, Guillermo O'Donnell, and Arturo Valenzuela. *Issues in Democratic Consolidation*. Notre Dame, IN: University of Notre Dame Press, 1992.

Marks, Gary and Larry Diamond, eds. *Reexamining Democracy*. Newbury Park, CA: Sage, 1992.

Olson, Mancur. *The Rise and Decline of Nations*. New Haven, CT: Yale University Press, 1982.

Olson, Mancur. *Power and Prosperity*. New York: Basic Books, 2000.

Putnam, Robert D. *Making Democracy Work*. Princeton, NJ: Princeton University Press, 1993.

Tsebelis, George. *Veto Players: An Introduction to Institutional Analysis*. Princeton, NJ: Princeton University Press, 2002.

Wilensky, Harold, *Rich Democracies: Political Economy, Public Policy, and Performance*. Berkeley, CA: University of California Press, 2002.

Wilson, James G. *The Politics of Regulation in the United States*. New York: Basic Books, 1980.

ENDNOTES

1. See World Bank, *Entering the 21st Century: World Development Report 1999–2000* (New York: Oxford University Press, 2000), Table A.1, pp. 216–217.

2. Peter Flora and Arnold Heidenheimer, *The Development of Welfare States in Europe and America* (New Brunswick, NJ: Transaction Books, 1981); Arnold Heidenheimer, Hugh Heclo, and Carolyn Teich Adams, *Comparative Public Policy*, 3rd ed. (New York: St. Martin's Press, 1990).

3. Heidenheimer, Heclo and Adams. *Comparative Public Policy*, pp. 211–219.

4. *The Economist* (May 30, 1998): 19.

5. See, for example, Samuel Brittan, *The Economic Consequences of Democracy* (London: Temple Smith, 1977); Michael Boskin, *The Crisis in Social Security* (San Francisco: Institute for Contemporary Studies, 1978); Mancur Olson, *The Rise and Decline of Nations* (New Haven, CT: Yale University Press, 1982).

6. Steven C. Poe and C. Neal Tate, "Repression of Human Rights to Personal Integrity in the 1980s: A Global Analysis," *American Political Science Review* 88, no. 4 (December 1994): 853–872.

7. Simon Kuznets, "Economic Growth and Income Equality," *American Economic Review* 45 (1955): 1–28.

8. World Bank, *World Development Report: Infrastructure for Development* (New York: Oxford University Press, 1994), Overview, pp. 1, ff.

9. Peter Gourevitch in his book *Politics in Hard Times* (Cornell University Press, 1986) analyzes the policy responses of five Western industrial nations—Britain, France, Germany, Sweden, and the United States—to the three world depressions of 1870–1890, 1930–1940, and 1975–1985.

Gourevitch shows how these crises affected business, labor, and agriculture differently in each country; consequences for political structure and policy varied greatly. Thus the world depression of the 1930s resulted in a conservative reaction in Britain (the formation of a "National" government), a moderate left reaction in the United States (the "New Deal"), a polarization and paralysis of public policy in France ("Immobilisme"), a moderate social democratic reaction in Sweden, and a radical right and left polarization in Germany, leading to a breakdown of democracy and the emergence of National Socialism. While the causes of World War II were complex, the pacifism of Britain, the demoralization and defeatism in France, the isolationism of the United States, and the nihilism and aggression of Germany were all fed by the devastating worldwide economic depression of the 1930s.

10. Summarized in "States in Armed Conflict," produced by the Department of Peace and Conflict Research, Uppsala University, Sweden, at their website, www.peace.uu.se, consulted May 15, 2000. For a more complete account see Peter Wallensteen and Margareta Sollenberg, "Armed Conflict and Regional Conflict Complexes, 1989–97", *Journal of Peace Research*, 35, no. 5, (1998).

11. Ruth Leger Sivard, *World Military and Social Indicators* (Washington: World Priorities, 1993), p. 20.

12. Robert Jackson and Carl Rosberg, *Personal Rule in Black Africa* (Berkeley, CA: University of California Press, 1982).

13. See, among others, Guillermo O'Donnell and Philippe C. Schmitter, *Transitions from Authoritarian Rule: Tentative Conclusions About Uncertain Democracies* (Baltimore, MD: Johns Hopkins University Press, 1986); Samuel Huntington, *The Third Wave: Democratization in the Late Twentieth Century* (Norman, OK: University of Oklahoma Press, 1991); Terry Karl, "Dilemmas of Democratization in Latin America," in *Comparative Politics* (October 1990): 1–22; Nancy Bermeo, "Rethinking Regime Change," *Comparative Politics* 22, no. 3: 359–377; Giuseppe Di Palma, *To Craft Democracies* (Berkeley, CA: University of California Press, 1990); Gary Marks and Larry Diamond, eds., *Reexamining Democracy* (Newbury Park, CA: Sage, 1992).

14. Larry Diamond, "Toward Democratic Consolidation," *Journal of Democracy* 5, no. 3 (July 1994): 4–17; Lawrence Whitehead, "The Consolidation of Fragile Democracies," in Robert A. Pastor, ed., *Democracy in the Americas* (New York: Holmes and Meier, 1989); Samuel J. Valenzuela, "Democratic Consolidation in Post Transitional Settings," in Scott Mainwaring, Guillermo O'Donnell, and Arturo Valenzuela, *Issues in Democratic Consolidation* (Notre Dame, IN: University of Notre Dame Press, 1992); Scott Mainwaring, "Transition to Democracy and Democratic Consolidation: Theoretical and Comparative Issues," in Mainwaring, et al., *Issues.* Terry Karl and Philippe Schmitter, "Modes of Transition in Latin America," *International Social Science Journal* 138 (May 1991): 269–284. Larry Diamond, *Political Culture and Democracy in Developing Countries* (Boulder, CO: Lynne Rienner, 1994), ch. 1; Robert D. Putnam, *Making Democracy Work* (Princeton, NJ: Princeton University Press, 1993).

15. Daniel Lerner, *The Passing of Traditional Society* (Glencoe, IL: Free Press, 1958); Seymour M. Lipset, "Some Social Requisites of Democracy," *American Political Science Review* (September 1959): 69–105; Karl Deutsch, "Social Mobilization and Political Development," *American Political Science Review* (September 1961): 493–514.

INDEX